Environmental Crime in the United States

Environmental Crime in the United States provides an introduction to the laws that govern environmental crime, how these laws are implemented and enforced, and the impact they have had since their passing in the twentieth century and their continued applications.

Environmental crimes such as wildlife trafficking, over-fishing, artisanal mining, and deforestation are lucrative contributors to a global illicit trade market and sources of cheap resources for corporations to exploit. This book presents a review of U.S.-based laws and regulations regarding such environmental crimes at the state and federal level, combined with examples of international convention or trade agreements which can be prosecuted within the United States. It examines attempts to modify these laws, the exceptions granted to prevent enforcement, and the ability of political and social groups to address inefficiencies of the laws or their implementations. Both criminal and administrative laws are reviewed to assess how laws governing the environment compare to other areas of law that seek to protect and improve social well-being and public health; this includes a review of how environmental crimes overlap with general crimes, and how these crimes fuel illicit commerce while strengthening international crime syndicates. Trends such as the actions taken by non-governmental organizations and other entities other than law enforcement to stop environmental crimes such as poaching will be explained, with a discussion of how environmental crimes spurn illicit markets and provide lucrative schemes for international crime rings as well as corporations.

This book will be of great interest to students of environmental crime and justice, green criminology, environmental conservation, natural resource management, and environmental law.

Karen Clark is an Adjunct Faculty at the University of Arizona and the University of Nebraska, U.S.A. She earned a doctorate degree in criminology, law, and society from the University of California, Irvine, and has published numerous articles on environmental crimes, natural resource exploitation, and transnational crime trends.

Environmental Crime in the United States

Law and Enforcement

Karen Clark

Routledge
Taylor & Francis Group
LONDON AND NEW YORK

earthscan
from Routledge

Designed cover image: © Getty

First published 2024
by Routledge
4 Park Square, Milton Park, Abingdon, Oxon OX14 4RN

and by Routledge
605 Third Avenue, New York, NY 10158

Routledge is an imprint of the Taylor & Francis Group, an informa business

British Library Cataloguing-in-Publication Data
A catalogue record for this book is available from the British Library

ISBN: 978-1-032-14807-6 (hbk)
ISBN: 978-1-032-14805-2 (pbk)
ISBN: 978-1-003-24120-1 (ebk)

DOI: 10.4324/9781003241201

Typeset in Times New Roman
by codeMantra

Contents

1 Introduction to Environmental Crime

Nature provides an abundance of resources that are in demand and have the potential to be acquired and misused in a global economy that prizes limited supplies and rare commodities. Environmental crimes can take the form of criminal conspiracies that are employed to maximize the profit of natural resource exploitation. Generally, crime is often opportunistic and this is also true for environmental crimes. When commodity prices are high, when there is demand for a limited commodity and when there is competition for a dwindling resource, criminal groups can take advantage of these circumstances. Whether it is for trade in rhinoceros horn, demand for fish that exceeds legitimate supply, or supplying precious metals such as gold that is unlawfully extracted but in high demand for legitimate uses, natural resources provide ample opportunities for entrepreneurial illicit enterprises and motivated offenders.

This book employs the terms environmental crime and natural resource crime interchangeably. The difference between the terms is limited to environmental crimes that are not exclusively related to natural resources. Most environmental crimes are the exploitation of natural resources. Pollution is an environmental crime that is not the result of natural resource exploitation but is from industrial processes. The industrial process can be an illegal marijuana grow in a national forest which involves the widespread use of banned pesticides and herbicides that have long-term detrimental impacts on forest ecosystems. For this text, environmental crimes and natural resource crimes are both used to mean unlawful violations of environmental protections as proscribed by laws and regulations.

The status of environmental regulations can create a paradoxical effect. Regulatory laws such as the National Environmental Policy Act 1969 (NEPA), sets strict standards and has compelled guidelines for development or activities on federal lands. While some champion strict environmental regulations as a mechanism for preserving wildlife or conserving lands, there is often a deleterious effect from imposing and enforcing increasingly rigorous restrictions. As regulations increase costs of development, subversion of the laws is a mechanism employed to ensure profit. Government officials, while attempting to please activists or address political concerns, do not often display the same savvy that criminal groups do. Through strict regulations the government can induce businesses that operate lawfully to subvert laws.

DOI: 10.4324/9781003241201-1

There must always be a balance between the laws and the cost of business. Failing to recognize and account for this balance leads to business operators willing to take risks. Frequently the risks are minimal as many environmental enforcement mechanisms are lax. Enforcement is infrequent. When it is applied, usually the response by the government is to levy fines. These can be paid by larger operators who understand the costs of compliance, the costs of disregard for some environmental codes, and the profits available in the commodity market. Through government regulation, often smaller operators cannot stay in business or the U.S. market becomes uncompetitive in comparison to foreign markets. As an example, regulated logging in the United States increases the cost of timber locally and has the occasional effect of accelerating illegal logging overseas. As industries pursue cheap timber, a more expensive local commodity is usurped in the market by a cheaper product.

The nexus of demand of a product – such as fish or timber – in a global market, a sophisticated regulatory environment, inconsistent enforcement, corporate voluntary compliance agreements and large, multinational business entities make environmental crime an ideal setting for organized crime to flourish. Additionally, when smaller businesses or individuals are targeted for enforcement but larger entities are in voluntary compliance agreements, those who earn wages through natural resource commodity harvest, transfer, and sale feel resentment toward government officials including game wardens, forest rangers, and customs officials. The governmental laws and guidelines are often uneven. The federal government, through the U.S. Fish and Wildlife Department, strictly regulates commercial fishing fleets but does not regulate or oversee recreation fishing vessels. Recreation vessels can bring in significant quantities of fish and profit and can be used in smuggling operations since they are not regularly inspected and audited the way commercial vessels are. This gap in enforcement is exploited by criminal organizations.

There is persistent strain that results from conflicting demand for natural resources for exploitation and conservation of land and wildlife. When the United States government acts to reduce the effects of poaching in American territorial waters or lands, it employs conservation officers who enforce various hunting and fishing laws. Environmental activities such as hunting are lawful activities that can become illegal if done on private or protected land, during off-season or without permit. The environment, at best, is a complicated and difficult subject to regulate. Governmental rules and actions can create unintended consequences of inducements for organized crime that operates in an increasingly complex global market with high demand pressures and escalating profits.

This textbook will serve as a reference to those seeking to understand global crimes, transnational crime, natural resource exploitation, and the enforcement of these crimes within the United States. The chapters in this text will highlight various laws, regulations, contemporary cases of overfishing, wildlife trafficking, illegal mining, whaling, deforestation, and illegal waste dumping. To understand how these crimes evolved to their current status, there will be a review of how laws and regulations addressing natural resource exploitation were formed. Each of the major legislative acts was instituted as a consequence of an environmental misfortune. Substantive air pollutants that made it challenging for residents to find their way through thick smog caused by smokestacks and an inversion layer in Donora, Pennsylvania in 1948 and fires in the Cuyahoga River, Ohio, sparked by passing trains due to the elevated levels of industrial pollutants in the environment, brought the awareness of environmental harms to the public's attention. Biologist Rachel Carson's book *Silent Spring* provoked curiosity about the links between environmental regulations and potential hazards to wildlife and, by extension, the human environment.

Definitions and Laws

In the United States, the Environmental Protection Agency (EPA) defines environmental crimes as: "a negligent, knowing or willful violation of a federal environmental law. 'Knowing' violations are those that are deliberate and not the product of an accident or mistake" (Environmental Protection Agency, n.d.). Often environmental crimes are accompanied by other crimes such as fraud, conspiracy, corruption, and violations of labor laws to include those under the authorities of Occupational Safety and Health Administration (OSHA) and Mining Health and Safety Administration (MHSA).

Initially laws relating to the environment were dispersed throughout various authorities: agriculture, workplace safety regulations, mining regulations, environmental regulations under both public and private law, and criminal code enforcement. What substantiates criminal code within environmental law is the offender's intent or negligence by failing to abide by a permitting process. A judicial body must be convinced that a wrongdoer intended or knowingly violated an environmental law for it to be considered a felony violation. There are many instances where industrial accidents occur or brokers file importation paperwork incorrectly without intent. Although there may be significant environmental harm as a result, these are not crimes under the law. They may be violations of civil or administrative law. Explanations of the laws governing environmental violations will be covered with a survey of criminal violations relating to the most commonly applied statutes.

Various units within the Department of Agriculture and the Environmental Protection Agency enforce congressionally enacted legislation regarding the conservation, commercial use, and protection of animal and plant species. As a consequence, parsing out environmental laws that prohibit illegal trade, harvest, or collection of natural resources can become a complicated and bureaucratic process. Unlike the most common federal criminal violations, most of the criminal cases pursued by the Department of Justice against violators rely on regulatory schemes that put limits on legal trade. All of the topics covered in the text have a lawful component. Even trade in rhinoceros horn and elephant ivory can be lawful under strict guidelines even though both are under general bans of importation and exportation.

It can be confusing as to which laws address environmental crimes since they can occur when either an illegal act occurs – such as a large scale marijuana grow in a national forest – or when a lawful act is conducted unlawfully – such as when fish stocks are imported under a false label, mislabeling the fish to bypass quota or catch requirements. Fishing, mining, timber harvesting, purchase and transportation of wildlife, dumping of industrial waste, and whaling are all legal activities but can become unlawful when conducted in protected areas or when protected species are harvested. These activities can also become a crime when importation or origination documents are filed fraudulently to conceal the nation of origin or the species harvested.

Since many of the environmental crimes occur as violations of harvesting limits or the harvesting of protected species, those who push for enforcement are often those who are employed within the commodities enterprises. Industry groups make demands and elevate agendas for the protection of their industries through enforcement of environmental protections. The domestic timber industry suffers when timber is illegally harvested and imported into the United States (USAID, n.d.). The illegal harvests undermine the legal market. Similarly, illegal marijuana grows on federal public lands undermine the lawful marijuana market (Sykes, 2022). There are other implications such as that the overfishing of various regions or seas creates risks of population collapse endangering longevity of legal fish markets.

Contemporary cases of natural resource exploitation can be scrutinized as environmental crimes based on laws starting in 1900 with the Lacey Act (16 U.S.C. 3371 et seq.) and the largest environmental laws passed in the 1960s. Contemporary environmental crimes are natural resource crimes. These crimes can be viewed similarly to other corporate, international, or organized crimes as they occur at this scale. Accordingly, environmental crimes can be compared to other commodity crimes such as drugs, human, or weapons trafficking.

Conservation Enforcement

Simply creating protected areas such as national parks or conservation ranges has proven insufficient to stop compromise to ecosystems or to protect effectively wild flora or fauna. This is true both overseas and within the United States. There are ample case studies of poaching on U.S. National Park Service land and the destruction of miles of national forests due to large scale marijuana grows. The United States has not sufficiently invested in conservation agents to enforce conservation lands and to protect natural resources such as public lands (Swan, 2016). Across the United States there are approximately 765,000 full-time and 44,000 part-time law enforcement officers between state, local, and federal agencies. In contrast, the entire nation has almost 8,000 conservation officers – that includes state and federal officers combined (Swan, 2016). The State of California has 200 game wardens for a population of thirty-eight million people and nearly one million acres of state-owned forests (UCANR, n.d.).

Deficits in law enforcement resources are compounded through the multi-jurisdictional issues that environmental crimes often present. While the Environmental Protection Agency (EPA) has a mandate to ensure human health and the environment, the jurisdiction its enforcement division has is limited to the investigation of criminal activity that threatens human health or the environment.

This parameter is interpreted as an intentional violation of a federal environmental law. The EPA has both an administrative as well as criminal enforcement division. The criminal enforcement division is staffed by federal agents who receive the same basic training as all other federal agents but are given additional training in enforcing environmental regulations. Violations can occur through negligence by an operator who has environmental obligations, such as a water treatment facility. The manager or owner of the facility has to maintain the productive operation of the facility lest he be charged with an environmental regulation. In criminal courts this occurs when an organization or facility has received multiple violation notices yet does not resolve the issue causing an environmental code breach.

Enforcement of trade regulations that prohibit the importation of poached animals or plants is conducted by both the Department of Homeland Security, which oversees borders and ports, and through the Department of Agriculture, which oversees plants and animals. Thus, large scale environmental crimes such as those conducted by organized crime groups often involve co-ordination of multiple agencies. The United States Postal Service Office of the Inspector General frequently plays an enforcement role in environmental crimes if products or live animals are transported via the U.S. mail. Federal and state wardens and rangers that oversee the safeguarding of protected lands and waterways are tasked with enforcing state and federal laws regarding animal and plant protections.

State agency departments that specialize in public health often identify environmental law violations. Agencies such as the Department of Toxic Substance Control in California or Department of Environmental Quality in Arizona frequently come across environmental code violations as they receive tips from the public. The aforementioned agencies and those like it across the country work with local businesses and the public to ensure pollution controls are enforced through required testing of air, soil, and water samples.

Beyond the larger government agencies, port and transportation law enforcement such as railroad police, a special jurisdiction police within the United States, participate in cases where poached or illicit goods are shipped across state and federal borders. Private shipping companies such as FedEx and United Parcel Service (UPS) have their own investigative units to coordinate with law enforcement agencies when illegal transfers are suspected.

Tribal governments work with state and federal agencies to address environmental crimes that occur on Indian lands or involve Indian companies or enrolled tribal members. Tribal governments may have their own environmental laws but they cannot conflict with federal law. They can be stricter than federal law but not more lax. The federal government has final authority on environmental code enforcement on tribal lands.

Military properties have strict environmental regulations that are enforced through military law enforcement agents. Often this occurs through the Naval Criminal Investigative Service, Army Criminal Investigations Division or the Air Force Office of Special Investigations. Typically, military commanders who govern the property will request the assistance of the EPA in criminal enforcement of criminal environmental violations.

Enforcement of Environmental Crime Statutes

The confluence of the licit and the illicit market complicates investigations of environmental crimes. All activities covered in this text – from overfishing to waste dumping – are reflective of lawful activities, in this case fishing and waste disposal. Hence a labor-intensive investigative process is required to convict criminally or cite administratively organizations that have business licenses, adaptive processes of purchase, banking and product transfer that cross the lines between illegal and legal, and valid paperwork comingled with invalid paperwork. Prosecutors have to convincingly demonstrate intent: there was a conspiracy by a group of people and businesses who collaborated with the intent of violating the Lacey Act or some other environmental statute. When organized crime groups merge and start to traffic in both narcotics and timber, it becomes easier to prosecute them on the possession or sale of narcotics as this act represents a strict liability a crime.

Simply possessing or selling a regulated natural resource product is enough for the conviction for protected or prohibited species. This can occur with elephant tusks as ivory trade is banned in most nations. With regard to overfishing or illegal fishing, it becomes incumbent upon the government to demonstrate fishing permits were invalid, identification of the species of fish collected, the amount of fish collected, the approximate time frame, and location of the catch. It is a burdensome process that requires substantive investigative and scientific resources. Unfortunately states and the federal government are insufficiently supplied in this area. In part, this is why organized crime has become so prolific in their involvement, capture, and expansion within the illicit market in wildlife trade (Thompson, 2019).

The lack of enforcement resources is a problem throughout the world. In a globalized marketplace, there is greater permeability for commodity transfer as the volume of goods traded throughout the world increases each year. With increased population sizes, expanding middle classes in Asia, South America, and Africa, and with it increased demands for goods and services, the amount of cargo and natural resources passing through international ports can easily obscure the transfer of illicit goods or the illicit transfer of licit goods.

Governments struggle to balance supply and demand. Without effective policies environmental crimes can proliferate such as the harvesting of protected timber and overfishing – each multi-billion-dollar industries. Governments cannot simply make commodities legal without regulatory guardrails. The proliferation of illegal marijuana grows on public lands shows us that state governments' failures to create regulatory schemes that are achievable and realistic with a well-supported compliance mechanism leads to burgeoning illegal enterprises that cause substantive environmental damage. States like Oregon, California, and Colorado which legalized marijuana consumption and sales have had to confront massive illegal grows that have diverted millions of gallons of water from riparian systems and municipal water supplies (Cagnassola, 2021; Felbab-Brown, 2021; Selsky, 2021; USDOJ, 2015). Environmental damage caused by the illegal grows of what is now a lawful product demonstrates that simply creating laws or making the illicit licit is insufficient. To promote environmental sustainability and conservation, governments need to grapple with both the licit and the illicit. In many areas of crime, governments need to balance enforcement with other competing political and budgetary concerns. For environmental crimes, governments have to consider implications from delving into complex markets where there is persistent high demand, limits of governmental enforcement, and incentives that promote law abidance by various industries.

Environmental and Animal Offenses that Are not Environmental Crimes

There is a separation between domestic and wild species of plants and animals. The laws that address the care of domestic species to include agricultural production of livestock are not included in environmental regulations. Conversely, pollutants from agricultural production such as pesticide runoff into riparian systems and inappropriate disposal of animal carcasses or illegal dumping of animal waste can violate environmental laws such as the Clean Water Act. The environmental laws govern the soil, air, and water and the source point of the pollution must be identified. The presence of animals or crops as a part or cause of the pollution is not addressed by environmental codes.

Animal welfare is governed via the Animal Welfare Act of 1966 (7 U.S.C. 2143). The Animal Welfare Act oversees animal care for any animal used in food production, research, zoos, animals used for entertainment or competition such as rodeos, circuses, or dog shows, pet breeders, animal transporters, animal brokers, and pet stores or wildlife dealers. The United States Department of Agriculture administers the Animal Welfare Act via the Animal and Plant Health Inspection Service (APHIS). This agency also oversees the Lacey Act which prohibits importation of protected plant and animal species into the United States. Violations of the Lacey Act can be either criminal or civil. Substantive cases have been adjudicated against large corporations for violations of the Lacey Act. Two of the cases will be highlighted in Chapter 10 which focuses on deforestation.

Domestic species tend to be covered under property laws. There are sets of laws that govern access to and use of natural resources that are not under criminal or federal codes. Natural resource laws are governed by state or local governments. A person who owns land may not have access to mineral or water rights on the land or a person may have trees on private property that cannot be removed if they are protected. Property laws widely varied in both what a landowner can do in terms of removal of natural resources or development as well as what a person can do if they access land that they don't own, such as a cattle rancher who has a grazing permit on public lands.

Even if there is environmental damage under these laws, the violations will more than likely be adjudicated through an administrative procedure. Other violations can be adjudicated through civil litigation if there are contractual violations. Additionally, environmental damage can occur through other law violations, namely the Antiquities Act of 1906 and the Archeological Resources Protection Act of 1979 (ARPA) (Pub.L. 96-95; 16 U.S.C. §§470aa–470mm; 93 Stat. 721) which protects

American Indian artifacts on public lands. ARPA is defined as grave-robbing, looting, pot-hunting, vandalism, and other forms of damage to or defacement of archeological sites. Any of these activities can create significant compromise to sensitive ecological systems but rarely are environmental codes invoked as ARPA violations – like narcotics – are a strict liability crime. In other words, if a person possesses an artifact taken from a protected archeological site, simple possession is all that is required to substantiate the crime.

The investigation and prosecution of ARPA is more straightforward than environmental code violations as substantiating intent is not required under ARPA. Lastly, tribal law enforcement can enforce tribal laws that protect Indian lands and Indian artifacts taken from archeological sites under the Native American Graves Protection and Repatriation Act of 1990 (NAGPRA) (Pub.L. 101–601; 25 U.S.C. 3001–3013;104 Stat. 3048–3058). While these crimes may seem unrelated to large scale environmental crime such as ivory poaching, organized crime groups that engage in trading weapons in exchange for illicit minerals also participate in a global trade of stolen antiquities (Charney, 2018; Interpol, 2020). American Indian pots that are several hundred years old have been found being purchased by museums and private collections in Europe even while the tribe associated with the pottery proclaims the artifact as stolen (BBC, 2013; Domonoske, 2016).

Some of these items can sell for hundreds of thousands of dollars. ARPA violations are big business for organized crime and the illicit global market. The connection between trade in poached animal products and stolen antiquities has been established through object laundering schemes. Laundering is a method to trade illegal goods in legal markets through transactions that obscure the identity, origination point, and terminus point for the illegally obtained item. Laundering correlates strongly with stolen objects, such as currency, weapons, antiquities, and art. Poached animals can be laundered by labeling them as products of legal sport hunting.

Detection of these crimes is similar to environmental crimes as they may not be discovered until long after the crimes have been committed. Environmental crimes can occur in remote or rural areas that overlap with where antiquities are commonly located. The antiquities, in this case American Indian artifacts, are often located on public and tribal lands. Similarly, poaching and other environmental crimes like large scale illegal marijuana grows regularly occur on public lands in remote or rural communities. Opportunities for both crimes occur in the same or similar physical environments.

Antiquities and poached animals and plants have tremendous value because they are rare. The more endangered the animal or plant, the older and scarcer the antiquity, the more likely it is that organized crime groups will seek them out. The same methods outlined earlier, of documentation fraud, mislabeling products, and exploiting and corrupting officials, in this case art and antiquities brokers, apply to poached animals and antiquities equally. Both purveyors of stolen antiquities and poached animals and their products garner illicit items from small, localized groups who are opportunistic in their acquisition of regional contraband. Often it is members of the local community who use rudimentary tools to collect the antiquity or animal that cause environmental harms in their pursuit of quick profit. The small group then sells the item to a medium size enterprise that acts as a broker for the larger, more organized criminal network.

Similar to environmental criminal enforcement, those who enforce ARPA, NAGPRA, and the Antiquities Act typically require coordination between multiple law enforcement agencies. Tribal police, state police, Bureau of Land Management agents, Immigration and Customs Enforcement under the Department of Homeland Security, U.S. Forest Service, U.S. Fish and Wildlife Service, and the National Park Service police organize task forces to investigate crimes under these acts. While the EPA and enforcement agents from the Department of Agriculture are excluded from participation in these task forces, the prosecution of ARPA cases falls under the same division under the U.S. Department of Justice: Environmental and Natural Resources Division. The National Environmental Policy Act (1970) (42 U.S.C.A. §4321 et seq.), the Clean Air Act, the Clean Water Act, and hazardous waste laws under Comprehensive Environmental Response, Compensation, and Liability Act (CERCLA) are covered by this federal prosecution unit. So, while ARPA, NAGRPA, and Antiquities Act violations are not environmental crimes, there is overlap between the offenders, their methods, public land agencies, and the prosecutors involved in these cases and environmental crime cases. This is important for intelligence gathering operations even if the commonalities between them in terms of charges filed are disparate.

Industrial Pollution

Chapter 9 will cover industrial pollution and waste. Much of the modern environmental movement began in the United States during the late 1960s. There was considerable pollution that was notable in the air, waterways, coastal regions, lands, and various urban areas where industry had predominated for decades. The incident at Love Canal provoked public interest in hazardous waste and the ineffectiveness of the EPA in addressing it.

In 1942 in Love Canal, New York, the Hooker Chemical Company began filling an abandoned canal with 22,000 tons of hazardous waste that was packed in 55-gallon drums. The land was sold to the Niagara Falls School Board in 1953. Eventually the land was used for a housing development. In 1975 and 1976 substantial precipitation fell and caused hazardous waste storage containers to rise to the surface soil. Soon thereafter the contaminant began spreading throughout the town. The off-gassing of the hazardous material caused in-ground pools to elevate. By 1978, the state of New York declared a state of emergency and relocated 238 families from the area (Beck, 1979).

In 1980, the EPA sent two officials to the area to assess the level of toxicity in the community. Out of every 36 residents tested, 11 tested positive for chromosomal abnormalities due to toxic exposure. The residents raged against the government for failing to protect them. As a result, they took the two EPA officials hostage and refused to release them until the federal government declared the area a federal state of emergency. The federal government complied with the demand, eventually relocating an additional 710 families.

The long-term effect of the Love Canal incident was the formation of the Superfund Site program. This incident spotlighted toxic waste as a persistent and too often hidden problem resulting from years of under-regulated industries. It led directly to public demand of environmental regulatory enforcement and broader environmental awareness. Unfortunately, incidents such as the toxic waste release in Love Canal led to distrust of government. This ironically also enhanced environmental activism due to suspicions of unknown effects of chemical and waste exposure.

In 1970 the Clean Air Act was passed. In 1972 Congress passed both the Clean Water Act and the Ocean Dumping Act in attempts to curtail dumping of chemicals and industrial waste into rivers, streams, and coastal waters. These new laws entailed criminal enforcement provisions which had been lacking in previously established environmental laws. While the new laws as written could only impose criminal violations at the misdemeanor level, it was the first time a criminal violation was included in environmental regulations.

Later, the Resource Conservation and Recovery Act of 1976 (RCRA), 42 U.S.C. §6901 et seq. (1976), enabled the EPA to control hazardous waste. The law governs the generation, transportation, storage, treatment, and disposal of hazardous waste. This law has provisions for criminal violations at the felony level. The government passed these laws to ameliorate public concerns about public health. Laws were the result of social demand and recognition that the laws which had been relied upon were insufficient to address decades of industrialization.

Structure of the Text

Chapters in the text will highlight laws and case studies on the most common environmental crimes: overfishing, illegal mining, illegal timber harvesting, whaling, and wildlife trafficking. These crimes involve large scale trades and various statutes and represent civil as well as criminal violations. While the scope of these events is international, the United States provides a nexus for all the aforementioned categories of environmental crimes.

Chapter 2 of the text covers an array of theories: economic, criminological, and bureaucratic theories. As environmental crimes fall under civil, criminal, and administrative legal systems, multiple theories can address motivations and causes. Many environmental crimes are similar to white collar crimes whereby an individual exploits his/her position within lawful industries to conduct corrupt or illegal trades.

Chapter 3 of the text addresses some of the most impactful and larger environmental laws. Many were passed under the administration of President Richard M. Nixon. One of the oldest laws in the nation is the Lacey Act. Passed in 1900, this act was implemented to prevent the trafficking and taking of game animals across state lines. This law is uniquely centered in enforcement by the U.S. Fish and Wildlife Service.

Chapter 4 covers illegal, unreported, and unregulated fishing which challenges global fish stocks. While much of illegal fishing occurs outside of U.S. waters, the importation of illegally sourced and purposefully mislabeled fish is a recurring concern that various law enforcement agencies are tasked to address. Illegal harvesting of various fresh water and marine species is addressed through state conservation agencies. Examples of both federal and state enforcement and legal cases are covered in this chapter.

Chapter 5 covers wildlife trafficking. The methods of wildlife trafficking are highlighted in the chapter as well as a review of the types of criminals most likely to engage in this activity. Wildlife trafficking is a global phenomenon. The United States is the second largest consumer of illegal wildlife products, after China. The United States is also a pass-through nation for illegally harvested animal products. Various federal agencies are responsible for addressing this complex crime. Investigative methods of wildlife trade enforcement are covered.

Chapter 6 covers mining in the United States. Some of the most environmentally harmful mining occurs outside of the United States. Reports are replete with labor exploitation, environmental harms, abusive mine owners and corruption of local government officials. Yet, demand for mining products is rapidly accelerating due to legislative action to increase the use of electronic vehicles and the diminishment of fossil fuel production. This stimulates greater demand for mining. Much of the mining expansion hasn't occurred in the United States, due to bureaucratic inertia and political opposition to local mining. As a consequence, the United States imports metals and minerals that originate from illegal mines. Within the United States, environmental crimes coincide with labor violations within the domestic mining industry. This chapter will highlight cases relating to environmental crimes within the United States.

The final chapters cover whaling, forestry, and pollution. Chapter 7 addresses whaling. Although the United States does not engage in whaling, there are cases where American Indian tribes have recently been permitted to kill whales within United States' waters. The permitting was completed by the State of Washington and approved through international agreements. This case highlights the complexity of international treaties, domestic permitting, and divergence of law based on group preferences. It is detailed in this chapter. The following chapter covers some of the most prominent environmental crimes in the United States. The chapter addresses crimes within forests. There is not a lot of illegal timber harvesting in the United States. Similar to illegal mining, unlawfully harvested timber products are imported to the United States. The timber products are mislabeled so that they enter within the larger trade process. Other crimes that happen within U.S. forests include the illegal cultivation of marijuana. This is occurring at such a scale that it is creating long-term impacts on the forest ecology. The role of organized crime is highlighted. Lastly, the topic of pollution is covered in Chapter 9. Air and water pollution are the main focus of this chapter. Discussion of hazardous waste is included in this chapter.

Illegally sourced timber and fish are brought into the United States by corporations that work to usurp laws. Trafficked wildlife is poached in the United States for export overseas as well as importation of foreign poached species brought illegally into the United States. Illegally mined metals and precious metals are imported into the country and brought into the legitimate supply chain. Lastly, international organized crimes that engage in these illegal trades also engage in trade of other items trafficked into the United States: narcotics, weapons, and sex trafficking victims. Natural resource exploitation is merely one of many businesses that organized crime operate.

Environmental crimes are one element within organized crime that infiltrates financial systems throughout the world. The United States, as the primary driver of global commerce, sets the standards through its laws and enforcement. The exchange of commodities that are universally traded are impacted by American standards even if the federal government isn't directly involved. Thus, this text will approach the predominant forms of environmental crimes that occur today while explaining the laws and legal actions that attempt to address them within the United States.

References

BBC (2013, December 9). Native American Hopi artefacts sold at Paris auction. http://bbc.com/news/world-europe-25306834.

Beck, E. (1979). The Love Canal tragedy. *Environmental Protection Agency*. https://www.epa.gov/archive/epa/aboutepa/love-canal-tragedy.html.

Cagnassola, M.E. (2021, September 17). Marijuana farms accused of stealing water in Oregon as region faces extreme drought. *Newsweek*. https://www.newsweek.com/marijuana-farms-accused-of-stealing-water-oregon-region-faces-extreme-drought-1630251.

Charney, N. (2018, July 13). How the sale of stolen antiquities funds organized crime. *CNN*. http://cnn.com/style/article/europol-illegal-antiquities-organized-crime/index.html.

Domonoske, C. (2016, May 25). Native Americans protest a planned auction of sacred objects in France. *National Public Radio*. http://npr.org/sections/thetwo-way/2016/05/25/479445188/native-americans-protest-planned-auction-of-sacred-objects-in-france.

Environmental Protection Agency (n.d.) Basic information and enforcement. https://www.epa.gov/enforcement/basic-information-enforcement

Felbab-Brown, V. (2021). Pot, water theft, and environmental harms in the US and Mexico. *Brookings Institution*. http://brookings.edu/articles/pot-and-water-theft-and-enviornmental-harms-in-the-us-and-mexico.

Interpol (2020, May 6). 101 Arrested and 19,000 stolen artefacts recovered in international crackdown on art trafficking. http://interpol.int/News-and-Events/News/2020/101-arrested-and-19-000-stolen-artefacts-recovered-in-international-crackdown-on-art-trafficking.

Selsky, A. (2021, September 17). Illegal marijuana farms take West's water in "blatant theft": The grows are adding strain during a severe drought. *The Denver Post*. http://denverpost.com/2021/09/17/illegal-marijuana-farms-western-drought/.

Swan, J.A. (2016, October 27). Thin green line: The heroic work of game wardens. *American Forests*. https://americanforests.org/article/thin-green-line-the-heroic-work-of-game-wardens.

Sykes, D. (2022, December 23). Marijuana's black market is undercutting legal businesses. *CNBC*. https://cnbc.com/2022/12/23/marijuana-black-market-undercuts-legal-business.html.

Thompson, R. (2019). Illicit mining: Threats to U.S. national security and international human rights. *Federal Bureau of Investigation*. https://www.fbi.gov/news/testimony/illicit-mining-threats-to-us-national-security-and-international-human-rights-120519.

United States Agency International Development (USAID) (n.d.). Illegal logging and deforestation. https://usaid.gov/biodiversity/illegal-logging-and-deforestation.

United States Department of Justice (USDOJ) (2015, October 8). Confronting wave of illicit marijuana cultivation, federal, state and local authorities discover and destroy major marijuana grows in locations across Colorado. http://justice.gov/usao-co/pr/contronting-wave-illicit-marijuana-cultivation-federal-state-and-local-authorities.

University of California Agriculture and Natural Resources (UCANR) (n.d.). California forests. *Forest Research and Outreach*. https://ucanr.edu/sites/forestry/California_forests/.

2 Environmental Crime Theory

Introduction

Environmental crimes, like many crimes, can be analyzed through the lens of various academic theories. Due to the nature of many environmental crimes as a consequence of global trade, business operations, or regulatory violations, economic theories apply as often as criminological theories. Criminology theories are rooted in sociological theories but are more specialized as they focus on the nexus of social structures and values as a reflection of societally agreed upon rules that are formalized through government. The sociological and criminological theories will be highlighted along with the economic theories as they apply to environmental crimes.

Looking through the historical establishment of economic theories in the 17th century, there were numerous writings about nature. One of the early positions of economists and philosophers of the 17th century was that man is not in a position to evaluate the worth and value of nature. Man did not create nature and therefore cannot impose a worth or even accurate assessment of nature. The concept of environmental crimes reflects the values of nature imposed upon it by society. Environmental laws are created by those who hold certain views and impose monetary values on goods that are transported and traded. Social inquiry and observation infused within a shared ethical framework create environmental laws in the same manner that other laws are created; thus, an evaluation of law formation and legal theories can be applied to any legal category.

Green Criminology

The field of environmental or natural resource crime has not established its own theoretical perspectives. What is generally referred to as green criminology, environmental criminology, conservation criminology, or environmental justice tends to reflect and be a subset of critical criminology. Broadly, green criminology follows the concepts of biocentrism and ecocentrism. Biocentrism is a theory developed by Robert Lanza who posited that the universe is created by conscious beings which means that the universe is a living organism (Lanza and Berman, 2010). This theory was developed from a romanticized notion that all living things

DOI: 10.4324/9781003241201-2

must be considered equally. In criminology this idea was expounded upon by Harold Barnett who in 1999 wrote "The Land Ethic and Environmental Crime" which was published in Criminal Justice Policy Review (Barnett, 1999).

Barnett's ideas stem from environmentalist Aldo Leopold who published "A Sand County Almanac" in 1949. From this text, Barnett relies on the land ethic of Leopold, "a thing is right when it tends to preserve the integrity, stability, and beauty of the biotic community" (Leopold, 1949). Barnett evaluated the orthodox tenets of environmental laws – that they addressed nature as a source of human economic opportunities – and challenged them to shift from environmental harm that is sanctioned by law and environmental harm that is not sanctioned by law. Barnett's work imposes upon environmental laws which constrain human endeavors a form of ethics as described by Leopold.

Barnett extrapolates that a system of ethics can be derived from science. He believed that landowners would "recognize the realities of interdependency" with the land thus causing them to accept "self-imposed limits on their behavior" (Barnett, 1999). Barnett invokes Sutherland's Differential Association theory to Leopold's land ethic to shift behavior. He underscores Sutherland's understanding of group norms as a strong influence that could elicit behavior changes. An obvious problem with this idea is that biotic systems are not stable or static. Humans would consistently need to re-adapt to ecological fluctuations. A second and perhaps more obvious problem with applying Leopold's land ethic is that one of the underlying premises, "to preserve the beauty of the biotic community" is anything but scientific. There is no reliable objective metric which can be applied to fulfill this portion of Barnett's and Leopold's shared idea.

The second and the most common green criminology theory, ecocentrism, is based on critical theory, which is to say it is an extension of Marxist, feminist, and social ecology theories. Critical theory is often referred to and used interchangeably with post-modern theory. These theories rely heavily on a concept of universal rights, harm, and reparations (Benton, 1998; Brisman & South, 2014; Lane, 1998; Lynch, et al., 2017; Manes, 1990; Rivers & Gibbs, 2011). In the view of critical criminologists, nature becomes an exploited object whose own rights are not respected and when harm occurs that harm is passed onto the most vulnerable and exploitable. In the words of critical criminologists Stuart Henry and Dragan Milovanovic, criminology has to be aware of social constructions whose relations of power are relations of harm (Henry & Milovanovic, 1991). For the environment this means that there should be other views of the relationship between human society and the environment. This critical theoretical view is currently popular in criminology, but it is not the focus of this text. While critical theoretical approaches can be found in many social science and ecology texts, for the purpose of understanding and applying environmental laws, this text will focus on contravention of U.S. statutes.

Critical theoretical applications often move beyond statutes to include an assessment of what may or may not violate existing environmental regulations in order to assess impact of race, gender, or other statuses. The majority of current social science texts reflect critical theories and impose them onto interpretation of statutes, criminal events, and law enforcement. This academic approach is disparate from the realities of the U.S. court system, the work of park, forest and conservation rangers, and the economic incentives of transborder crime. Social post-modern theories are not reflected in data and do not apply to the context of natural resource exploitation cases that are adjudicated in various courts. Most environmental criminology texts, often referred to as green criminology, are an expansion of post-modern theories, incorporating concepts of race, sex and gender, and selected historical artifacts removed from context, to promote a theoretical construct onto environmental concerns. Texts such as *Green Criminology* written by Lynch, Long, Stretesky, and Barrett (2017) focus on the political construct of environmental justice. This is not a field within criminology as it is outside the boundaries of laws and regulations. It is based on the premise that capitalism is a source of disorganization and makes the claim that all environmental harms are the consequence of political structures of power and capitalist economies. Texts such as these are not criminological texts as they do not focus on the history and applications of environmental laws by natural resource conservation officers within the United States. All current texts in environmental crime and green criminology follow the same pattern. All integrate post-modern critical theories and impose them onto various crimes as a method to interpret social and legal transactions alongside allegations of disparities (McClanahan & Brisman, 2021; Nurse, 2016; White, 2014). As this text is not focused on politics, post-modern theory, critical race theory, and the political creations of social and environmental justice, none of these texts is referenced. This text will focus on statutes and their violations. For this reason, orthodox criminological theories will apply.

Some theories which are well suited to the topic are based on economics. Since much of environmental crime is the consequence of demand as well as ineffective regulatory schemes, underfunded policing, and limited punishment, this chapter will highlight some of the criminological and legal theories that apply to the influencing factors of natural resource crime.

Economic Theories

Natural resources are commodified, which entails the valuation of a resource in monetary terms. The resource, now a commodity, is placed into a system of trades and is exchanged for money. The commodification of natural resources can turn them into valuable global resources in a system of international trade. This transition of the resource into a saleable product can lead to the value of the commodity fluctuating with the trade markets. There is no fixed amount of goods or supply as the demand fluctuates regardless of availability of supply on the market. There are ample resources available for fishing and timber harvest, but the demands reflect preferences which fluctuate.

> In some ultimate sense, the earth has a finite amount of each resource but, even when that amount may be enough to last for centuries or millennia, at any given time the amount that is economically feasible to extract and process varies directly with the price for which it can be sold.
>
> (Sowell, 2015)

The value of a product is a higher value than the rate of money one pays for raw material and there is still cost in the transformation of raw material into a product. Also, the value of goods increases as there are more restrictions on the movement and trade of the goods (Whalen, 2010). The financial incentives of trading a product increase substantially when there is greater restriction of the availability of the goods on the market. The commodification of the rare is often embodied in the trade of endangered species. The rarity and the clandestine transfer and increased violations with the mislabeling of goods to pass through customs, increases the cost of the good, the value of the good and the demand for the good. In economic terms, "money, as the embodiment of value, is the mediating term in the interchange of use-values, while use-values are mediating terms in the movement of money" (Levine, 1978).

The value of the goods reflects the demand and availability whether it is the sale of mislabeled timber, poached fish, or illegally mined gold. The value of these goods is reflective of the restrictions placed on these items by regulations in addition to the demand on the market. If the government limits the amount of timber imports from a specific region, mislabeling of timber can occur to subvert the government's restrictions. In this way, government policy incentivizes crime as the demand for the product exceeds the government's artificially reduced supply (Tierney, 2000). Several governments throughout the world have tried to reduce the availability of rhinoceros horn by criminalizing importation of the product. While this has a substantial effect, it ignores the reality that there is still a demand for the product and no alternative has been created to redirect the demand. In a free market economy, alternatives shift supply without shifting demand. Governments and conservation workers have not created an alternative, such as the harvest and sale of deer antlers to replace the rhinoceros horn, to significantly alter the remaining demand.

With corruption of African leaders who abet the trade of rhinoceros horn, no elimination of trade in rhinoceros horn will likely occur in the near future (Kassa, et al., 2019). Economic theories focus not only on the criminals' behavior, but on the government's actions, as both the creator of incentives for and against crime. Some may assume that a corrupt government leads to greater shadow economies, but that is not always the case. "Theoretically, the relationship between corruption and the shadow economy is unsettled" (Dreher & Schneider, 2010). This statement reflects research in high-income nations such as the United States that have large scale enforcement apparatus to serve as checks within a regulatory scheme. In low-income nations, economic models demonstrate that corruption and shadow economies complement each other. Those who trade in illicit goods such as endangered species pay bribes to officials to ensure their actions are not detected by official regulatory authorities (Dreher & Schneider, 2010; Hindriks, et al., 1999).

Supply and demand

This theory is straightforward and applies to whaling, mining, fishing, and wildlife trade. There is demand for the product thus suppliers develop methods, often times breaching regulations, to meet demand. The supply may be legal but illegally obtained, as happens in poaching. The supply may be illegal at all times such as trade in elephant tusks. The supply may be legal but illegal in its transfer such as mislabeling of products to subvert quota limits. Lastly the supply can be legal but garnered illegal as in unauthorized mining operations. Since there is global demand for raw material and for materials that are limited in the availability, governments can restrict their trade as the U.S. does through ratification of the Convention on International Trade in Endangered Species of Wild Fauna and Flora (CITES) or through expansive inspection activity at ports to ensure products are properly labeled such as through Federal Insecticide, Fungicide, and Rodenticide Act (FIFRA).

The Convention on Biodiversity, a multilateral treaty signed in the Rio Earth Summit in 1992, whose aim was to promote sustainable development and signed by 150 nations, has accomplished limited results. When it comes to fish species, this Convention has not been effective. The failure of the convention with regard to the oceans is due to overfishing. Overfishing is the greatest threat to fish species throughout the world (FAO, 2016). Overfishing results from the presence of fish in the ocean and high demand for fish for consumption throughout the world. As long as there are financial incentives to trade in fish, and there are fish in the seas, there will be commercial large scale fishing due to unremitting demand. Fish provide the predominant source of protein for 35% of the world's population (Link & Watson, 2019). Researchers from the National Oceanic and Atmospheric Administration (NOAA) reviewed 64 marine ecosystems and found that those in the tropics, particularly in Southeast Asia, had the highest rates of overfishing (NOAA, 2019). Supply shifts in where the fish are sourced mirrors the economic constructs of supply and demand. The persistent demand for fish creates a market for farmed fish. Farming fish creates its own environmental impacts such as waste, effluent, and discharge of chemicals collecting on the seabed below the fish frames. There is an immediate impact on sediment dwelling creatures and complications for the regional waters such as sea lice and other diseases. "Farmed fish account for 70% of all farmed animals worldwide" (Pellman-Rowland, 2017). Between 2013 and 2021 salmon farming created $47 billion in negative externalities as measured in pollution and the processing of fish meal and fish oil from wild caught fish used to feed the farmed salmon (Just Economics, 2021). Modern aquaculture demonstrates trade-offs that are persistent in use, trade, and exploitation of natural resources.

Tragedy of the Commons

In 1968, Garret Hardin, an ecologist, published an article called "Tragedy of the Commons" in the journal, *Science* (Hardin, 1968). The tragedy of the commons is an economic and ecological challenge in that individuals have incentives to use a shared resource, thus, presenting an expense for other individuals. In shared resource systems, such as the ocean, there is no means to prevent any individual from maximizing his/her short-term benefit regardless of long-term consequence. In the example of the oceans as a common, tragedy of the commons is observable. Fishing companies maximize their fishing catch, especially when they offload their catch in a port that does not conduct inspections, has sufficient inspections, or has corrupt port regulators. If the United States fishing companies uphold fishing limits imposed by U.S. regulators, but fishing companies from China, Indonesia, and Norway do not abide by fishing moratoriums or limits, then the fish population can become depleted or compromised. The world's fishing industry suffers from the tragedy of the commons. Approximately 100 million tons of fish are taken from the world's oceans each year (FAO, 2016; Pellman-Rowland, 2017). The attitude that pervades many fishermen and fishing companies is, "if I don't catch these fish, someone else will" (Pires & Moreto, 2011).

International agreements such as CITES (Convention on International Trade in Endangered Species of Wild Fauna and Flora) may reduce the global trade of some prohibited items such as elephant tusks but CITES cannot regulate trade within a nation like China. Large scale economies like China can generate enough demand that international regulatory schemes become ineffectual. In the United States, the government has been responsible for both increasing the over-exploitation of a resource such as lobster (*Homarus americanus*) and cod (*Gadus*), while also effectively protecting resources such as eels (*Anguilla rostrata*). Government policies are inconsistent with regard to conservation of species due to the myriad of priorities across different industries and special interest groups. Adding that government policies shift every four to eight years depending on who wins presidential elections, leads to challenges for long-term forecasting of resource populations. Lastly, government catch quotas are not always sufficient for long-term conservation goals (Nijman, 2010; Pires & Moreto, 2011).

Moral Hazards

Moral hazards can develop when an organization increases risk exposure through a transaction in order to maximize profit even when the entity may not have to absorb the repercussions of taking that risk. If that business is engaging in a risky transaction, it may do so if someone else has to absorb the negative consequences. In economics, the transaction is the consequence of information asymmetry. The imbalanced information often stimulates the company to take even greater risks. Classic examples are people who are insured taking greater risks when they are driving than those who aren't insured. Also, the banking system in 2008 which was "too big to fail" relied on taxpayer funded bailouts. Essentially profit was privatized while risk was placed onto the taxpayer. In fishing, this is measured in illegal, unreported, and unregulated fishing (IUU) which is estimated to be 20–30% of the global catch (Pramod, et al., 2014). Opaque supply chains and food processing offshore enable imports into the United States with virtually no likelihood of being identified (Pramod, et al., 2014). This is an example of a moral hazard within natural resource trade.

In natural resources, moral hazard applies to poaching and mislabeling of natural resources such as timber or fish. Those who collect species en masse without regard to the capacity of the species to reproduce and sustain its population engage in a moral hazard. The poacher or the importer who mislabels fish or timber may suffer as the number of available stock in the future diminishes. The ecological system suffers the moral hazard. Additionally, conservation groups that work to promote biological diversity spend funds to recuperate forests or fish stocks. The cost of the biological species lost is often borne by those who depend on the ecosystem as a whole, by conservation groups who invest funds in recovery of lost ecosystems, and those who use those natural resources for immediate survival.

Another example of moral hazard is outlined in Chapter 8 on forestry. The chapter highlights, among other topics, illegal marijuana grows in national forests. Due to the proliferation of illegal grows water wells on private lands in northern California are contaminated with banned pesticides and herbicides that were banned decades ago due to these chemicals' persistent neurotoxicity (Battaglia, 2022; Medel, et al., 2022). The inhabitants of northern California who use private water wells for their water sources are being exposed to toxins as a result of the illegal marijuana grows on public lands. The neurotoxin exposure is a moral hazard borne by California residents whereby organized crime members profit from the illegal grows.

Another moral hazard that is common within environmental laws is the promotion of regulatory schemes by non-profit organizations. When environmental organizations are able to impose greater restrictions and regulations on industries such as mining, timber, agriculture, and chemical manufacturing, an immediate consequence is that the increased costs shouldered by industry are often passed to consumers. Additionally, smaller companies that operate at higher costs due to economies of scale are often driven to closure. The moral hazard of increased rules and regulations is that smaller business and consumers pay the costs of the regulatory schemes.

There is also a paradoxical effect. The environment may or may not benefit from the new regulations, but consumers and commerce are directly impacted by consolidation. A smaller group of interested parties has a more direct effect on governmental regulations. An example of this is the use of ethanol, a corn product, in fuel. The production of ethanol was supposed to reduce U.S. dependence on foreign fuel sources and reduce greenhouse gases. In 2006, a study published by the Proceedings of the National Academy of Sciences demonstrated that the use of ethanol does not substantially reduce the use of gasoline, reduce greenhouse gas emissions, and does not reduce U.S. dependence on foreign fuel sources (Hill, et al., 2006). The negative effects of government mandated ethanol fuel sources increased corn production that caused increased runoff of pesticides and fertilizers where corn is grown. Growing corn for ethanol is not a net benefit to the nation or the environment; yet the Congressional officials have not rescinded the ethanol mandate (Runge, 2016). The reason is that ethanol is an effective topic employed in political campaigns in states like Iowa where corn is grown. This political yielding to a small interest group creates ineffective policies despite a lack of significant evidence that the policy is environmentally productive. Political actors are far less effective at reducing environmental harms than enforcement of environmental laws that were established for decades. The reason is that environmental laws are clearly delineated, such as a specified fine or imprisonment for importation of an endangered species, whereas projections of environmental outcomes based on political interests are conveyed as universally beneficial even when there is insufficient evidence to support it. In the case of ethanol, use of E85 fuel in "flex-fuel vehicles may increase ozone-related mortality, asthma and hospitalizations by 4% compared to gasoline" (Jacobson, 2007).

Say's Law

Jean-Baptiste Say (1767–1832), a French economist, wrote in "Treatise on Political Economy" that when a majority of a population is employed, there will be a demand for products. Effectively he wrote that "supply creates its own demand" (Sowell, 2015). In many ways we can see this with the demand for goods such as wildlife products, specific fish, and preferred timber products. As wealth has accelerated globally and worldwide poverty has effectively been reduced, demands for products has consistently increased. Today 10% of the global population live in extreme poverty (UN, n.d.) In 1990 the total global population living in extreme poverty was 35% (World Bank, 2017). In China, 966 million people were living in poverty. By 2013, that number had fallen to 71 million (World Bank, 2017). As the middle and upper classes of China have expanded, so has the demand for products such as bear bile and ivory. Say's Law, in this case, would imply that production comes first and demand follows. Since wildlife products are available on the market, there is a demand for these items. Under Say's Law, the demand does not precede the supply; the supply stimulates the demand. There are many individuals with discretionary income; therefore, a status or culturally important item becomes desirable and in demand. In many cases of environmental crimes, this classic macroeconomic theory may well apply.

Legal Theories

Focusing on economic growth and development as a cause of environmental harm is often a misplaced idea. The legal system has expanded the rights of nature through expanding environmental protections through civil, administrative, criminal, and property laws. The laws are expanded through state legislatures, federal Congress, and through legal precedent in court.

Foundational arguments that nature should have equal rights to man were based on a legal argument of who should have legal standing to speak on behalf of nature. In legal cases, a person who brings a case to trial has to be a party to the case, in other words, that person should show that s/he was harmed as a direct consequence of someone's actions or neglect. The argument that nature should have rights was posited in a law article entitled, "Should Trees Have Standing?" by Christopher D. Stone published in Southern California Law Review in 1972. This article was a reaction to a legal case that went to the U.S. Supreme Court, *Sierra Club v. Morton* (1972a and b). This case was brought by an environmentalist group, the Sierra Club, against the U.S. Secretary of the Interior Rogers Clark Ballard Morton. The Sierra Club was attempting to block the development of a ski resort in the Sequoia National Forest in the Sierra Nevada Mountains. The U.S. Court of Appeals in California as well as the U.S. Supreme Court decided that the environmental organization did not have legal standing in the case as it had not been injured (405 U.S. 727 (1972)).

Stone's legal argument in the law review journal was that there were other instances in which non-human entities were enjoined by legal rights: corporations, joint ventures, municipalities, and ships. Stone, therefore, argued that ecosystems and trees could also have rights. This idea later became accepted by legal scholars and became a pivotal argument in the environmental movement. The limit of this argument is that it is separate from animal rights. Ecological rights could be extended to groups like the Sierra Club but a specific species' rights could not. In the case, *CEASE (Citizens to End Animal Suffering and Exploitation), Kama, et al. v. New England Aquarium (1993)*, at issue was the right of a dolphin, Kama, born in captivity at Sea World, then transferred to the New England Aquarium in Boston, Massachusetts. The dolphin, Kama, did not fit into the aquarium so it was transferred to a U.S. naval installation where it was used in sonar capabilities studies. The animal rights group CEASE sued the aquarium. The U.S. District Court ruled that in the Marine Mammal Protection Act, Congress did not grant status to the animals specifically; therefore, CEASE did not have standing to sue as the animal rights group did not suffer "injury in fact" and the dolphin didn't have an individual right (Doyle, 1996).

Environmental laws are in a different context than other form of laws as there is a baseline understanding that law by itself doesn't address issues of conservation, ecological processes, or species sustainability. These constructs are decided through biologists who specialize in topics like marine fisheries or through political special interest groups operating as environmental non-government organizations (NGOs). Representatives from the NGOs tend to demand more results from legal systems, neglecting to recognize that many environmental problems are the result of diffuse and multiple causes over time and that the environmental group may not always have legal standing to sue.

Even when injured parties are identified, events that are diffuse and not directly causal are hard to prosecute in a court of law. The case of Toms River, New Jersey is a classic example. In this case, industrial waste was secretly dumped in the 1970s onto a three-acre parcel of land, known as Reich Farm (Sucato, 2001). In 1971, over 4,500 drums of chemical waste were illegally dumped on the property (New Jersey Health, n.d.). There was a spike in childhood cancer in the 1980s and 1990s. Scientists suspected styrene-acrylonitrile trimer (SAN trimer). Years of studies on SAN trimer indicated that the substance did not cause cancer in rats. As a consequence, after decades of research into various industrial compounds, none are found to be causal to the cancer cluster. The residents of Toms River, New Jersey are no closer to definitive answers as to the cause of the cancer today than they were years ago (Nazaryan, 2013).

Criminal Justice Theories

Bureaucracy Theory

In 1969, Donald Cressey wrote in *Theft of the Nation*, that organized crime is a bureaucracy with divisions of labor, hierarchy, codes of conduct, and sanctions within the organization for malfeasance by members (Cressey, 2009). Cressey's ideas are based on sociologist Max Weber's 1905 theory of bureaucracy explained in his text *The Protestant Ethic and the Spirit of Capitalism* (Weber, 2013). Bureaucracy is the term applied to a structure and administrative process of an organization where there are known rules, processes, procedures, and delineation of authority in order to reduce complexities of how a bureaucracy functions. Unlike most property and street level crimes, which are open to everyone, most roles are not filled by any criminal. The positions are specialized in their tasking as well as the selection of who fulfills each role. In a bureaucracy, positions are defined by their role and who can fulfill the role in a similar way.

The theory applies to organized crime networks that prevail in weak states. Historically, organized crime groups existed prior to the formation of a strong state: Sicilian Mafia, Hong Kong Triads, Japanese Yakuza, and Russian Organized Crime. In modern China, organized crime operates through bribery and control of regional political offices, far removed from the centralized government in China. Organized crime follows bureaucratic theory in that it pursues various profitable enterprises efficiently and can fluctuate to maximize profit through adapting to transit crime (Kleemans, 2013).

Traditionally, organized crime controlled a local enterprise such as prostitution or numbers running and, in the case of environmental crimes, waste dumping (this will be covered in Chapter 9). By the twenty-first century, organized crime has moved into the realm of transnational crime. Most crimes that organized crime engages in are transit crimes: drug smuggling, weapons trafficking, human trafficking, and wildlife trade.

Transit crimes are far more sophisticated than most other crimes in that it compels sophisticated logistics, money transfers that are electronic, and capacity to conceal activities from port and customs authorities. Currently, organized crime groups are more profitable in transit crimes that transcend jurisdictions and do not require corruption of local officials or law enforcement.

> Transit crime does not require corruption. In fact, it may benefit from reliable government and an excellent infrastructure for the transportation of legal (and illegal) goods, a transit country such as the Netherlands being a prime example. This means that foreign criminal groups have better opportunities to operate in these open, developed economies than in isolated areas.
>
> (Kleemans, 2013)

The modern organized crime group operating in environmental crimes is able to transfer large, expensive commodities such as rhinoceros horn and elephant ivory, or import large amounts of fish that are either a protected species or from protected waters, or provide the sophisticated coordination of various operators across more than one continent required by the extraction of timber that is moved across multiple jurisdictions. Movement and trade across multiple jurisdictions require proficiency in understanding importation laws, restrictions on goods, and dexterity in responding to supply and demand.

Deterrence Theory

Criminal penalties resulting from prosecution of environmental crimes cannot become simply another cost of doing business. They must be substantive enough for criminal actors to acknowledge risk that is not easily offset through the commission of the crime. Generally, criminal punishment, due to insufficient inspection and enforcement, presents limited risk for environmental crimes. Consequently, the level of deterrence tends to be low for the poachers, endangered species importers, and illegal mine operators. In criminological theory, one of the original and most impactful theories was written by the philosopher Cesare Beccaria in 1764. Beccaria wrote a text called *On Crimes and Punishment* in which he states that individuals have free will and choose their actions. He emphasized the rule of law, proportionality, lenience, and rationality in the legal process. While Beccaria was initiating criminological theory, his emphasis was on penology – how people should be punished for their crimes.

One of the most impactful aspects of this revolutionary text was Beccaria's declaration that punishment "must be swift, severe, and certain" (Beccaria, 2016). Beccaria's belief was that people were motivated to commit crime via a calculation of pleasure acquired through its commission versus the pain one would experience from being caught and prosecuted. The legal system must balance motivation for crime with a consequence that has an impact that creates more pain than the reward is worth. If the punishment is "swift, severe, and certain" then a person is far less likely to commit a crime. The government must create a legal environment in which the criminal fears the results of the crime commission. Beccaria's theory came to be known as "classical theory" in criminology as it was part of the classical school of thought which included Voltaire and Jean-Jacques Rousseau in France and Jeremy Bentham in England. It led directly to the concept of deterrence and deterrence theory. A person who abides by the law for fear of repercussions, regardless of how remote, is experiencing general deterrence. If laws are routinely enforced there is general deterrence for the majority of the population. If criminal penalties are enhanced each time a person commits a crime, the person experiences specific deterrence. This reflects an individualization of punishment.

Differential Association Theory

Edwin Sutherland, an early criminologist, wrote his seminal work, *Criminology*, in 1924. Prior to Sutherland's work, crime was associated with economics or biological and psychological causes. Sutherland was the first to proclaim that crime is the consequence of learned behavior. He chose to view crime through proximate causes that can be observed. Sutherland argued that a person's social circle and environment influences his values. A person often has to learn how to commit a crime: techniques, timing, location, and methods. An individual's friends or those who share relationships with him can dispense technical information but also values.

If an individual hears messages about crime that are favorable and messages that law abidance is unfavorable, and highly values the person providing these messages, it is more likely that the individual will become a criminal. Elevated intensity, duration, and frequency of messages from a trusted and valued source enable an individual to prioritize law violations over law abidance. In this manner, individuals learn criminal behavior in the same way other behaviors and values are learned. Societal norms are not shared equally across all of society. Some will absorb positive messaging about deviant behavior and this will be the norm within that individual's social network. A person can learn and adapt the attitudes of those they admire, respect, and emulate. Thus, the social norm that people follow rules and laws is overtly rejected by those who do not share those values. Under Sutherland's Differential Association Theory, law violation is a choice that reflects a value system that rejects law abidance. People choose to commit crime as a consequence of learned behavior from those whose opinions, behaviors, and attitudes are shared with the criminal offender. Since the majority of environmental crimes require planning and directed execution, applying theories reflecting social learning seems an appropriate fit.

The principles of Edwin Sutherland are:

1. All criminal behavior is considered to be a learned behavior.
2. Criminal behaviors are learned through the interactions that one person has with others through variable communication processes.
3. The principle component of the learning process for criminal behaviors occurs within the intimate personal circles and relationships of the individual.
4. The learning process for criminal behavior can include many different components. This may include specific techniques that can be used to commit a crime. It may include specific motives and rationalizations. It can also include the attitudes which are necessary to go against what is considered a societal norm.
5. The direction of motives and drives is learned from the favorable or unfavorable interpretation of the legal codes which exist in that person's jurisdictions.
6. People choose to become criminals because there is an excessive number of favorable conclusions to violating the law compared to the unfavorable conclusions that they are able to determine.
7. Differential associations can be extremely variable. They may vary in intensity, priority, duration, and frequency.
8. The process of learning criminal behaviors through association involves the same mechanisms that people use for all other types of learning.
9. Criminal behavior may be an express of generalized values or needs, but it is not explained by those needs since non-criminal behaviors have the same requirements.

(Siegel, 2019)

Organized Crime Theory

Illegal enterprise theory is one of the prominent theories that applies to organized crime. It demonstrates similarities between legal and illegal enterprises.

The organized crime members can be viewed as rational, profit-focused entrepreneurs, who are involved in activities that, though illegal, are a response to supply and demand. While governments constrain and make trade of specific goods illegal, such as trade in elephant ivory, the demand doesn't go away simply because a governing body decided to make the product illegal. The trade continues, but the cost of the trade increases due to higher risks, which compels higher prices and draws in entrepreneurs who are willing to assume the risks. The organized crime operator often exploits criminogenic asymmetries, meaning they garner profits by exploiting differences between laws and regulations of different jurisdictions (Passas, 1999).

The original focus of organized crime theories was based on gambling, running numbers, and loan sharking. These are predominantly small, local enterprises. Most organized crime theorists and researchers focus on a local organized crime group rather than a transnational organized group that transfers goods such as rhino horn, illegally harvested timber, or mislabeled fish. These environmental crimes involve multiple jurisdictions over extended periods of time. Also, environmental crime, when it comes to illegally harvesting timber, plants, and/or animals in conservation areas, often involves bribery of officials in the affected country. Transacting with corrupt officials is reflective of organized crime origins and prevalence. Organized crime thrives where there is weak central government and lax enforcement of laws. The Sicilian Mafia and Japanese Yakuza – which existed prior to a strong centralized nation-state of modern Italy and Japan – both developed in locations and times when there was weak government (Paoli, 2003; Varese, 2011). This continues to be true in locations where illegal timber (in Asia and Africa) and ivory (in Africa) are harvested. With regard to fishing, studies demonstrate that organized crime is able to poach much further from littoral waters and act as professional poachers since they have technology and equipment for large scale harvests in deeper waters. In contrast, local poachers tend to be opportunistic and poach along the coastline (Pires & Moreto, 2011; Saffron, 2002)

Merton's Strain Theory

In 1938, Robert Merton applied Emile Durkheim's (1893) ideas of anomie, which is a foundational idea in classic sociological theory, to criminology. Durkheim's idea of anomie is social instability that results from a breakdown of values and norms (Siegel, 2019). Merton expanded the idea of anomie and it became a framework for a category of social and criminological theory known as strain theory. Strain Theory views society as a cohesive group as the majority of the people adhere to laws. The strain in society is created when some members of the society commit crime when there are insufficient legitimate opportunities for them to achieve success goals of a society. According to this theory there is a "strain" between the goals and means to achieve those goals. As argued by Merton, there are three assumptions to this theory: there is a cohesive set of norms in society, the norms are agreed upon by society, there are agreed upon reactions to deviance of the norms. These assumptions are based on social conditions rather than individual decisions.

Merton's ideas are broken down into five assumptions referred to as social adaptation:

> Conformity: individuals embrace conventional social goals and have or pursue legitimate means to obtain the goals. Thus, they choose to conform. This group is law abiding.
>
> Innovation: individuals embrace conventional social goals and lack legitimate methods of achieving the goals. Thus, they choose to violate laws. This group is most commonly associated with criminality.
>
> Ritualism: individuals gain pleasure from practicing traditional ceremonies regardless of whether there is a goal or a purpose. This category is reflected not only in religious groups, but also feudal societies, college fraternities, and clubs.
>
> Retreatism: individuals reject goals and methods of attaining those goals in society. This category is associated with drug users, cultists, and transient populations.
>
> Rebellion: individuals in this category choose to substitute goals or methods with alternative goals or methods. Examples within this category include alternative lifestyles such as polygamous families, or terrorists that seek to replace conventional social structures and rules with a separate set of structures and rules.
>
> (Shram & Tibbets, 2020; Siegel, 2019)

The problem with applying this theory generally is that for each person who commits crime there will be many people in the same economic class that do not choose to commit crime. This theory enables policy makers to overestimate crime in the lower socioeconomic classes and underestimate crime in the middle and upper socioeconomic classes. In terms of environmental crimes, there are game wardens, customs officers, and executives in companies like Gibson Guitars that knowingly imported endangered woods that were purposefully mislabeled, electing to commit crimes despite adequate incomes and status in their social circles.

Other complications in applying strain theories are that it relies on economics as the foundational argument which does not explain violent crime. It also does not explain many environmental crimes. It doesn't explain greed in cases where a fish importer, who already has legitimate income and legitimacy within society, may choose to mislabel imported fish that are a protected species in order to maximize profit. The theory also denies the reality that there are opportunities for income and legitimacy for those who work toward conservation, whether that is in the form of working as a game warden, conservation advocate for non-profits that promote conservation areas, or as a tour guide in an ecological preserve.

Rational Choice Theory

In 1979 Lawrence Cohen and Marcus Felson developed a theory that assumes that there will always be people who are willing to commit crime, regardless of their motives (greed, revenge, self-promotion within gangs, etc.). Under their theory what stimulates the crime is a combination of three factors that are present at one time: a motivated offender, a suitable target without the presence of a capable guardian. The capable guardian can be in the form of parental supervision, alarm systems, security guards, police officers, watchful neighbors, camera and surveillance systems, or simply the presence of other people (Kitteringham & Fennelly, 2020). This crime theory reflects opportunistic crime which encompasses substantive amounts of crime. While this theory often is applied to street crime, such as burglary, and juvenile crimes, as juveniles commit crime when they are not supervised by adults, it also applies to white-collar crime. In the context of environmental crime, mislabeling of fish and other animal and plant species including timber, poaching, and deforestation that accompanies illegal marijuana grows on forest lands, occur within the context of a motivated offender, suitable target, and a sustained absence of an effective guardian. Many environmental crimes are committed in response to demand for a natural resource product or products grown unlawfully on public lands, with a profit as the key motivation. The likelihood of being caught and prosecuted for such crimes is quite small.

Offenders are attracted to these crimes through opportunities such as living or working proximal to lands and seas where there are high demand products. There are lucrative markets for the products derived from natural environments creating the motive of greed. While some criminologists argue that poverty is a motive for greed, this is demonstrably untrue. Impoverished urban neighborhoods tend to have access to more money and programs than impoverished rural environments yet the urban neighborhoods have much higher rates of crime than rural communities (NCJRS, 2017). This may be reflected in social learning theories such as Sutherland's differential association theory or due to routine activities theory as there are more capable guardians in a rural setting as community members don't enjoy the anonymity that comes with urban living. In rural communities most people tend to know each other and interact on a personal rather than anonymous level. This enhances the presence of capable guardians.

In environmental crimes such as exportation of endangered species or their parts, this action is conducted through an expansive system of trade where customs officers inspect a small portion of goods imported. Other environmental crimes, such as deforestation, illegal fish catches, illegal marijuana grows on public lands, illegal mining, and illegal dumping, often occur well outside areas that are monitored or surveilled. The likelihood of being caught committing these crimes is substantively lower in remote locations that have limited enforcement agents. For these crimes, routine activities theory can apply.

Various Forms of Environmental Crimes Enforcement

The United States employs criminal sanctions to enforce environmental standards. While some may find this ideal as a method to induce deterrence, a more effective method to prevent environmental crimes and promote environmental standards is the application of audits. Enforcement that involves fines and civil penalties for violations and demanding recompense for federal funds spent on remediation of harmed environments are effective tools in punishing criminal offenses under the Natural Resources Division of the U.S. Department of Justice Environmental Enforcement Section.

With an increase in enforcement via the Natural Resources Division, which was created in 1981, the federal government collected large criminal fines and civil penalties to offset public expenditure for the mitigation of environmental damage. Criminal enforcement reduces moral hazard. In the 1990s there were some of the most impactful environmental crime cases prosecuted by the EPA. They include the Exxon Valdez accident in Alaska whereby the company paid a $125 million fine and an additional $500 million in punitive damages as a consequence of an accidental release of 10.8 million gallons of crude oil in 1989 in violation of the Clean Water Act, the Refuse Act of 1899, and the Migratory Bird Treaty Act (Rohrman, 2008). Additionally, four top executives of the Iroquois Pipeline Operation Company pled guilty to violation the Clean Water Act during construction of a 375 miles natural gas pipeline from Ontario, Canada to Long Island, New York. The company agreed to pay $22 million in criminal fines and civil penalties. The company was also required to rehabilitate thirty wetlands and streams in upstate New York. The construction permit issued by the U.S. Army Corps of Engineers required that the pipeline company restore all affected wetlands. The company failed to do so, causing harm to the wetlands' capacities to hold water (Environmental Protection Agency, 1996).

The federal government recognizes the limits of the enforcement division of the EPA and augments enforcement which is a lengthy and costly process with voluntary compliance imposed through regulations imposed on companies in industries such as manufacturing and agriculture. Individual cases of environmental harm such as the Iroquois Pipeline Operating Company are highlighted by activists and the media to indicate the inefficiencies of voluntary compliance; however, compliance programs prevent environmental harms on a broad scale. Compliance requires industry representatives to routinely file environmental compliance reports to governmental agencies. Compliance programs often compel multiple permits and documentation submission throughout the operationalization of a project such as a pipeline construction.

Disrupting processes through compliance benchmarks mitigates environmental harm before projects are complete. Identifying mislabeled fish and punishing the importer may be a deterrent to other fish importers but it doesn't spare the fish that were illegally caught and transferred. Compliance programs, such as the Commercial Vessel Compliance Program operated by the U.S. Coast Guard, compels fishing vessels to be inspected for vessel safety. Additionally, the Coast Guard employs outreach, training, dockside examinations, and at-sea boardings to ensure that vessels operate at standards. This program mitigates injuries and death at sea as well as environmental hazards caused by vessel damage and losses at sea.

Additionally, the government has a high standard and legal burden to enter and inspect private property. Many of the crimes relating to pollution involve inspection of private property. EPA officials are required to obtain administrative search warrants to enter private property for audit and investigative activities. This process takes time and compels government officials to collect substantial evidence to persuade a federal judge that the agency should search for evidence of a crime. There have been several environmental criminal cases where evidence was suppressed because soil and water samples were collected without consent of a company, violating the Fourth Amendment. In the case of *Boliden Metech, Inc. v. United States*, 695 F. Supp. 77 (D.R.I. 1988), Boliden Metech, Inc., a company that reclaimed precious metals, was accused of releasing polychlorinated biphenyls (PCBs) into nearby land and riparian systems. EPA officials collected soil and water samples without consent of the company. The federal court ruled that the data derived from the collected samples could not be used since the company's Fourth Amendment rights were violated. The company did not consent to state officials collecting material from their property. There was no administrative warrant issued at the time the samples were collected; therefore, two of the three counts the EPA had against Boliden Metech, Inc. were dismissed by the court as a consequence.

Criminal enforcement happens after the crime occurs. It can only prevent crimes through deterrence but the effect of deterrence is limited, particularly in parts of the world where poaching and illegal catches are common. As long as there is high demand, there will be individuals or companies that are willing to provide supply. The criminological theories explain motivations for crimes whereas the legal structures can create obstacles through punishment and compliance programs. The government's capacity to broaden enforcement through civil, administrative, and criminal law systems enable more efficient environmental protections than strict reliance on criminal codes.

Conclusion

Various theories can be used to explain environmental crimes. As there are various types of environmental crimes, different theories will apply. The range of crime relating to environmental laws and regulations often cross jurisdictions, and involve multiple people, some knowingly and intentionally while others incidentally. The theories relating to economics and organized crime appear to be aligned more closely with the movement of animals, plants, and their parts across the globe, while local dumping of pesticides might align more with rational choice theory. Some crime theories apply while others present challenges as a clean fit. Enforcement of state regulations relating to capture and sale of animals and plants is more aligned with other regulatory enforcement such as the sale of alcohol or cigarettes. Applying criminological theories or economic theories does not assist judicial decisions as most environmental crimes are strict liability crimes: if a person is in possession of a prohibited item, the person is guilty through possession. Mislabeling hazardous waste, pesticides, timber products, or imported fish can be examples of strict liability crimes but most often these offenses are handled administratively through regulatory agencies.

Most environmental crimes are handled through administrative and civil courts; thus, the application of criminal theory may be less significant in this category of crimes than other categories of crime. Theory informs policy and research; thus, theories are important in trying to explain what motivates individuals to commit crimes. For those interested in preventing environmental crimes, studying economics of commodities may be more beneficial than individual motives since most environmental crimes require planning and preparing logistics. Simply preserving lands or waterways in the form of conservation areas is insufficient to protect species and ecosystems. Demanding reduced consumption resulting from governmental dictums does not seem to substantively reduce harvest and trade of the targeted good. Theories that combine understanding of economics and organized crime will likely be the most productive in generating directed policy to mitigate environmental crimes.

Discussion Questions

1. Which category of theories is most applicable to explain environmental crimes – economic or criminal? Explain why.
2. Sutherland's Differential Association Theory shows us that not everyone shares the same values. Those who choose to commit crime due so because they associate their values with law violating behavior. Is this theory sufficient to explain wildlife trade or poaching?
3. Criminal behavior can be explained by various theories. Does one type of theory lend itself to environmental crime?
4. Can environmental crimes be explained by rational rejection of state requirements due to the costs imposed by governmental regulatory schemes?
5. What explains why government agencies are less likely to fund enforcement of environmental crimes?

Further Reading Recommendations

1. Hussen, A. (2018). *Principles of environmental economics and sustainability: An integrated economic and ecological approach* (4th ed.). Routledge.
2. Landsburg, S.E. (2012). *The armchair economist: Economics and everyday life.* Free Press.
3. Lilly, J.R., Cullen, F.T., & Ball, R.A., (2018). *Criminological theory: Context and Consequences* (7th ed.). Sage Publications.
4. Mixon, F.G. (2019). The modern theory of bureaucracy. In *A terrible efficiency.* Palgrave.
5. Payne, B.K. (2021). *White-collar crime: A systems approach* (3rd ed.) Sage Publications.

References

Barnett, H. (1999). The land ethic and environmental crime. *Criminal Justice Policy Review, 10* (2), 161–192.

Battaglia, R. (2022, December 15). Pesticides from illegal cannabis are contaminating California waterways, survey says. *Jefferson Public Radio.* https://ijpr.org/environment-

energy-and-transportation/2022-12-15/pesticides-from-illegal-cannabis-are-contaminating-california-waterways-survey-says.
Beccaria, C. (2016). *On crimes and punishments.* Transaction Publishers.
Benton, T. (1998). Rights and justice on a shared planet: More rights or new relations. *Theoretical Criminology, 2* (2), 149–176.
Brisman, A. & South, N. (2014). *Green cultural criminology: Constructions of environmental harm, consumerism, and resistance to ecocide.* Taylor & Francis.
Cressey, D. (2009). *Theft of the nation: The structure and operations of organized crime in America.* Routledge.
Doyle, M.A. (1996). *CEASE v. New England Aquarium*: Standing to challenge marine mammal permits. *Ocean and Coastal Law Journal, 2* (1). https://digitalcommons.mainelaw.marine.edu/oclj/vol2/iss1/7.
Dreher, A. & Schneider, F. (2010). Corruption and the shadow economy: an empirical analysis. *Public Choice, 144* (1–2), 215–238.
Environmental Protection Agency (1996, May 24). PA Iroquois Pipeline Co. to pay second largest environmental penalty ever. https://epa.gov/archive/epapages/newsroom_archives/newsreleases/dda8ede-4015b99318525646c00509072.html.
Hardin, G. (1968). The tragedy of the commons: The population problem has no technical solution; it requires a fundamental extension in morality. *Science, 162* (3859), 1243–1248.
Henry, S. & Milovanovic, D. (1991). Constitutive criminology: The maturation of critical theory. *Criminology, 29* (2), 293–316.
Hill, K., Nelson, E., Tilman, D., Polasky, S., & Tiffany, D. (2006). Environmental, economic, and energetic costs and benefits of biodiesel and ethanol biofuels. *Proceedings of the National Academy of Science.* https://pnas.org/doi/pdf/10.1073/pnas.0604600103.
Hindriks, J., Muthoo, A., & Keen, M. (1999). Corruption, extortion and evasion. *Journal of Public Economics, 74* (3), 395–430.
Jacobson, M.Z. (2007). Effects of ethanol (E85) versus gasoline vehicles on cancer and mortality in the United States. *Environmental Science and Technology, 41* (11), 4150–4157. https://doi.org/101021/es062085v.
Just Economics (2021, February). Dead loss: The high cost of poor farming practices and mortalities on salmon farms. https://Justeconomics.co.uk/health-and-well-being/dead-loss.
Kassa, S., Costa, J., & Camargo, C.B. (2019). Corruption and wildlife trafficking: Exploring drivers, facilitators and networks behind illegal wildlife trade in East Africa. *Basel Institute on Governance.* https://baselgovernance.org/sites/default/files/2019-07/WP30_CorruptionandIWT_0.pdf.
Kitteringham, G. & Fennelly, L.J. (2020). Environmental crime control. In *Handbook of loss prevention and crime prevention* (6th ed., pp. 207–222). http://doi.org/10.1016/B978-0-12-817273-5.00019-3.
Kleemans, E.R. (2013). Theoretical perspectives on organized crime. *Oxford handbook of organized crime.* Oxford University Press. https://doi.org/10.1093/oxfordhb/9780199730445.0.13.005.
Lane, P. (1998). Ecofeminism meets criminology. *Theoretical Criminology, 2* (2), 235–248.
Lanza, R. & Berman, B. (2010). *Biocentrism: How life and consciousness are the keys to understanding the true nature of the universe.* BenBella Books.
Leopold, A. (1949). *A Sand County almanac.* Oxford University Press.
Levine, D.P. (1978). *Economic theory.* Routledge.
Link, J.S. & Watson, R.A. (2019). Global ecosystem overfishing: Clear delineation within real limits to production. *Science Advances, 4* (6). DOI: 10.1126.sciadv.aav0474.

Lynch, M., Long, M., Stretesky, P.B., & Barrett, K.L. (2017). *Green criminology*. University of California Press.

Manes, C. (1990). *Green rage: Radical environmentalism and the unmaking of civilization.* Little Brown and Company.

McClanahan, B. & Brisman, A. (2021). *Green criminology.* Mdpi AG.

Medel, I.D., Gabriel, M.W., Wengert, G.M., Filigenzi, M.S., & Clifford, D. (2022). Passive monitoring of soluble pesticides linked to cannabis cultivation: A multi-scale analysis. *Water Quality Research Journal, 57* (4), 233–246. https://doi.org/10.2166.wqrj.2022.101.

Nassaro, M.R.F. (2017). Wildlife trafficking in the state of São Paolo, Brazil. In D. Rodríguez Goyes, H. Mol, A. Brisman, & N. South (Eds.), *Environmental crime in Latin America: The theft of nature and the poisoning of the land* (pp. 245–260). Palgrave Macmillan.

National Criminal Justice Reference Service (NCJRS) (2017). Urban and rural victimization. https://ncjrs.gov/ovc_archives/ncvrw/2017/images/en_artwork/Fact_Sheets/2017-NCVRW_UrbanRural_508.pdf.

National Oceanic and Atmospheric Administration (NOAA) (2019, June26). New indicators could help manage global overfishing. https://fisheries.noaa.gov/feature-story/new-indicators-could-help-manage-global-overfishing.

Nazaryan, A. (2013, May 24). A town plagued by water. *New Yorker.* https;//newyorker.com/tech/annals-of-technology/a-town-plagued-by-water.

New Jersey Health (n.d.). Toms River Township childhood cancer investigation. *Department of Health.* https://nj.gov/health/ceohs/enviornmental-occupational/hazardous-waste-sites/ocean/dovertwp.shtml.

Nijman, V. (2010). An overview of international wildlife trade from Southeast Asia. *Biodiversity & Conservation, 19* (4), 1101–1114.

Nurse, A. (2016). *Green criminology and environmental justice.* Sage Publications.

Paoli, L. (2003). *Mafia brotherhoods: Organized crime, Italian style.* Oxford University Press.

Passas, N. (1999). Globalization, criminogenic, asymmetries and economic crime. *European Journal of Law Reform, 1* (4), 399–423.

Pellman-Rowland, M. (2017, July 24). Two-thirds of the world's seafood is over-fished: Here's how you can help. *Forbes.* https://forbes.com/sites/michaelpellmanrowland/2017/07/24/seafood-sustainability-facts/?sh=68794751bbf.

Pires, S.F. & Moreto, W.D. (2011). Preventing wildlife crimes: Solutions that can overcome the 'tragedy of the commons.' *European Journal of Criminal Policy and Research, 17* (2), 101–123.

Pramod, G., Nakamura, K., Pitcher, T.J., & Delagran, L. (2014). Estimates of illegal unreported fish in seafood imports to the USA. *Marine Policy, 48*, 102–113. https://doi.org/10.1016/j.marpol.2014.03.2019.

Rivers III, L. & Gibbs, C. (2011). Applying a conservation-criminology framework to common-pool natural-resource issues. *International Journal of Comparative and Applied Criminal Justice, 35* (4), 327–346.

Rohrman, D.G. (2008). The crime and punishment of the Exxon Valdez. *Frontiers in Ecology and the Environment, 6* (6): 339.

Runge, C.F. (2016). The case against more ethanol: It's simply bad for the environment. *Yale Environment 360.* https://e360.yale.edu/features/the_case_against_ethanol_bad_for_environment.

Saffron, I. (2002). *Caviar: The strange history and uncertain future of the world's most coveted delicacy.* Broadway Books.

Shram, P.J. & Tibbetts, S.G. (2020). *Introduction to criminology: Why do they do it?* (3rd ed.). Sage Publications.
Siegel, J. (2019) *Essentials of criminal justice* (11th ed.). Cengage Publishing.
Sowell, T. (2015). *Basic economics: A common sense guide to the economy* (5th ed.). Basic Books.
Stone, C.D. (1972a). Should trees have standing? Toward legal rights for natural objects. *Southern California Law Review*, 450.
Stone, C.D. (1972b). *Should trees have standing? Law, morality and the environment.* Oxford University Press.
Sucato, K. (2001). What's wrong in Toms River? *New York Times*. https://nytimes.com/2001/12/16/nyregion/what-s-wrong-in-toms-river.html.
Sutherland, E.H. (1924). *Criminology*. J.B. Lippincott Company.
Tierney, J. (2000). A tale of two fisheries. *New York Times Magazine*, 38.
United Nations (n.d.). Global Compact. http://unglobalcompact.org/what-is-gc/our-work/social/poverty.
United Nations Food and Agricultural Organization (FAO) (2016). The state of the world fisheries and aquaculture. Contributing to food security to food security and nutrition for all.
Varese, F. (2011). *Mafias on the move*. Princeton University Press.
Weber, M. (2013). *The Protestant ethic and the spirit of capitalism*. Routledge.
Whalen, C. (2010). *Naked economics: Undressing the dismal science.* W.W. Norton & Company.
White, R. (2014). *Green criminology*. Routledge.
World Bank (2017). Sustainability development goals atlas. http://datatopics.worldbank.org/sdgatlas/archive/2017/sdg-01-no-poverty.html.

3 Laws and Regulations

Introduction

This chapter covers the most commonly applied domestic environmental laws. Some of the laws, such as the Lacey Act which passed in 1900, have long histories of promoting conservation. The federal government has a range of laws to enhance environmental protection. The laws reflect the primary legal systems within the U.S.: administrative law, criminal law, and civil law. Through the creation of regulations and statutes within the three legal systems, diverse approaches are employed to address environmental safeguards. Environmental laws can be enforced by various agencies and directed through regulatory processes to prompt compliance.

Most environmental laws passed in the 1970s under President Richard Nixon. This occurred in a period where there was broad restlessness across the country, largely driven by a discontent relating to the Vietnam War, distrust in government accompanied by significant spikes in crime, and unemployment. Following on from the 1960s, when there were many years of protests that took place and the welfare programs initiated under former President Lyndon Johnson promoted some groups over others while the general population was in a sustained state of economic malaise, there was a sustained backlash against the government. President Nixon, a conservative Republican, was the primary driver of many ideas that in the twenty-first century would be considered liberal. President Nixon drove the passing of the National Environmental Policy Act (NEPA) 40 C.F.R. Parts 1500–1508, in 1970 to be followed by the passing of the Clean Air Act, 42 U.S.C. §7401 et seq. and the Clean Water Act, 33 U.S.C. 1251 et seq. two years later. Reaction to pollution was the main driver of the formation of environmental policies. Under these new acts and the development of a new agency, the Environmental Protection Agency (EPA), citizens were afforded the right to sue polluters and those who would exploit, damage, and/or alter land or natural assets held as commons.

The 1970s reflected an inflection point for not just the United States but also England, as countries that had been steeped in a sustained self-content status during the prosperous post World War II years confronted economic and social tumult. The affluence of the post-war years enabled the United States and England to realize that, as they were satisfied with their prosperity, foreign competitors and previous enemies had not only drawn near but in fact had started to surpass the economic

DOI: 10.4324/9781003241201-3

and manufacturing positions of the world's leading nations. Japan, Germany, Saudi Arabia, and soon China would quickly compete against and sometimes outpace the economics of the United States. The turbulence of the 1970s partly facilitated the ability for other nations to outcompete the United States. Yet despite the backdrop of political upheaval, the environment was broadly addressed through the creation of a plethora of laws that would be enforced through a nascent EPA. Support for the pollution controls was so pervasive and popular that children's programming on television played commercials sponsored by the U.S. Forest Service with Woodsy Owl who reminded children, "Give a hoot, don't pollute." This fashionable government campaign reminded Americans that they had a personal responsibility to care for the environment just as the government started flexing its muscles to constrain and punish polluters. The environmental laws of the 1970s were not the first environmental laws but they were the first environmental laws that came with criminal penalties. The first environmental law, the Refuse Act of 1899, 33 U.S.C. §407, which prohibited dumping of waste into navigable waters without a permit, created a standard that the federal government could enforce. It was the first federal regulation to address pollution directly at a national level.

Environmental issues which most concerned most citizens were air pollution and water pollution. While addressing these concerns, the government also addressed issues of human health to include the regulations of pesticides, waste water, drinking water, hazardous waste, and remediation of polluted lands from industrial wastes. As political movements at the time included the first Earth Day celebration on April 22, 1970, government officials expanded federal capacity to regulate chemicals and, later, construction on all federal projects. Some of the first in a series of environmental laws in the early 1970s were a reaction to well-publicized events: Donora Smog in Pennsylvania and Cuyahoga River fires in Ohio. These events prompted legislative reactions in the form of the Clean Air Act and the Clean Water Act.

History of the Clean Air Act (CAA)

On October 26, 1948, fog descended into Donora, Pennsylvania. Donora is situated on the banks of the Monongahela River. Cold air came down from the hills and created an inversion layer that prevented warmer air from escaping. Smoke that was normally released from the town's two mills, the American Steel & Wire Co. and Donora Zinc Works which employed the majority of the town's population, was unable to escape the inversion layer (Davis, 2002; Peterman, 2009). The mills burned coal in their furnaces to make steel and zinc products. The release of the material from the smokestacks hung low in the air as the mills continue to operate through the unusual weather event. While fog was not uncommon in the Monongahela Valley, the duration of the cold air causing pressure and trapping in the warm air for a sustained duration was an unusual occurrence.

To create steel, furnaces are maintained at 2,000 degrees. The mills in Donora used as much coal as all of the residents in Pittsburgh. "Fumes from the mills, coke ovens, coal stoves and zinc furnaces were often trapped in the valley by the surrounding hills" (Davis, 2002). Since the townspeople of Donora had confronted smog and days of heavy smoke before, they continued their daily activities unabated. The schoolchildren participated in Halloween festivities under a yellow haze (Peterman, 2009). Within two days the police department began receiving calls about individuals who had gotten lost and residents who were finding it difficult to breathe (Davis, 2002; Peterman 2009). Those who were not sent out of Donora via ambulance were unable to depart as the smog was so thick that they were unable to drive safely. Reports by the local newspaper declared that the air was so thick that the town officials ordered the streetlights to be lit during the day to assist pedestrians and the mills were ordered to cease operations to prevent further accumulation of trapped pollutants.

The two regional hospitals, Monongahela Memorial and Charleroi-Monessen Hospitals, became overrun with patients and the community town center was converted into a morgue. Twenty residents died during the five days of the inversion. It is estimated that thousands had fallen sick from inhaling pollutants. A storm moved into the valley on Halloween, October 31, 1948, thus clearing much of the pollutants that had accumulated close to the ground. The inversion layer broke enabling smoke to be released into the atmosphere.

Four years later, London, England, experienced intense smog which became known as London's Great Smog of 1952. Heavy fog is not unusual in London and there had been a long history of coal and soot permeating England's largest city. In 1853 Charles Dickens started his story, *Bleak House*, with a description of black rain: "Smoke lowering from chimney-pots, making a soft black drizzle, with flakes of soot in it as big as full-grown snow-flakes – gone into mourning one might imagine – for the death of the sun" (Dickens, 1993). It was in London that Dr. Harold Des Voeux coined the term "smog," a combination of smoke and fog (Daley, 2016).

The Great Fog occurred because on December 5, 1952 the winds stopped. The normal condition of a cold, damp fog sat listlessly atop the smoke released from traffic, coal heated homes and businesses, industrial production that employed coal furnaces, smoke billowing from ships at port, and trains that crossed London. The amount of smoke accumulation accompanied by the impenetrable heavy winter fog created smog so thick that parents placed their children in face masks; flights destined for and from Heathrow airport were canceled as were the normal bus transports. Like Donora, the fog stayed near the ground for five days. But unlike Donora, which only had a population of 14,000, London with its large population suffered a loss of 4,000 people who perished during the Great Fog (Daley, 2016).

The tragic events of Donora and London created the impetus for the Clean Air which passed in 1956 in London, England and in the United States the Air Pollution Control Act of 1955 was passed. The American legislation directed research of air pollutants and, in 1970, President Richard Nixon signed the Clean Air Act which gave the federal government the right to regulate outdoor air pollution from multiple sources.

The Clean Air Act (CAA) was revised in 1977 and 1990. Its original passage was during a period when there was a national environmental movement that saw the approval of several environmental protections and the development of the Environmental Protection Agency (EPA). The 1977 modification of the CAA reflected the federal government's attempt to address acid rain. Acid rain was a well-known environmental problem in the 1970s and 1980s. Acid rain is defined as any precipitation, including fog or snow, that is more acidic than the normative range of water molecules. Surface water has a typical range of 6.5 to 8.5 on a pH scale. On a pH scale, 7 measures as neutral. Acid rain is noted as having a pH range of 4.0 to 4.5. It is caused by nitrogen oxides and sulfur oxides mixed with rain. Emissions from volcanoes, wildfires, some form of manufacturing, and diesel exhaust mix with precipitation in the air to form acid rain. The range of acid rain, which concentrated in the northeastern United States due to the historic manufacturing sites, led to drops in fish population in some rivers and streams and defoliation in some forests.

The 1990 modification was written to address the stratospheric ozone layer concerns that were highlighted in the Montreal Protocol. The Montreal Protocol, an international agreement, addressed ozone depleting substances: chlorofluorocarbons (CFCs) and halons. These substances were often used as coolants in refrigerators, air conditioners, and fire extinguishing systems. The EPA regulates the importation, exportation, handling, and disposal of halons 1211, 1301, and 2402 and equipment containing them in order to limit their release. The production of CFCs and halons has been banned within the U.S. since 1994 (EPA, 2022c).

The Clean Air Act enabled the EPA to establish air quality standards for specific, common and widespread pollutants. The EPA sets air quality standards for particulate matter, ozone, sulfur dioxide, nitrogen dioxide, carbon monoxide, and lead. Each state was required to develop environmental standards that are enforceable and meet the federal guidelines. Additionally, Congress authorized the EPA to monitor 188 toxic air pollutants. These pollutants are known or are suspected to cause harm to human health or serious harm to the physical environment. The pollutants are those that are involved in industrial processes. Examples of toxic air pollutants are: benzene which is found in gasoline, perchloroethylene which is emitted from some dry-cleaning businesses, and methylene chloride which is found in paint strippers and other solvents. Other commonly monitored toxic air pollutants include dioxin (bleach), asbestos, mercury, and lead (Environmental Protection Agency, 2022a).

Examples of Clean Air Act Violations

On September 12, 2019, the EPA entered a legal settlement with Performance Diesel Inc., a company that sold after-market products that would facilitate the subversion of emissions controls on heavy duty diesel trucks (Environmental Protection Agency, 2019a). The agreement between Performance Diesel Inc. and the Environmental Protection Agency prevented further sales of products that would subvert emission controls on diesel engines and the company agreed to pay a fine of $1.1 million for its profiteering from the sale of products that violate the Clean Air Act.

On August 13, 2021, the EPA entered a legal settlement with Advanced Flow Engineering, Inc. This company was alleged to have marketed, sold, and distributed after-market parts used to subvert Clear Air Act devices that are manufactured in engines to limit the release of air pollutants. The company agreed to pay $250,000 in fines for the sale of devices that would defeat emissions controls. Officials in the company submitted in the settlement that the company was in violation of Section 203(a)(3)(B) of the Clean Air Act, 42 U.S.C. §7522(a)(3)(B) for each product it sold. Part of the settlement included orders that the company would not technically support or warranty any product used to subvert emissions controls. Additionally, the company's marketing material had to scrub any statement referencing the sale or promotion of gear that would impede emissions controls and provide formal notice to all authorized dealers who sold their products that the company had entered a formal agreement with the EPA due to its violations of the Clean Air Act (Environmental Protection Agency, 2021c).

On September 15, 2021, the EPA entered a legal settlement with Xtreme Diesel Production LLC (XDP). Between January 1, 2015, and May 31, 2017, XDP manufactured, sold, and offered to sell at least 27,000 aftermarket devices designed to defeat emission controls on diesel pickup trucks.

> XDP allegedly manufactured, sold and distributed products designed to disable or bypass exhaust gas recirculation (EGR) systems that are on diesel pickup trucks. XDP also marketed and sold other EGR delete kits, empty exhaust pipes (a.k.a., "straight pipes"), and electronic tuning devices ("tuners") that disable filters, catalysts, EGR systems, and other critical emissions control devices equipped on diesel pickup trucks.
>
> (Environmental Protection Agency, 2021a)

These emissions control devices were installed on motor vehicles' original equipment by manufacturers in order to comply with Clean Air Act emission standards. XDP's aftermarket products were designed for use with numerous models of vehicles, including diesel trucks manufactured by Ford, GM, and Dodge. Accordingly, the EPA alleges that each act of manufacturing and each sale constitutes a violation of Section 203(a)(3)(B) of the CAA, 42 U.S.C. §7522(a)(3)(B) (EPA, 2021a). These violations led to an agreed settlement with the EPA which led XDP to pay a $1.125 million fine.

Water Pollution

Cleveland, Ohio has been one of the most industrial locations within the United States throughout the late nineteenth century and well into the late twentieth century. Historical records indicate that by 1837 Cleveland had four iron foundries which produced steam engines, locomotives, stoves, and iron for construction. In addition, Cleveland was a center for carriage makers, flour mills, and household goods manufacturing such as pottery, soap, candle, and rope manufacturing. One of the prominent reasons for the flourishing development of industry was Cleveland's location: on the banks of Lake Eerie and the mouth of the Cuyahoga River. The confluence of these fresh water systems was pivotal in transportation of the goods into commerce. From the 1930s and well into the 1960s Cleveland was a venue for parts manufacturing and assembly for the motor vehicle industry based in Michigan. Cleveland ironworks continued to create iron for vehicles and construction (Latson, 2015). Throughout the development of manufacturing and large scale industrialization the Cuyahoga River was an accessible and expedient location for discarding factory waste. The Cuyahoga River had caught on fire more than ten times in the previous century (National Park Service, n.d.).

The Cuyahoga River was so polluted by the late twentieth century that sewage and waste in the river water caught fire thirteen times since 1860. In 1952, the Cuyahoga River experienced its most expensive fire with over one million and a half dollars' worth of damage (Blakemore, 2023; Strandling & Strandling, 2015). The 1952 fire was caused by an unintentional release of oil from an oil refinery situated on Kingsbury Run, a creek that ran behind the refinery and emptied into the Cuyahoga River at the Great Lakes Towing Company boat repair yard (Boissoneault, 2019; Strandling & Strandling, 2015). This river fire engulfed tow boats, a bridge at Jefferson Street, and nearly reached the Standard Oil Refinery. Firefighters battled the blaze from fireboats. Descriptions of this fire and the battle against it were published in the *Time* magazine article which used images from a fire that occurred years later in 1969 (Rotman, n.d.).

There was another river fire in 1969 which was much smaller than the fire of 1952 but it became infamous due to the national coverage provided by an article about the fire in the popular *Time* magazine. The magazine article brought attention to the bizarre event even though no one in the region was surprised by the fire.

> Railroad bridges near Republic Steel trapped debris in the river, causing it to pile up. Oil on the water added to its flammability. A flare tossed from an overpassing train likely provided the spark that ignited the debris. The fire lasted for less than a half hour and resulted in minor damage to the railroad bridges.
>
> (National Park Service, n.d.)

This small river fire that only took twenty minutes to put out received national attention, triggering a disproportionate reaction as the national sentiment had turned toward environmental activism. In 1962, Rachel Carson had published *Silent Spring*, a text covering the ill effects of pesticides, specifically dichlorodiphenyltrichloroethane, more commonly known as DDT. Given the national public interest in environmental impacts and concerns that had become popular news enabled the enhanced attention on the 1969 Cuyahoga River fire. This fire has been heralded as a catalyst for the passage of the Clean Water Act of 1972. This act was initially passed to regulate waterways of the nation through imposing water quality standards and restrictions of chemical dumping into riparian systems.

It is unclear how much the Cuyahoga River fire of 1969 affected the formation of the Clean Water Act but the *Time* magazine coverage was exploited by other press such as *National Geographic*, which ran a cover story called "Our Ecological Crisis" on the cover of its December 1970 issue. The first Earth Day took place on

April 22, 1970, a date that was supposed to correlate to the spring equinox in a nod toward renewal. This political movement was given tremendous media coverage in a fawning and positive way and has continued to receive affirmative coverage to this day (Adler, 2002; Boissoneault, 2019). Although the river continued to be polluted with industrial waste, by 1970 there were no more fires on the Cuyahoga River. The fixation on the Cuyahoga River by environmental activists and the press came at the end of a century of pollution, long after the neighboring residents had grown accustomed to the pollution and had already begun to address some of the most substantive sources of pollution, namely spills from the nearby oil refinery (Rotman, n.d.).

Clean Water Act

The Clean Water Act (CWA) developed the parameters for regulating pollutant discharges into the United States' waters and regulating quality standards for surface waters. The basis of the CWA was a 1948 law known as the Federal Water Pollution Control Act. This Act was restricted and expanded in 1972 and became known as the modern "Clean Water Act." Under the CWA the Environmental Protection Agency regulates pollution control programs such as setting wastewater standards for manufacturing and agricultural industries. The EPA developed national water quality criteria recommendations for pollutants that are discharged into surface waters such as rivers, streams, ponds, and creeks. Additionally, the CWA made it illegal to discharge without a permit any pollutant from a point source into navigable waters. Point sources include pipes, ditches, and ships. The government's operationalization of the CWA from a program-based platform that addressed pollutants and sources separately into a broader watershed management approach.

During periods of excessive rain, municipal and other sewage systems may not be able handle the overburden of water volume leading some of the water runoff and untreated sewage to overflow from the sewage system. The combination of rainwater and effluence, often referred to as wastewater, discharging directly into the nearest body of water is considered point source pollution. It can cause harm to environmental and human health. Government officials address wastewater through the National Pollutant Discharge Elimination System (NPDES). This system provides guidelines for inspections when there are incidents of non-compliance and violations. There are various forms of inspections such as combined sewer overflow inspections, sewage sludge/biosolids inspections, focused compliance inspections, follow-up inspections, significant industrial user inspections, sanitary sewer overflow inspections, stormwater inspections, municipal separate storm sewer system inspections, and concentrated animal feeding operation inspections. Industry managers are required to operate within these guidelines.

Examples of Clean Water Act Violations

In 2022, Cleveland Cliffs Burns Harbor, a steel mill facility which produces as much as five million tons of raw steel per year in Burns Harbor, Indiana, was cited for release of cyanide and ammonia nitrogen release beyond its permitted effluence into the Little Calumet River (Environmental Protection Agency, 2023a). The discharge caused fish kills in the river as well as beach closures for seven days along the Indiana Dunes National Lakeshore. Several days of discharge occurred in August of 2019 due to a failure of a pump system. The facility alerted the EPA's emergency response team as well as the Indiana Department of Environmental Management response team. As a result of the discharge, Cleveland-Cliffs worked to upgrade its wastewater system at its steel manufacturing and finishing facility in Burns Harbor, Indiana. CCBH is required to maintain a newly installed cyanide treatment system to reduce cyanide at the facility to maintain compliance with NPDES permit effluent limits.

The company was obligated to pay a $3 million fine that was split between the federal government and the state of Indiana. Additionally, the company paid $10,025.37 to the Environmental Protection Agency for the cost of the cleanup and $37,650 to the Indiana Department of Environmental Management for its share of the cleanup costs (Environmental Protection Agency, 2023b).

On January 26, 2017, the Department of Justice on behalf of the Environmental Protection Agency filed a complaint in federal court in Colorado, against the City of Colorado Springs. The complaint highlighted the failure by the city to fund its stormwater management system and alleges that the city mismanaged its stormwater management system since 2002. According to public documents:

> Colorado Springs' storm sewer system covers an area of almost 200 square miles and consists of 389 miles of storm sewer mains; 118 miles of privately owned sewer lines; 250 miles of ditches/channels; 13,243 inlets; 1,459 manholes; 72 ponds; 693 major outfalls; and 1,316 minor outfalls. The storm sewer discharges to Fountain Creek and several of its tributaries. Fountain Creek flows north to south, bisecting Colorado Springs and eventually flowing into the Arkansas River near Pueblo, Colorado, which is about 40 miles south of Colorado Springs. Major tributaries of Fountain Creek in Colorado Springs include Monument Creek, Camp Creek, Cheyenne Creek, Shooks Run, Sand Creek, Cottonwood Creek, and Pine Creek.
>
> (Environmental Protection Agency, 2021b)

The city agreed to pay a $1 million fine as a civil penalty to the Environmental Protection Agency. Instead of paying a fine to the state of Colorado, the city of Colorado Springs agreed to construct $1 million worth of environmental projects that will safeguard water quality into the Arkansas River (Environmental Protection Agency, 2021b).

As these cases show, companies and municipalities can violate environmental safeguards to avoid costs. This is a pattern of how companies in the past operated before there were environmental regulations. Companies would indiscriminately dump waste into streambeds or rivers with the oft repeated phrase, "dilution is the solution to pollution." The actions by companies and municipalities are a function of cost versus benefit. The cost of law abidance is an operational cost which does not enhance the service or products sold. It is merely a sunk cost to the company. This is a problem of economics that the government does not formally recognize. The federal government provides funds for tribes to create and operationalize pollution controls. To ensure that all environments are safeguards, the federal government should consider enhanced funding to municipalities and counties that cannot afford to comply with all federal regulations.

Comprehensive Environmental Response, Compensation, and Liability Act (CERCLA)

On December 11, 1980, the Comprehensive Environmental Response, Compensation, and Liability Act (CERCLA), commonly known as the Superfund site program, was passed by Congress. This law created a tax on the petroleum and chemical manufacturers in order to fund cleanup of toxic sites. The law expanded the federal government's authority in order to respond directly to releases or potential releases of hazardous substances that have the potential to harm people and/or the environment. According to the EPA, over a five-year span $1.6 billion is collected via the tax imposed on the chemical and petroleum industries. The taxes are saved in a trust fund which is referred to as the Superfund. This money in this program is used to clean former, abandoned, or hazardous waste sites that are not well controlled.

Example of CERCLA Violations

The Foster Wheeler Energy Corporation (FWEC) is responsible for the Church Road trichloroethylene (TCE) superfund site. Between 1953 and 1984, FWEC operated in Mountain Top, Pennsylvania, where FWEC manufactured large pressure vessels employed in oil refineries, electric utility plants, and the shipping industry as TCE is a common degreaser and industrial cleaner. The manufacturing process led to soil and groundwater contamination through leakage of trichloroethylene. Remediation through groundwater extraction and treatment took place on the former FWEC facility starting in 1993. Groundwater contamination was identified in residential water wells and public water systems. The site is not listed on the National Priorities List; instead it is listed on the Superfund Alternative Approach. This approach, a program under the EPA, enables companies to enter into agreements to clean up superfund sites. The same investigations and cleanup schedules are imposed by the EPA, but the agency is spared some resource expense as the agreement is entered voluntarily before the EPA imposes one on the company. The Church Road superfund site is significant and still requires cleanup even though the company started remediation in 1993. According to the EPA, whose officials conducted an intermediate cleanup assessment in 2018, officials from FWEC will continue to pay for cleanup and reimburse the EPA $950,000 for its cleanup costs (Environmental Protection Agency, 2022b). The consent decree, signed on February 27, 2018, specifies the payment and the commitment by FWEC to continue to pay for future cleanup costs.

National Environmental Policy Act (NEPA)

The National Environmental Policy Act (NEPA), 40 C.F.R. Parts 1500–1508, initiated the concept of environmental impact statements (EIS) and environmental assessments (EA) that developers and government agencies must address when planning and requesting permits for development. According to the EPA:

> Section 102 in Title I of the Act requires federal agencies to incorporate environmental considerations in their planning and decision-making through a systematic interdisciplinary approach. Specifically, all federal agencies are to prepare detailed statements assessing the environmental impact of and alternatives to major federal actions significantly affecting the environment.
> (Environmental Protection Agency, 2022d).

NEPA was formed to alter how the federal government including the military conducted development and production. There are many instances in which this law has been subverted by criminal actors. The law, which may appear to be rudimentary, is actual the cause of much consternation in the development and construction industries.

Under NEPA, all companies engaging in development, production, or expansion of a facility on federal property must comply by filing an environmental assessment. These statements require tremendous resources in terms of cost and time from a construction, mining, or development company. Before any activity begins, there must be an assessment of the environment, an explanation of the development and its potential impacts to the environment, in addition to a description and explanation of possible alternatives to the development. A company planning on development must propose alternative actions in addition to the actions it is proposing. The cost involved in this process is so extensive that it increases the costs of each project. In order for a company to receive a permit to develop, mine, or expand a facility, there must be an environmental assessment which then is reviewed by the Bureau of Justice Assistance (BJA). If officials at the BJA determine the environmental assessment is sufficient, they issue a document known as a "Finding of No Significant Impact" (FONSI). This document states that the company has explicitly outlined all mitigation efforts to reduce environmental impact of a worksite. If a FONSI is not issued, the company must complete an environmental impact statement (EIS). This process is very complicated when it comes to use of chemicals, developing near or within a river that is designated as part of the Wild and Scenic River System, a designated wildlife area, a proposed wildlife area, or near an aquifer recharge system. NEPA and the filing of EIS can take years for a mining company, an agricultural company, or a manufacturing company. This cost is parlayed into the cost of the product affecting consumers years later.

NEPA is enforced through citizen lawsuits. NEPA can be subverted when large companies file for exemptions under NEPA. Both of these common occurrences make NEPA one of the most inefficient and least appreciated environmental laws. It is burdensome to comply with and it is easily used to cause costly delays through civilian lawsuits against companies who file for permits. For environmental activists, filing NEPA lawsuits has become commonplace. This law has had a profound impact on industry and has much to do with industry's low opinion of government regulations as "job eliminators."

Toxic Substance Control Act (TSCA)

The Toxic Substances Control Act (15 U.S.C. §2601 et seq. 1976) was enacted by Congress to provide legal authority for the Environmental Protection Agency to require records, reporting, testing requirements, and restrictions relating to the use and/or discharge of chemical substances or compounds. Manufacturers that plan to create or manufacture new chemical mixtures or compounds are legally required to provide notice to the EPA prior to initiating chemical production. If a chemical compound is labeled as a "substance of concern" or is going to be used in a manner not originally intended, then the chemical producer is obliged to record or file notice with the EPA as to the new use, discharge, release, or exposure. Pesticides, cosmetics, items qualifying as food, and pharmaceutical products are excluded from this act as well as the jurisdiction of the EPA (Food and Drug Administration, 2022).

Senator Tom Udall (D-New Mexico) wrote a new law to update this act. In 2016, the Frank R. Lautenberg Chemical Safety Act for the 21st Century was passed as Public Law 114–182. It was the first major environmental legislation in more than two decades. What prompted the revision was that the EPA could not regulate asbestos under the original act (Daly, 2022). Because there was so much litigation in the courts relating to asbestos, members of Congress felt compelled to regulate the substance which had cost the government so much in law suits (asbestos had long been used in ship building and in the insulation of homes, particularly those in military housing units). The effectiveness of the updated version of the TSCA may be limited as there is a provision in the law which limits the states' capacity to test chemicals for their safety. The new law states that if the EPA is testing a chemical's safety or toxicity, then the states cannot. State officials must wait for the results from the EPA before they take action on the chemical. While this may seem reasonable, the EPA only tests about 25 chemicals per year. There are 8,000 synthetic chemicals in use and only 1,000 have been vetted by the EPA (Scialla, 2016).

Example of TSCA Violations

The Environmental Protection Agency along with the Department of Justice entered into a national settlement with Home Depot U.S.A. Inc. resolving violations of the EPA's Lead Renovation, Repair and Painting (RRP) Rule at home renovations completed by contractors hired by Home Depot. Additionally, the states of Rhode Island, Utah, and Massachusetts, that also operated EPA-authorized RRP programs, joined the federal Department of Justice in the legal agreement.

Home Depot, which is based in the state of Georgia, entered into a legally binding agreement with the federal government via the District Court for the Northern District of Georgia. The settlement compels Home Depot to implement a national program that trains and audits any company which hires workers or contractors to become certified in lead-safe work that will prevent distribution of lead dust and paint chips during home renovation operations. Home Depot was ordered to pay a $20.75 million penalty. This became the largest civil penalty for violations under the Toxic Substances Control Act. From the total penalty, $50,000 will go to Rhode Island, $750,000 will be paid to Utah, and $732,000 will go to Massachusetts (Department of Justice, 2020).

Federal Insecticide, Fungicide, and Rodenticide Act

The Federal Insecticide, Fungicide, and Rodenticide Act (7 U.S.C. §136 et seq.) was passed in 1996. This act granted the federal government the right to oversee all distribution, use, and sale of pesticides. This act is meant to ensure the level of safety of pesticide products in foods, the environment, and human health. There are many examples of the misuse of this act, mainly through the importation of pesticides that are banned by the EPA. These products tend to be applied to illegal marijuana grows as noted in Chapter 8, forestry. Much of the trouble that companies get into with FIFRA violations involves violations of the Clean Water Act. FIFRA violations rarely occur alone. Even in the case of the application and illegal importation of banned pesticides, the primary violation tends to be other environmental and criminal statutes. When companies run afoul of FIFRA, it is often in the mishandling of the products or the illegal disposal of these regulated products.

Examples of FIFRA Violations

Examples of violations of the Federal Insecticide, Fungicide, and Rodenticide Act (FIFRA) include the violations by Wal-Mart. When Wal-Mart was cited by the Environmental Protection Agency for violations of the Clean Water Act, it was also cited for violations of FIFRA since the company did not have appropriate training and operational plans for the distribution, transfer, and storage of pesticides. The law was modified in 1981 to require all pesticides to come in child-resistant packaging so that a child five years old or younger would not be able to open the package in addition to having the words "danger," "caution," or "warning" on it. The labels cannot have imagery of candy, children, pets, flowers, or eating utensils as the EPA considers this to be confusing to a child.

On July 24, 2019, the Environmental Protection Agency announced that it entered into a legal agreement with the Stepan Company of Northfield, Illinois. The Stepan Company distributed pesticides. Officials from the company allegedly mislabeled pesticides in order to ship them. Officials from the EPA stated that pesticides were illegally labeled and sold eighty-nine times by Stepan Company. For these violations, the Stepan Company was ordered to pay $612,718 in fines for violations of FIFRA (EPA, 2019b).

E-bay, an online based e-commerce company in San Jose, California, has been put under several consent decrees by the EPA, including one in June of 2020 and another in June of 2021, for selling, offering to sell, and distributing 170 prohibited pesticides on its website (Environmental Protection Agency, 2022e). The pesticides in question included dichlorvos (DDVP), an organophosphate insecticide that is under numerous prohibitions and restrictions within the United States. The prohibitions were due to the threat the insecticide presents to human health. This class of pesticides, those which contain brodifacoum, prevents coagulation of the blood and is associated with several cases of toxicity in individuals due to its ingestion or exposure.

Safe Drinking Water Act (SDWA)

The Safe Drinking Water Act was passed in 1974 to protect public drinking water systems. The EPA established standards for various contaminants that can be found in public drinking water. A modification of the law in 1986 expanded the contaminant list to over ninety contaminants that are evaluated and monitored. Approximately 87% of the U.S. population receives drinking water through public water systems (University of Michigan, n.d.) The EPA does not have authority over private wells or water systems that serve less than twenty-five people. Since the expansion of the law, the EPA has authority to monitor public drinking water systems' sources such as rivers, springs, reservoirs, lakes, and groundwater wells. Tap water must meet standards set by the EPA, which created stricter standards in 1996.

The standards are based on measures of safety and risk. The EPA identifies contaminants that may be present and establishes parameters for when they may pose a risk to public health through an assessment of the volume and frequency of the contaminant's presence in the water system or water source. The target level for each contaminant is set below the threshold of when the contaminant may pose a risk to human health. EPA officials then set maximum limits based on the target levels. The limits are enforceable. In order to facilitate enforcement, the EPA advises municipal and public water systems on the latest technology for removing contaminants. Where the cost of technologies may be prohibitive for some water systems, the EPA specifies methods for water treatment for the elimination or reduction of contaminant levels. To assist with treatment and contaminant removal, the EPA provides financial grants to water systems that cannot sufficiently fund training or purchase of equipment.

States can enforce the water standards as does the EPA; enforcement often includes administrative orders, legal action, or fines against utility companies. Recently the EPA began evaluating the effects of microbial contaminants such as cryptosporidium and started to appraise derivatives or byproducts of drinking water disinfection treatments. Additionally, common contaminants that can be naturally found in groundwater well systems such as radon and arsenic may be in water that is not disinfected. Water supplies in geological formations where these elements organically occur are considered vulnerable ground water sources and can be found in aquifers or private well systems.

Criminal violations of the Safe Drinking Water Act include willful violations of injection control (42 U.S.C. 300h-2(b)) and tampering with public water systems (42 U.S.C. 300i-1). The willful violations of injection control can lead to three years of imprisonment and/or fines as specified under 18 U.S.C. 3571. Relevant regulations fall under 40 C.F.R. 144–149 (Underground Injection Control Program). The Underground Injection Control Program specifies how a company can inject hazardous waste into the ground. States must comply with this provision to safeguard water systems. Under this program, the EPA can issue grants to ensure the protection of water supplies by states or utilities.

Any person who tampers or attempts to tamper with a public water system is subject to criminal penalties of ten years of imprisonment for attempt to tamper and twenty years of imprisonment for tampering with a water system. Additionally, fines may be levied as expressed in 18 U.S.C. 3571. A judge may impose a fine of up to $1 million for tampering with a public water system or up to $100,000 for threatening or attempting to tamper with a public water system. Relevant regulations fall under 40 C.F.R. 141–143 (National Primary Drinking Water Regulations).

Federal agencies that violate the Safe Drinking Water Act can be fined $32,500 per violation per day. Officials of the EPA do not need to provide public notice prior to imposing fines against violators of the SDWA. The EPA has emergency powers under the SWDA in order to respond to events that present substantial or imminent threat to public health. In this circumstance, EPA officials only engage if the local or state authority has failed to engage or take action.

SDWA subsection 1449(a), 42 U.S.C. §300j-8 allows citizens to file a civil action against a federal agency that violates any rule or requirement under the SDWA. If a state attorney general office has filed a case against the alleged offender the citizen cannot file an additional civil action. SDWA subsection 1449(b), 42 U.S.C. §300j-8 specifies the exclusion of citizen action if a state agency has already filed against the alleged violator of the SDWA.

SDWA violations tend to be at the municipal level and can be the result of corruption, mismanagement, or underfunding of municipal water supplies. Most water violations take place under the Clean Water Act. This law, while it has substantial provisions for criminal enforcement, is not one of the most often criminally enforced laws. There are many civil lawsuits against the government for its violations of SDWA on military bases. In those cases, military personnel and officials are not criminally prosecuted. The water systems are fouled due to negligence not due to intentional subversion of drinking water requirements. In 2022, class action attorneys began amassing clients due to drinking water contamination that occurred at the Marine Corps base, Camp Lejeune in North Carolina. It is estimated that families living on the base between August 1, 1952, through December 31, 1987, could have been exposed to benzene that was leaked into the water systems. Sustained exposure to benzene can cause kidney, bladder, or liver cancer, adult leukemia, Parkinson's disease, Non-Hodgkin's lymphoma, multiple myeloma, and aplastic anemias (U.S. Department of Veterans Affairs, n.d.).

Emergency Planning and Community Right-to-Know Act (EPCRA)

The Emergency Planning and Community Right-to-Know Act, 41 U.S.C. 116 (EPCRA) and codified through 40 CFR Chapter I Subchapter J Sections 302, 355, 370 and 372, was passed in 1986 as a reaction to a chemical fog release that took place in Bhopal, India. The law compels several industries such as chemical manufacturing to publicize information about their use and release of chemical waste through steam, fluid, or solids. The EPA operationalized public transparency through the creation of a Toxic Release Inventory (TRI). This inventory has been used by various state agencies to create pollution monitoring systems and geographic databases to track pollutants and study their impacts on local populations. The goal of the law was to prepare local and state health departments and environmental toxic substance control agencies to respond in case of a chemical spill or release.

The Union Carbide plant in Bhopal, India was owned and operated by an American Company, Union Carbide based in Danbury, Connecticut, and the company Union Carbide India Limited. On December 3, 1984, methyl isocyanate (MIC) gas was leaked from the pesticide manufacturing plant, killing 3,800 people and injuring approximately 11,000 people (Taylor, 2014). Unknown at the time, a disgruntled employee, intent on spoiling a batch of pesticide production, added water to one of the chemical tanks. This caused a reaction that led to the gas leak (Taylor, 2014). Union Carbide paid $470 million to residents of Bhopal in 1991. In 2007, the Indian Supreme Court affirmed that the payment was fair and appropriate. This incident led to two events: the creation of the Community Action Response Center (CAER), that is sponsored by the Chemical Manufacturers' Association, and the passing of the EPA's Federal Superfund Reauthorization. The CAER's mission was to prevent industrial accidents and create coordinated plans to respond to incidents when they occur. The Federal Superfund Reauthorization created a network of local emergency planning councils. This program enables corporate officers to coordinate with local agencies to create plans to respond to environmental emergencies.

Through the Superfund program under CERCLA robust databases have been created. Through various remediation sites, government officials as well as public health and academic researchers have been able to collect information on the chemicals that are the most likely to be present in Superfund sites. The most commonly listed chemicals on the TRI are: aldrin (an organochlorine insecticide that is used in pesticides such as DDT), arsenic, barium, benzene, cadmium, carbon tetrachloride (an organic compound used in fire extinguishers and as a precursor to refrigerants), chlordane (used in pesticides), chloroform, chromium, cyanide, 1,1 – dichloroethene (a volatile organic compound that is used to create flexible material such as plastic wrap, coating for pipes and is used in the manufacturing of flame retardants for textiles), 1,2 – dichloroethene (a.k.a. ethylene dichloride – one of the most commonly used compounds, it is used to extract lead from fuel, fumigate textiles, create adhesives, degrease metals, amongst hundreds of other uses), lead, mercury, methylene chloride (a.k.a. dichlormethane – naturally found in wetlands and volcanos, it is used to decaffeinate coffee as well as an aerosol spray propellant), naphthalene (synthetic PAH used in products such as mothballs and found in cigarette smoke), nickel, pentachlorophenol (used as a disinfectant and pesticide), polychlorinated biphenyls (PCBs, used as a coolant for electric equipment and in the lining of food cans), polycyclic aromatic hydrocarbons (PAHs – naturally occurring in coal, crude oil, gas, wood, and gasoline), tetrachloroethylene (a.k.a.

perchloroethylene, it is used to dry clean products), vinyl chloride (formerly used in refrigerants, most commonly used to make polyvinyl chloride or PVC pipes), xylene (used as a solvent in chemical sprays, aviation fuel and gasoline, and solvents in paints), and zinc.

The law is intended as a mechanism for the government to recover costs of cleanup and remediation of a site. Companies may also subvert this regulation by relocating manufacturing to locations with less stringent environmental safeguards and remediation requirements. The incident at Bhopal, India did not reduce the amount of manufacturing overseas. Quite the reverse, U.S. based companies which manufacture overseas have greatly expanded since the Union Carbide event in Bhopal.

Resource Conservation and Recovery Act (RCRA)

The Resource Conservation and Recovery Act established parameters and rules regarding the transportation and disposal of hazardous and non-hazardous waste. In effect, RCRA is the federal government's waste management program. States have their own rules and agencies to address the handling of hazardous waste. Most follow the federal guidelines but some such as Hawai'i and California have more strict guidelines than the federal system. States can have stricter rules but these cannot be more lax than the federal rules.

In 1984, RCRA was amended through the passage of the Hazardous and Solid Waste Amendments (HSWA). Changes included additional rules for land disposal of hazardous waste, through land disposal restrictions. In 2016, EPA officials implemented a General Improvements Rule. This rule changed the requirements for container labeling, enhanced EPA notifications, and expanded contingency plan requirements. When the EPA modifies or creates new rules under RCRA, the rule cannot be enforced in a state with an authorized plan until the state adopts an equivalent rule. If the new RCRA rule is more strict or rigorous than existing RCRA regulations, the state is entitled to one year to adopt an equivalent rule. If action is required through the state legislature because state law needs to be modified to accommodate the new rule then the state has two years to adopt and raise their standards to match the federal criteria. In Iowa and Alaska, the federal government implements RCRA rather than state agencies so the rules in those states are implemented immediately.

Overall, the goals of the rules under RCRA are to protect human and environmental health; reduce the amount of waste being produced; ensure that waste is handled appropriately through a set of guidelines, restrictions, and rules; and to conserve natural resources. Two industries that are heavily monitored under these rules include the military and the oil/gas exploration industry. Both these industries create large volumes of waste that has the potential to be hazardous waste. In addition, agriculture, mining, and manufacturing may create large volumes of both hazardous and non-hazardous waste. Companies involved in these industries obtain permits under RCRA that specify how the waste will be collected, treated, stored, recycled, and/or disposed. The permits under RCRA are legally binding documents under 40 CFR Parts 124 and 270.

If there are violations of the rules or the permit agreements, corrective actions are issued by the EPA to the company. The corrective actions include site inspection, characterization of the site which determines the level of impact of the waste on the environment, interim actions which may include actions such as diverting or altering water supply if contamination is present, remediation plans implemented through a corrective measures study, and corrective measures implementation. These steps require tracking and notation of reaching targets throughout the process. Lastly, a long-term plan is implemented to mitigate any further hazardous waste exposure.

The federal government, as a result of Superfund sites, requires companies to demonstrate financial stability whereby the cost of remediation and plant closure will be paid by the company. In order to demonstrate this stability, the company must show that it has six times the estimated cost of closure and post-closure remediation costs. The laws regulating the cost of cleanup and the financial requirements of permitted companies can be found in Subtitle C RCRA §§3001–3023.

The costs of cleanups are so high, that instances of criminal activity, and often organized crime in New Jersey, New York, and Pennsylvania, were known to purposefully not label waste that was hazardous. As the labeling of hazardous waste increases the cost of dumping the waste, there are several instances of hazardous waste being improperly disposed. Other violations include exceeding maximum limits on hazardous waste, storing more than one type of waste in a waste container, failure to keep waste containers closed at all times, failure to inspect hazardous waste storage areas, using damaged hazardous waste containers and not having proper documentation on transportation of hazardous waste. The waste hauling industry in the aforementioned states has a reputation of having organized crime involvement. The data on organized crime's involvement is inconsistent. It is explained in detail in Chapter 9.

Endangered Species Act and the Lacey Act

The Endangered Species Act and the Lacey Act are covered in the chapters that cover wildlife, fishing, and forestry. These acts promote wildlife and wild flora conservation through restrictions and regulatory schemes that address the trade, sale, and collection of wild species. The Lacey Act is the oldest environmental law in the United States. It was passed in 1900 as a reaction to the overhunting of game birds and decline in the population of native birds in addition to stopping "injurious species" from entering the United States without a permit (Macdonald, n.d.). As noted by the Smithsonian Institution, the last passenger pigeon (*Ectopistes migratorius*) recorded in the wild was in Pike County, Ohio in 1900 (Smithsonian Institution, n.d.). These laws, as most of the environmental laws, were adopted as a result of well-publicized problems or events. Sometimes the events are minor but the popular sentiment spurs actions by the government. Environmental laws are often supported broadly by the general population which makes them straightforward to pass by politicians who want credit for accomplishing tasks. Unfortunately, government agencies such as the EPA continue to expand regulatory schemes, this increases financial burdens on industries and becomes a complicated set of rule-making for the states. Governments tend to expand rather than retract their power. Creating and increasing rule-making makes it harder for smaller companies to operate, harder for individuals to follow all of the rules, and creates challenges for enforcement. While the EPA expands its rule-making, the number of enforcement agents and investigators does not increase. This creates a gap between enforcement and violations whereby the violators calculate the likelihood of being caught as compared to the financial reward of the law violation. Nowhere is this more prominent than in the areas of wildlife trafficking, illegally forestry, illegal mining, and illegal fishing. The Endangered Species Act and the Lacey Act are the most effective and useful tools to address these violations. The laws and their enforcement are emphasized in Chapters 4, 5, 6, and 8.

Conclusion

The laws created by Congress have addressed specific fields within chemical industries and applications. In part, this was a reaction to the text *Silent Spring* by Rachel Carson. She drew attention to the impacts of widespread use of DDT, an insecticide developed during World War II. Government officials advanced chemical development, particularly in the field of herbicides and pesticides. During the period of the Vietnam War, Agent Orange was a chemical used as a defoliant. Chemical derivatives of Agent Orange became fundamental elements in herbicides. The origination of these chemical compounds stimulates public fear. Use and application of these chemicals became highly regulated, in part to allay public apprehension. Government agencies are responsible for keeping strict oversight on these products so that they do not become problematic. The aim is to prevent environmental harm through coordination with industry rather than reacting to environmental risk through criminal law.

Discussion Questions

1. How did the Donora Smog event cause the public to demand environmental pollution controls?
2. Why did so many people in Ohio tolerate long-term industrial pollution prior to the national attention to the Cuyahoga River fire?
3. Why don't members of the press cover routine cases relating to environmental regulation and instead focus on major events?
4. If Rachel Carson were writing today, do you think her book, *Silent Spring*, would have the same impact as it did when she published?
5. The Lacey Act was a response to species collapse of domestic species. Do you draw any parallels between the intention of this act when it was written and wildlife crime today?

Further Reading Recommendations

1. Crane, J. (2014). *The environment in American history: Nature and the formation of the United States.* Routledge.
2. Davis, F.R. (2014). *Banned: A history of pesticides and the science of toxicology.* Yale University Press.

3. Worster, D. (1994). *Nature's economy: A history of ecological ideas.* Cambridge University Press.
4. Wright, D.A. & Welbourn, P. (2002). *Environmental toxicology*. Cambridge University Press.

References

Adler, J.H. (2002). Fables of the Cuyahoga: Reconstructing a history of environmental protection. *Fordham Environmental Law Journal, 14* (1), 89–146.

Blakemore, E. (2023, October 4). The shocking river fire that fueled the creation of the EPA: When Cleveland's Cuyahoga River burned, the nation noticed. *History*. https://www.history.com/news/epa-earth-day-cleveland-cuyahoga-river-fire-clean-water-act.

Boissoneault, L. (2019, June 19). The Cuyahoga River caught river at least a dozen times, but no one cared until 1969: Despite being much smaller than previous fires, the river blaze in Cleveland 50 years ago became a symbol for the nascent environmental movement. *Smithsonian Magazine*. https://www.smithsonianmag.com/history/cuyahoga-river-caught-fire-least-dozen-times-no-one-cared-until-1969-180972444/.

Daley, J. (2016, November 21). Researchers dive into the science of London's deadly fog. *Smithsonian Magazine*. https://smithsonianmag.com/smart-news/researchers-figure-out-science-behind-londons-deadly-fog-180961138.

Daly, M. (2022, April 5). EPA rule would finally ban asbestos, carcinogen still in use. *Associated Press*. https://apnews.com/article/business-health-united-states-enviornment-environment-82341b509d0398c2bbfcd00ea28af69b.

Davis, D.L. (2002). When smoke ran like water: Tales of environmental deception and the battle against pollution. Basic Books.

Department of Justice (2020, December 17). Home Depot to pay $20,750,000 penalty for nationwide failure to follow rules for conducting renovations involving lead paint. https://justice.gov/opa/pr/home-depot-pay-20750000-penalty-nationwide-failure-follow-rules-conducting-renovations.

Dickens, C. (1993). *Bleak House*. Wordsworth Editions.

Environmental Protection Agency (EPA) (2023a, May 23). Air Quality – National Summary. https://www.epa.gov/air-trends/air-quality-national-summary.

Environmental Protection Agency (EPA) (2023b, February 23). Cleveland-Cliffs Steel LLC and Cleveland-Cliffs Burns Harbor LLC Settlement. https://epa.gov/enforcement/cleveland-cliffs-steel-llc-and-cleveland-cliffs-burns-harbor-llc-settlement.

Environmental Protection Agency (EPA) (2022a, December 19). Initial list of hazardous air pollutants with modifications. https://epa.gov/haps/initial-list-hazardous-air-pollutants-modifications.

Environmental Protection Agency (EPA) (2022b, November 16). Agreement addresses TCE cleanup at Foster Wheeler Energy Corp/Church Road TCE site in Pennsylvania. https://epa.gov/agreement-addresses-tce-cleanup-foster-wheeler-energy-corpchurch-road-tce-site.

Environmental Protection Agency (EPA) (2022c, October 27) Halons program. https://epa.gov/ozone-layer-protection/halons-program.

Environmental Protection Agency (EPA) (2022d, October 26). What is the National Environmental Policy Act? https://epa.gov/nepa/what-national-environmental-policy-act.

Environmental Protection Agency (EPA) (2022e, July 20). Amended stop sale, use, or removal order issued to Ebay, Inc. https://epa.gov/enforcement/amended-stop-sale-use-or-removal-order-issued-ebay-inc.

Environmental Protection Agency (EPA) (2021a, September 19). Xtreme Diesel Performance, LLC., Clean Air Act Settlement information sheet. https://epa.gov/enforcement/xtreme-diesel-performance-llc-clean-air-act-settlement-information-sheet.

Environmental Protection Agency (EPA) (2021b, September 15). Colorado Springs Settlement information sheet. https://19january2021.snapshot.epa.gov/enforcement/colorado-springs-settlement-information-sheet_html.

Environmental Protection Agency (EPA) (2021c, September 12). Advanced Flow Engineering, Inc., Clean Air Act Settlement information sheet. https://epa.gov/enforcement/advanced-flow-engineering-inc-clean-air-act-settlement-information-sheet.

Environmental Protection Agency (EPA) (2019a, September 12). Performance Diesel, Inc., Clean Air Act Settlement information sheet. https://epa.gov/enforcement/perfomance-diesel-inc-clean-air-act-settlement-information-sheet.

Environmental Protection Agency (EPA) (2019b, July 24). EPA settles case against Stepan Compan for selling misbranded pesticide. https://epa.gov/newsreleases/epa-settles-case-against-stepan-company-selling-misbranded-pesticide.

Food and Drug Administration (FDA). (2022, March 2). FDA authority over cosmetics: How cosmetics are not FDA-Approved, but are FDA-Regulated. https://fda.gov/cosmetics/cosmetics-laws-regulations/fda-authority-over-cosmetics-how-cosmetics-are-not-fda-approved-are-fda-regulated.

Latson, J. (2015, June 22). The burning river that sparked a revolution. *Time*. https://time.com/3921976/cuahoga-fire/.

Macdonald, B. (n.d.) The Lacey Act's injurious wildlife list helps prevent harm to and from wildlife. *U.S. Fish and Wildlife Service*. https://fws.gov/lacey-acts-injurious-wildlife-list-helps-prevent-harm-and-wildlife.

National Park Service (n.d.). The 1969 Cuyahoga River fire. https://nps.gov/articles/story-of-the-fire.htm.

Peterman, E. (2009). A cloud with a silver lining: A killer smog in Donora, 1948. *Pennsylvania Center for the Book*. https://pabook2.libraries.psu.edu/palitmap/DonoraSmog.html.

Rotman, M. (n.d.). Cuyahoga River fire: The blaze that started a national discussion. *Cleveland Historical Society*. https://clevelandhistorical.org/items/show/63.

Scialla, M. (2016). It could take centuries for the EPA to test all unregulated chemicals under a new landmark bill. *PBS Newshour*. https://pbs.org/newshour/science/it-could-take-centuries-for-epa-to-test-all-the-unregulated-chemicals-under-a-new-landmark-bill.

Smithsonian Institution (n.d.). The passenger pigeon. https://si.edu/spotlight/passenger-pigeon.

Strandling, D. & Strandling, R. (2015). *Where the river burned: Carl Stokes and the struggle to save Cleveland*. Cornell University Press.

Taylor, A. (2014, December 2). Bhopal: The world's worst industrial disaster, 30 years later. *The Atlantic*. https://theatlantic.com/photo/2014/12/bhopal-the-worlds-worst-industrial-disaster-30-years-later/100864.

University of Michigan (n.d.). U.S. water supply and distribution fact sheet. https://css.umich.edu/publications/factsheets/water/us-water-supply-and-distribution-factsheet.

U.S. Department of Veterans Affairs (n.d.) Camp Lejeune water contamination health issues. https://va.gov/disability/eligibility/hazardous-materials-exposure/camp-lejeune-eater-contamination.

4 Unregulated, Unreported, and Illegal Fishing

Introduction

One of the greatest concerns in conservation science is the unregulated, unreported, and illegal fishing across the world. The United States has strict regulations on commercial fishing. Unfortunately, U.S. ports are often used as transit ports for illegally harvested or mislabeled fish that are captured in international waters and shipped across the globe. Fish and seafood represent a fungible commodity in high demand in international markets. The chapter will survey cases that relate to the U.S. as a pass-through for international fishing as well as domestic cases of illegal fishing and domestic harvesting for internal consumption.

Unregulated, unreported, and illegal fishing generates approximately $15 billion to $36 billion in profits to criminals and criminal enterprises. This global problem impacts fish stocks, local economies where the local diet is dependent on fishing, and marine ecosystems. Worldwide threats to fish stocks include: fishing in protected areas or during closed seasons, catching protected fish species, fishing without proper licenses, and purposefully mislabeling fish catches. The United States imports approximately 5.3 billion pounds of seafood each year with an estimated value of $18 billion (NOAA, 2019a).

Overfishing has a long history, dating back at least to 1376 when King Edward III of England banned trawling on the bottom of rivers (British Sea Fishing, n.d.). Throughout history indigenous societies exploited animal populations to the point of near collapse or collapse. The Aleuts brought the sea otter population on the Aleutian Islands to near collapse 2000 years ago (Simenstad, et al., 1978). The goal of fisheries within the United States is to manage the fish stocks so that the fish populations are sustainable while generating maximum yield for fishermen. This enables fisheries management to ensure the maximum catch occurs while perpetuating the fish population for the next season. The federal government's goal is to create *optimal yield* defined as calculating fish populations in addition to impacts on fishermen and their families. Overfishing, defined by the National Oceanic and Atmospheric Administration (NOAA) Office of Sustainable Fisheries, is when the stock status via the annual rate of catch is too high (Rosenberg, 1996). Overfished is defined as the stock status if the population is too small. These two stock statuses are considered the primary threats to the oceans' animal populations. It is

DOI: 10.4324/9781003241201-4

defined as catching too many fish in a short period of time. Commercial fishing companies capture tons of fish at a time in large nets. This causes the capture of many animals and fish which aren't intended to be caught and processed and is a leading cause of shark and ray population reductions (Dulvy, et al., 2021). They're referred to as *bycatch* and are often discarded. The wholesale catch of tons of sea creatures including the intended fish species but captured in an indiscriminate way leads to capture of the breeding population.

> Beginning in the late 1950s and early 1960s, the United Nations, along with certain countries and organizations, began efforts to regulate fishing internationally. However, little was really accomplished until the 1970s, when many nations declared 200-mile exclusive economic zones (EEZs) out from their shorelines.
>
> (Blackford, 2008)

The fish population may become compromised as it may become too depleted to recover if immature fish aren't populous enough to later reproduce and sustain the population. There are various claims about how some fish stocks are overfished. The data is inconsistent as many fisheries are understudied or unstudied. The range of overfishing claims vary from a claim of 30% of fish stocks are overfished to 93% of fish stocks are overfished (Dulvy, et al., 2021; FAO, 2020; Pontecorvo & Schrank, 2014). A span of this size makes it challenging to create a scientific guideline for fishing fleets. Additionally, the guidelines for commercial fishing companies do not apply to recreational fishing fleets while limited scrutiny is focused on recreational fishing companies. Recreational fishing is often left out of data and analysis on fisheries yet there have been studies demonstrating that fish which are bred for recreational fishing are often deposited into protected waters.

> Two species used as fishing bait, *Squalius carolitertii* (chub) and *Phoxinus phoxinus* (minnow), are expanding in running [protected] waters. *Oncorhynchus mykiss* (rainbow trout) was also detected and is likely to have been introduced for angling or from fish farm escapes … Through the application of a social survey, it was found that unlike other population groups, anglers in the region significantly preferred stocking over environmental improvement for the management of fish populations.
>
> (Fernández, et al., 2019)

Most of the scrutiny of fish stocks falls on the commercial fishing industry and oceanic stock as opposed to freshwater fisheries. This serves to create ire within the fishing industry that is trying to sustain fishing careers, community, and industry as recreational fishing often provides cover for illegal activity as it is governed and regulated less.

Commercial Fishing Methods

Global fishing is a $400 billion per year industry (FAO, 2020). "For 2019, U.S. commercial and recreational saltwater fishing generated over $255 billion in sales impacts, contributed $117 billion to gross domestic product, and supported 1.8 million jobs in the U.S. marine fishing sector and across the broader economy" (NOAA Fisheries, 2022). Methods of capturing fish have created a threat to fishing stocks throughout the world. The various types of commercial fishing enable commercial seafood companies to catch tons of fish per year in addition to unintentional catch of other sea creatures as bycatch. The most common forms of commercial fishing are pelagic trawling, otter trawling, beam trawling, pair trawling, purse seining, dredging, long-line fishing, gill nets/drift nets/ tangle nets, and lobster/crab nets.

Pelagic trawling involves dragging a large net through the middle of the water column in order to capture the fish that most commonly inhabit this portion of the ocean. This includes the species of mackerel (*Scombrus scombrus* for the most common and commercially significant Atlantic mackerel, a relative of the tuna) and herring (*Clupea harengus harengus* for the more commonly caught Atlantic herring or *C. harengus pallasii* for the Pacific herring). These valuable and commonly traded commercial catches are captured with pelagic trawling methods which don't cause much environmental damage as the nets pass through the central columns of the sea and stay off the sea floor. But the nets used in the pelagic trawling method can be large enough that the net can hold four tons of fish. Some of the most commonly caught fish are captured with bottom trawling, that is dragging the large nets along the sea bottom.

Famously, cod (*Gadus morhua*, the most common commercial fish, the Atlantic cod), haddock (*Melanogrammus aeglefinus*), sole (*Solea solea*, a fish closely related to halibut and flounder), and plaice (*Pleuronectes platessa*) are all caught using bottom trawling. All of these valuable fish species which have had significant roles in economic systems in Britain, the United States, and other nations, have had their populations challenged and reduced through the use of bottom trawlers that capture so many fish at once. They have also created substantial damage to sea floors and impacted sponges, coral, and sea plants by resuspending sediment via rototilling the seabed (USGS, 2016).

Otter trawling is the most common form of trawling. It involves dragging a net that is held open with large steel boards that are called otter boards. The fish tend to swim into the back end of the net as the net moves quickly through the seawater. This method can be less impactful to fish that are not intended to be caught as the mesh size of these nets tends to be larger, thus allowing smaller fish to pass through unimpeded.

Beam trawling involves the dragging of nets on either side of the vessel. Each net is held open by a large metal beam and chains or metal slides are attached to the net system to stir up the sea floor. The majority of commercial beam trawlers use two beam trawls towed from derricks projecting over each side of the vessel. Beam trawling is more commonly used in sea habitat that is rockier or has deep sand. This method of trawling is used to stir the desired flatfish, namely sole and plaice species, from the sea floor.

Pair trawling employs two ships to drag the same net. The net size is typically one mile long, with an entry of 60 (65.6 yards) by 120 meters (131 yards). The size of the net is so large that it can hold ten 747 Boeing jumbo jet aircraft. By pairing the fishing vessels, the net moves faster, less fuel is used by the vessels as each ship has less drag weight, and the combination of the vessels enables a larger catch than each vessel would catch on its own. Historically this method created large bycatches of marine mammals such as whales and dolphins which led to its ban in many waterways such as European seas.

Purse seining draws a large net in a circle around a school of fish. A large net that spans one thousand meters across and goes down 250 meters can capture many fish in a small period of time. This is the most common way to capture large schools of fish such as tuna and sardines. If the net is relatively small, limited damage will be done but with large nets, the amount of fish that can be captured is substantial. Entire schools of fish can be captured at once. This method tends to have significant captures of bycatch such as sea turtles, dolphins, whales, and sharks.

Dredging is used to tow metal cages along the sea floor to capture oysters, scallops, and mussels. Metal teeth are used to scrape along the shellfish beds to scrape them off the sea floor. The cages catch the animals scraped by the dredging technique. As many as twenty cages can be dragged using a dredging technique. This method of commercial seafood capture causes considerable damage to the sea floor.

Longline fishing involves the dragging of long fishing lines from the back of a fishing vessel. The heavy lines have small live fish as bait hooked throughout the line which can stretch thirty miles from a vessel. Inadvertent catches of sea birds such as albatross is common with this method which is primarily used to catch tuna, swordfish, and marlin.

Gill nets, drift nets, and tangle nets are used by the dropping of a net that acts as a wall that captures any sea creature attempting to swim through its path. The drift nets are the least damaging as they drift alongside the vessel as it passes in the water. In large scale commercial use, there can be sizable bycatch. This method is the most commonly applied method of fishing for smaller scale commercial fishermen. Even without significant amounts of bycatch, the smaller scale fishermen inadvertently capture immature fish which should be left in the ocean to mature and reproduce. The net methods of fish capture are indiscriminate in their targeting. Additionally, nets which are left behind tend to catch fish for years after the net is abandoned by the commercial vessel. When this occurs, they are known as ghost nets.

Crab and lobster pots are the most environmentally sustainable form of commercial fishing as they are a collection of metal or wooden traps that are lowered to the seafloor. The lobster or crab is lured into the trap with bait and cannot escape once caught in the pot. If fish enter the pot and cannot escape, they can be released alive when the fishermen return to the pots. Environmental damage that can come from this commercial seafood capture is the abandoning of the pots by fishermen.

Governance and Regulation of Fishing within U.S. Waters

By 2017 the global commercial fishing industry generated $240.99 billion (Research and Markets, 2019). This commercial industry has many opportunities for fraud, exploitation, and disruption to the critical food supply market. To promote sustainable fisheries in the United States, Congress passed the Magnuson – Stevens Fishery Conservation and Management Act (MSA) in 1976. This law governs U.S. federal waters to promote biological and economic sustainability of the fish stocks and marine life. The goal of the law was to prevent overfishing, re-establish fish stocks that had been depleted through over-fishing in order to ensure a stable commercial fish market, and to protect the habitats where fish spawn, breed, hatch, and grow.

The MSA formalized U.S. waters as extending 200 nautical miles from the shorelines of U.S. territories and lands. The law established eight regional fishery management councils. The councils monitor and regulate areas that require conservation measures due to overfishing. The councils, which are comprised of voting and non-voting members, establish catch limits, develop priorities for re-establishing compromised fish stocks, and develop fish management plans for fish species that are federally managed. The eight regional fishery management councils are: North Pacific (Aleutian Islands, Alaska, and the Bering Sea), Western Pacific (American Samoa, Mariana, Hawai'i, and the Pacific Remote Island Area Fishery Ecosystem Plan [PRIA FEP - Howland Island, Kingman Reef, Jarvis Island, Baker Island, Wake Island, Johnston Atoll, Palmyra Atoll]), Pacific (California, Oregon, Washington, and Idaho), Gulf States (Louisiana, Mississippi, Alabama, Texas and the west coast of Florida), South Atlantic (North Carolina, South Carolina, Georgia, and the east coast of Florida through Key West), Mid-Atlantic (Maryland, Virginia, Pennsylvania, Delaware, New York, New Jersey, and a portion of North Carolina), New England (Maine, New Hampshire, Massachusetts, Rhode Island, and Connecticut), and Caribbean (Puerto Rico, U.S. Virgin Islands which includes St. John, St. Thomas, and St. Croix) (U.S. Regional Fishery Management Councils, n.d.).

All councils are required to address ten national standards as written into the law: general guidelines, scientific information, management units, allocations, efficiency, variations and contingencies, costs and benefits, communities, bycatch, and safety for life at sea.

The MSA was amended twice: 1996 and 2007. The Sustainable Fisheries Act of 1996 was passed to strengthen conservation efforts in an attempt to prevent overfishing and more effectively rebuild fish stocks. Metrics were implemented to estimate more accurately the overall health of the fish stock. The 1996 law strengthened bycatch laws, fishing vessel safety, and fishing communities. This is accomplished through the designation of essential fish habitat. This can include rivers, wetlands, coral reefs, and seagrasses. More specifically, coastal estuaries, canopy kelp, shallow corals, seagrass areas, and rocky reefs are targeted as they are areas where many fish species spawn, they are sensitive and rare ecosystems, as well as being subject to stress due to development.

The MSA Reauthorization Act of 2007 established annual catch limits, created market-based management systems that permitted catch shares, and most significantly, established greater cooperation between the United States and the international community to prevent illegal fishing. Nearly 80% of seafood consumed in the United States each year is imported. Therefore, it is critical that the federal government, via the National Oceanic and Atmospheric Administration (NOAA) which monitors fisheries, collaborate with foreign government agencies, private industry, and non-governmental organizations to reduce the likelihood of illegal fishing.

Illegal, Unreported, and Unregulated Fishing (IUU)

Illegal, unreported, and unregulated fishing occurs both in U.S. and international waters. Several points in the seafood collection and distribution provide opportunities for IUU fishing to occur. Examples include fishing in areas closed to fishing such as protected waters, fishing from unregulated vessels, failure to report on fish catches and bycatch, as well as transferring fish from fishing vessels to cargo ships to disclose the catch and distribution of fish and seafood such as scallops and crab.

The Chinese government has the world's largest commercial fishing fleet (Urbina, 2020). The Chinese government, like Norway, Iceland, South Korea, and Japan, subsidizes its fishing vessels which has created a fleet capable of catching more fish than their competition. It is estimated that China accounts for approximately 50% of the world's fishing activity (Urbina, 2020). Recently Chinese vessels were spotted in the waters of the Galapagos Islands, as a territory of Ecuador. An estimated 350–400 Chinese-flagged vessels overwhelmed the marine resources of Ecuador, thus causing Ecuadorian officials to request assistance from the U.S. Coast Guard (Borquez & Anand, 2022). "Eighteen of 22 violations of Chile's Nazca-Desventuradas Marine Park since 2016 were caused by Chinese vessels" (Borquez & Anand, 2022). The Chinese-flagged vessels then traveled to the waters controlled by the nation Chile. The Chinese-flagged vessels engaged in unregulated fishing, taking unknown quantities of fish from both protected marine areas as well as waters within the Exclusive Economic Zone of another sovereign nation without permit or authority (Ellis, 2020).

Methods employed to subvert monitoring of vessels include disabling of internationally required tracking devices, use of drift nets that are difficult to detect and the use of ship transfers whereby cargo is moved from one vessel to another while the vessels are both at sea. The transfer is conducted at sea to avoid accountability by port inspectors. The Chinese-flagged vessels, many of which fall under the state-owned China National Fisheries Corporation, have been fishing off the African coast. These vessels are frequently spotted in areas where fish stocks are already vulnerable (Herzinger, 2020; Myers, et al., 2022). Chinese-flagged vessels have fished in the waters of Sierra Leone, Gambia, Senegal, Mauritania, Guinea, and Guinea-Bissau. While in these nations' littoral waters, Chinese-flagged vessels have under-reported their catch, disabled mandatory tracking devices, misrepresented their locations, and employed bottom trawling methods that have been banned in some of these areas. Additionally, the Chinese vessels lacked permits and used illegal nets that prevented undersized fish from escaping (Pauly, et al., 2014). In 1985, the Chinese government had an estimated twelve vessels in African waters. By 2015, there were 450 Chinese-flagged vessels off Africa's coasts (Pauly, et al., 2014). This unregulated fishing presents a threat to the local fishing industry as well as threats to fish stocks and marine life in the region.

Data Concerns

In a November 2015 article in the local Monterrey, California press, it was revealed that the anchovy (*Engraulis mordax*) population had not been assessed for ten years by the NOAA fisheries (Schmalz, 2015). This created an opportunity for fishermen to catch large quotas of anchovies for years while the population was in decline. A preliminary assessment was conducted in 2011 by the Farallon Institute, but it was not concluded or available until the fall of 2015. By then the report showed the anchovy population along the eastern Pacific was in collapse (Davidson, et al., 2017).

Aside from failure to collect data in a frequency useful to population monitoring, data was collected in locations where the species was abundant, permitting officials to make the wrong estimation of the population totals. The fish population is not equally distributed along the coast. Failure to conduct sample assessments along the entire range of fish habitat led to an incorrect conclusion. This is a consistent reason why quotas are unreliable, commercial fishermen don't trust fisheries management, and why fish stock populations are not accurately assessed. It is also a reason to be skeptical of environmental and non-governmental reporting that pushes for moratoriums or substantive fishing restrictions. Government assessments of various fish stocks rely on insufficient or inadequate data to draw conclusions about the size and sustainability of a fishery. In a political climate of multi-layered regulations, high consumer demand, and a flaccid international response to Chinese-sponsored poaching on an industrial scale, those with substantial legal commercial fishing fleets can be lured into the illegal trade of selling illicitly harvested fish.

Better Control of Fish Populations

Fisheries management via NOAA Fisheries involves biologists conducting single species analysis. A more effective method might include collective evaluation of inter-species dynamics, fish habitats, fleet economics, and fishing communities. The government's approach has led to conflict and mistrust between those in the industry and NOAA officials. In the past, government quotas incentivized overfishing which led to the collapse of economically significant fish, such as cod (*Gadus morhua*). The cod stocks were so depleted that on July 2, 1992, a moratorium was placed on cod fishing in Canada (Smellie, 2021). The United States fisheries faced considerable cutbacks to cod quotas.

Drag netting increased harvests including bycatch of immature cod. Refrigerated ships also permitted vessels to stay at sea longer to harvest larger catches. The U.S. did not prohibit cod fishing at the same time due to political pressures from the New England fishing industry. Multi-generational history of cod fishing created an expectation of government permissiveness. Once the government finally limited cod fishing, vociferous condemnation of federal officials began. New Englanders blamed the government for destroying their industry, without recognizing their role (WBUR, 2014).

The story of cod is similar in the United Kingdom, which practiced unregulated cod fishing for more than 400 years in the North Sea (Blanchard, et al., 2005;

Cushing & Jenner, 1966; Davies & Rangeley, 2010; Mair, 1997). This led to the collapse of the cod stocks and conflict with Iceland as British commercial fishing fleets traveled to Icelandic waters to gather cod that had been depleted in British waters (Ingimundarson, 2003; Jackson, et al., 2004; Steinsson, 2016).

Shark Fishing

The only U.S. state to totally ban shark fishing is Hawai'i. All other states permit some form of shark fishing. The only shark fishing that is prohibited throughout the United States is species of shark that are listed as endangered species or listed on CITES (the Convention on International Trade in Endangered Species of Wild Fauna and Flora). While the United States, along with New Zealand, Australia, and Canada, has the most sustainable shark populations, recreational and commercial captures of sharks are permitted. The practice of shark finning is prohibited in all the aforementioned nations. Shark finning is the practice of cutting the shark fin from the body then dumping the shark body back in the ocean. This practice is common in Asia where shark fins are popular in cuisine and medicine. The popularity of shark fins has led to sharp declines in various shark populations throughout the world. It is estimated that shark populations have declined by 70% since 1970 (Einhorn, 2021). Sharks captured in the coastal waters of Central and South America are often finned then their fins are shipped to China and Hong Kong.

While shark finning was banned in the United States in 2010, the nation's ports often function as conduits to shark fins transferring from Central and South American nations to Asia. Reasons this occurs have to do with the complications of laws regulating seafood products. Bills of lading don't list endangered or illegal species. They tend to have wording such as dried fish, dried seafood, or shark fins. Only seventeen U.S. ports have inspectors that can inspect seafood, animals, and plant species but not all shark products are routed through these ports. If the shipment is labeled as "pass through," the shark products are not inspected. Pass through indicates that the United States is neither the origin nor the destination for the product; thus, the item passes through cargo transit ports without inspection.

Part of the issue is the overlap in regulation between wildlife and seafood. While twelve states have banned the shark fin trade, the U.S. federal government has not. According to the Shark Finning Prohibition Act of 1000 which is an amended version of the MSA, no person under U.S. jurisdiction can engage in the finning of sharks. Any shark fin that is aboard a U.S. fishing vessel must have a corresponding carcass. Under the Shark Conservation Act of 2010, the newest amended version of the MSA, all sharks brought to shore via a vessel must have their fins naturally attached. These fishing requirements do not apply to cargo that is in transit via U.S. territory. If it did, this would prevent the pass through of shark fins via U.S. ports. Ports can be airports such as those located in Atlanta, Georgia, or Memphis, Tennessee where large swaths of cargo are transferred. If the federal government banned all shark fin trades, all ports would have authority to inspect and suspend shark fin shipments. It is estimated that over 591–701 metric tons of shark fins were transferred via American ports between 2010 and 2017 (Murdock & Villanueva, 2019).

Another complication with the monitoring and prevention of shark fin trading is the number of agencies involved and the various ways different countries label cargo. While some nations label the specific shark and part, others create labels such as "frozen seafood" or "dried seafood." Some label the product as shark without labeling the species or part. This commercial international trade of sharks, shark parts, or seafood involves a multitude of federal agencies such as NOAA, U.S. Fish and Wildlife Service, National Marine Fisheries Service, the Food and Drug Administration, Department of Homeland Security, and various state agencies such as California, Texas, or Florida Departments of Fish and Game. Coordinated inspections and audits between these agencies need to be enhanced to ensure the United States is not enhancing the illegal trade of shark fins. Frequently traded shark fins often belong to vulnerable species: scalloped hammerhead (*Sphyrna lewini*), which is listed as critically endangered, and blue sharks (Prionace glauca), the most commonly overfished shark in the world, labeled as a threatened or near endangered species (Murdock & Villanueva, 2019). The case of shark finning exemplifies the complications with enforcing laws or regulations intended to prevent exploitation of fish stocks.

The Case of the "Codfather"

Carlos Rafael was the owner of Carlos Seafood Inc. based in New Bedford, Massachusetts. Carlos Seafood had a fleet of 32 fishing vessels operating through various independent corporate shells using 44 permits. The size of this company enabled Mr. Rafael to be one of the largest commercial fishing business owners in the United States with an approximate net worth between $10 million and $25 million derived from bringing in $34.8 million worth of fish to the docks of New Bedford each year (Farzan, 2019; Valencia, 2017). Mr. Rafael was perceived as a cod kingpin, often referred to as "the Codfather," which drew attention from other fishing companies. Carlos Seafood controlled 20% of the cod market even when the cod market was dwindling and causing financial hardships to those in the cod industry as the federal government cut the cod quota by 95% in 2014 (Kaufman, 2017).

Mr. Rafael has a history of law violations. In 1984, he was sentenced to six months in prison for tax evasion and paid $750,000 in back taxes. In 2001, Mr. Rafael pled guilty to forging sales receipts. Throughout these investigations, indictments, and charges, Mr. Rafael made public declarations claiming that the government was condemning him for his success and compared fisheries regulators to "Gestapo" (Farzan, 2019). In 2002, the Environmental Protection Agency was removing nine sunken vessels as part of a superfund cleanup. Mr. Rafael had a non-functioning ship, *Just a Girl*, which was leaking oil into the harbor. Instead of moving his vessel away so that the EPA could complete their work, he let his vessel sink; assuming the EPA would pay for the removal and cleanup of his boat. The EPA sent him a bill for the removal and cleanup of his vessel. He sued the agency and lost (Borrell, 2017). Not long after, a worker on one of his vessels, *Sandra Lee*, died of carbon monoxide poisoning. The U.S. Occupational Safety and Health Administration (OSHA) fined Mr. Rafael $46,000 for negligence (Borrell, 2017). This pattern of law violations and regulatory infringements did not slow as Mr. Rafael felt emboldened to commit more crimes as he increased his net worth and fishing capacity.

> "I am a pirate," Rafael told regulators during a federal fisheries management meeting, "It's your job to catch me." Over two decades, he racked up more than half a million dollars in fines for more than 30 federal fishing violations. His boats have been cited for overfishing, failing to throw back undersized fish and lobsters bearing eggs, having boats with secret coolers in them, blocking coast guard inspectors from boarding, failing to declare fishing trips, and filing false reports on his catch. For Rafael, it was just the cost of doing business. A couple of years ago, when the US Coast Guard boarded Rafael's boat the *Bulldog* in the Gulf of Maine, the trawl winch began unspooling, sending the net plunging into the ocean and out of sight. The feds suspected the winch brake had been released on purpose. They later retrieved the net and discovered it had an illegal liner designed to prevent undersized fish from slipping through the regulation mesh. The case is under investigation and the captain declined to comment for this article on the advice of his lawyer.
>
> (Borrell, 2017)

Between 2012 through January 2016, Mr. Rafael produced false declarations to the National Oceanic and Atmospheric Administration claiming he was catching haddock (*Melanogrammus aeglefinus*) which has a high quota, when his company was catching cod, sole, or other species that were under restrictive, lower quotas. Mr. Rafael misreported 782,812 pounds of fish. The Carlos Seafood Company offloaded the illegal catch by selling it directly to a buyer in New York in exchange for duffels of cash to conceal profits and the illegal catch by diverting it into the legitimate market. The Internal Revenue Service had evidence that much of the cash was smuggled into Mr. Rafael's native country of Portugal (U.S. Attorney's Office, 2017). Carlos Rafael pled guilty to twenty-eight offenses, including conspiracy, false labeling of fish, bulk cash smuggling, tax evasion, and falsifying federal records for which he was sentenced to forty-six months in prison, three years of supervised release, and ordered to pay a fine of $3 million and restitution to the U.S. Treasury of $108,929 (NOAA Fisheries, 2019b).

Seventeen of Mr. Rafael's former fishing vessel captains were also sentenced to various punishments. They each were suspended from serving aboard any federally permitted vessel while it is offloading seafood or fishing at sea. The range of suspensions varied from twenty days to two hundred days, which was based on the severity of the captain's participation in Mr. Rafael's violations. All were placed on probation periods ranging from one to three years in which they would be required to report to probation officers. A condition of probation is that if any new violation is incurred during the probationary period the captain would be permanently banned from obtaining a commercial operator permit, effectively banning the individual from commercial fishing (NOAA Fisheries, 2019b).

These punishments were hardly severe as Mr. Rafael managed to sustain his wealth. He was able to make millions of dollars when he sold off his fleet: "selling 12 groundfishing vessels and 27 of his permits to Blue Harvest Fisheries and six of his 11 scallops vessels to Quinn Fisheries. Other parts of his fleet were sold off to individuals" (Dunlop, 2021). The history of Mr. Rafael's fishing enterprises demonstrates that the federal government's punishment schemes are too lax to create disincentives or specific deterrence for wrongdoing in the fishing industry. No matter the amount of violations Mr. Rafael committed, no matter the complaints by other fishing companies, and no matter how many times Mr. Rafael went to prison or paid fines, the federal fishing laws and regulations did not restrict Mr. Rafael's fishing activities as captains of his fishing fleet continued to gather fish while Mr. Rafael served time in jail or paid fines.

The abundance of wealth Mr. Rafael procured reflects the vast sums available through illegal fishing. The failure to enhance or escalate punishment as would happen in other crimes which include enhancements for prior violations, fishing laws neither dissuade nor serve as a deterrent for individuals like Mr. Rafael who are intent on attaining as much profit as possible. The fines and monetary penalties did not recover the illicitly garnered funds which were sent overseas. The ownership of the vessels which were used to unlawfully catch protected species remained as Mr. Rafael's assets. If Mr. Rafael had committed drug smuggling via his vessels, the ships would have been seized, the U.S. government would have enjoined Portuguese officials to freeze and seize Mr. Rafael's assets overseas, and the captains would have served time in prison for their conspiracy to defraud the U.S. and its taxpayers. Since the penalties for fishing violations don't proximate narcotics violations, Mr. Rafael and his crew received minimal punishment for years of illegal behavior.

Other Illegal Fishing Cases

On May 6, 2021, Henry Danzing was sentenced in Key West, Florida for violations of the Lacey Act. He illegally harvested 529 pounds of demersal finfish in the Bahamas and transported the illegal harvest into the United States. Mr. Danzing did not have a license to fish or export fish in Bahamian waters. Mr. Danzing sold the illegally harvested fish in his café, the City Hall Café in Tavernier, Florida. The federal court in Florida ordered Mr. Danzing to forfeit his vessel, a thirty-foot Contender Tournament boat that will be used by the Royal Bahamas Defense Force to enforce fishing laws (U.S. Attorney's Office, 2021).

In a state case, the government of California pursued prosecution against Vallejo resident, Tam Tran, for harvesting 250 Dungeness crabs in state protected waters. The California Department of Fish and Wildlife (CDFW) received a tip from a commercial crabber that another individual set his crab pots in a marine reserve, North Farallon Island State Marine Reserve. This reserve serves to protect critical habitat for humpback and blue whales during their migration and is one of the largest nesting sites for birds in North America (Associated Press, 2022; Johnson, 2022). The islands, located thirty miles west of San Francisco, are under the strictest protections which include the prohibition of public visits to the islands

(Associated Press, 2022). Agents with CDFW located a string of 92 crab trap buoys in this reserve which surprisingly had commercial tags on them that were registered to Tran. Tran sold $60,750 worth of crab in San Francisco in 2021 and sold $65,669 worth of crab in the first five months of 2022 (Flores, 2022; Johnson, 2022). The district attorney's office alleges 365 violations. This would lead to a fine of $912,500 under California law.

Since December 2021, conservation officers from the California Department of Fish and Wildlife Marine Enforcement Division (CDFW) noted that crab cases are on the rise. Between December 2021 and March 2022, CDFW agents charged seven cases for illegal possession of undersize crabs by commercial crab fishermen (CDFW, 2022). Additionally, the CDFW officers found 120 crab traps that were used to illegally harvest crabs outside of the commercial season in order to illegally catch 8,322 pounds of crab (CDFW, 2022). The demand for and cost of crab incentivize illegal poaching of this commercially important natural resource.

Striped Bass

On February 19, 2009, five fishermen pled guilty in Maryland for illegally overfishing striped bass, known as rockfish (*Morone saxatilis*). The value of the illegal fish harvest was $2,900,269 (United States Department of Justice Office of Public Affairs, 2009). The five fishermen harvested striped bass with the intent of concealing their catch as the harvest of this species is strictly regulated. Each fisherman has a maximum annual quota for rockfish and is required to report the pounds of fish harvested each day on a Maryland state issued permit allocation card. In order to subvert strict regulations, the fishermen solicited and corrupted a public officer who facilitated their crime.

> According to their statements of fact, from 2003 to 2007, [Thomas] Crowder, [John] Dean, [Charles] Quade, [Thomas] Hallock and [John] Collins, with the help and assistance of a Maryland designated check-in station, falsely recorded the amount of striped bass that each harvested. In each year, the defendants failed to record some of the striped bass they caught. In addition, in each year the defendants recorded, and the check-in station certified on their Maryland permit allocation cards a lower weight of striped bass than was actually caught. The defendants and the check-in station operator would also falsely inflate on these records the actual number of fish harvested.
>
> (United States Department of Justice Office of Public Affairs, 2009)

The fishermen under-reported the weight of the fish and over-reported the number of fish caught, causing the state to issue additional tags. Seafood wholesalers provided cover to the fishermen by creating false receipts claiming the fish purchases were species other than rockfish. A consequence of this method of concealing the crime was that the state officials were unaware of real population value of the managed species. All fishermen in this case were charged with violations of the Lacey Act, with an additional charge against Hallock for fishing out of season.

On November 8, 2012, five fishing captains who operated charter fishing boats were convicted of poaching Atlantic striped bass (*Centropristis striata*) in violation of the Lacey Act. Each of the captains operated charters out of Rudee Inlet in Virginia Beach, Virginia. According to the Atlantic Striped Bass Conservation Act, passed by Congress in 1984, restrictions were imposed to the harvest of any Atlantic striped bass due to the fishery collapse (United States Department of Justice Office of Public Affairs, 2015). This law was passed to preserve a species that had been an important food source for those who reside in Atlantic states. By 1990, the federal government banned all fishing and harvesting of the Atlantic striped bass. All five captains, Jeffery S. Adams, Raymond Carroll Webb, David Dwayne Scott, William W. "Duby" Lowery, IV, and Nolan L. Agner, were also charged with destroying evidence to prevent seizure by law enforcement and lying to law enforcement officers.

Captain Nolan Agner was sentenced to pay a $3,500 fine and placed on probation for three years whereby he would have to have a vessel monitoring system device on any ship he owned or operated. Captain Jeffrey Adams was sentenced to three years' probation with the same requirement of having a vessel monitoring system. Captain David Scott was sentenced to pay a $5,600 fine and $1,900 in restitution to NOAA. Additionally, he was given three years' probation with the enhanced penalty of prohibition of participation in commercial fishing or charter fishing. Captain William Lowery was sentenced to thirty days in jail with a twelve-month supervised release post-incarceration. Additionally, Captain Lowery was required to surrender his captain's license to the U.S. Coast Guard and is prohibited from participating in the charter fishing industry for one year. Captain Raymond Webb was required to pay a $3,000 fine with an additional $1,000 fine to NOAA. He was sentenced to three years' probation with a requirement to acquire a vessel monitoring system to be applied to any vessel on which he works. (United States Department of Justice, 2013).

In February 2010, members of the United States Coast Guard boarded the *Lady Amaira*, a fishing vessel off the coast of North Carolina. The Coast Guard received a tip that this vessel was unlawfully harvesting Atlantic striped bass from federal waters in 2009 and 2010. The Coast Guard seized 90,000 pounds of Atlantic striped bass with an estimated value of $1.1 million. Consequently, thirteen commercial fishermen were charged with violation of the Lacey Act as well as falsely reporting the fish. The fishermen initially claimed that the fish were harvested in the state waters of North Carolina where Atlantic striped bass is legal. One of the fishermen, Dwayne J. Hopkins, was also charged with obstruction of a proceeding before a federal agency because he blocked Coast Guard members from boarding the vessel (United States Department of Justice Office of Public Affairs, 2015). All of the fishermen were licensed to fish state waters but not in federal waters. They falsified their reports to conceal their illegal catch. The fishermen charged in this case are Gaston Saunders Jr., Bryan Daniels, Ellis Leon Gibbs, Jr., David Saunders, Michael Potter, Steven Daniels, James R. Craddock, James K. Lewis, Joseph H. Williams, Dewey W. Lewis, Jr., Dwayne J. Hopkins, and John F. Roberts (United States Department of Justice Office of Public Affairs, 2015).

The aforementioned cases show the complications of enforcing conservation laws. The penalties often are too low to create deterrence. The differences between federal and state laws create opportunities for those seeking to subvert quotas or fishing moratoriums. The range of fishing laws and regulatory schemes across different regions complicates the enforcement as offenders can claim that they were unaware of changing quotas and the variation of regional restrictions. New England states have twenty-seven different managed species by limiting permits to commercial fishermen. This is one region in the country. The total number of regulated fish species is 479 in federal waters (NOAA Fisheries, 2019c). Each species has a limited catch that varies according to the latest federal assessment. Regulatory schemes create additional costs to commercial fish markets. The cost of the permits is too expensive for young fishermen so they work on senior fishermen's vessels rather than working their own boats or businesses.

These crimes demonstrate the challenges faced by biologists who manage fisheries in determining the amount of poaching when determining fish quotas is already an imprecise endeavor. The legitimate fishing industry relies on enforcement of conservation laws in order for the fisheries to remain sustainable. Poaching and the motivations to mislabel fish are too tempting in an environment where there is high demand and limited or complex enforcement actions.

Eels and Elvers

In early October 2016 seven men pled guilty in the federal court in Portland, Maine for violating the Lacey Act: Yarann Im, Mark Green, John Pinkham, Thomas Reno, Michael Bryant, George Anestis, and Thomas Choi (United States Department of Justice Office of Public Affairs, 2016). Their crimes involved the illegal harvest and sale of $1.9 million worth of juvenile American eels (*Anguilla rostrate*), also known as elvers. The elvers were illegally harvested in Massachusetts, New Jersey, Rhode Island, and Virginia. There is limited legal harvest of American Eels yet these aquatic species were sought for illegal catch and transportation to overseas markets.

Within the United States, elvers can only be harvested in Maine, South Carolina, and Florida. Elvers swim from coastal waters to river waters where they become adults in fresh waters. The migration pattern facilitates the illegal poaching as most of the poaching occurs in the river waters. The defendants had eel harvest licenses from Florida or Maine and claimed that all of their eels were harvested in the states that permit limited legal harvests. This was a method to demonstrate they were harvesting lawfully even though they were harvesting in states that prohibited all eel harvests. The three states that permit eel harvesting have strict enforcement of their laws in order to preserve the natural resource. The eels were harvested in states with less enforcement due to the fact that there is no permissible elver harvest.

Eels and elvers are harvested in Europe and Asia for human consumption but collapse of eel populations on those continents has led to new pressures on the American eel population. Elvers captured in the United States are exported to Asia where they are raised until they reach sexual maturity then are sold as food at a cost of $2,000 per pound. The case was a collaboration between New Jersey Division of Fish and Wildlife Bureau of Law Enforcement, Virginia Marine Resources Commission Police, Rhode Island Department of Environmental Management Division of Law Enforcement, the Atlantic States Marine Fisheries Commission, among others including the U.S. Fish and Wildlife Service.

Conclusion

These cases demonstrate the complexities of investigating and penalizing overfishing. There are dozens of regional and species-specific guidelines and rules. The burden for fishermen to abide by rules which can shift according to government sponsored assessments as well as the costs of permits and licenses incentivizes large scale commercial fishermen like Carlos Rafael. Smaller scale fishermen are the first to be pushed out of the industry. Fishing executives like Mr. Rafael are able to pay low level fines and continue to conduct commercial seafood harvests. The government's structure for enforcement relies heavily on state agencies and reports by those in the industry and results in limited enforcement.

Discussion Questions

1. Why don't environmental groups that push for reduced cattle and chicken production recognize the harms of fish consumption or the ecological harms from farmed fish?
2. The Codfather story reflects the lucrative trade of fish. Why aren't there more stories in the media about people like the Codfather?
3. What laws can be implemented or enforced to reduce the likelihood of someone becoming a Codfather?
4. The federal government has not effectively reduced the role of the United States as a pass-through nation. Which laws can be used to reduce the U.S.' role in this trade?
5. Why does the U.S. government not regulate recreational fishing?

Further Reading Recommendations

1. Clover, C. (2006). *The end of the line: How overfishing is changing the world and how we eat.* The New Press.
2. Greenberg, P. (2011). *Four fish: The future of the last wild food.* Penguin Books.
3. How many fisheries are overfished, and what does that mean? http://www.sustainablefisheries-uw.org/how-many-fisheries-are-overfished/.
4. Kurlansky, M. (2009). *The last fish tale: The fate of the Atlantic and survival in Gloucester, America's oldest fishing port and most original town.* Riverhead Books.
5. Sinclair, M. (2021). The National security imperative to tackle illegal, unreported, and unregulated fishing. Brookings Institution. http://brookings.edu/articles/the-national-security-imperative-to-tackle-illegal-unreported-and-unregulated-fishing/.

References

Associated Press (2022, May 30). State sues California fisherman in 'egregious' crabbing case. *CBS*. https://sacramento.cbslocal.com/2022/05/30/state-sues-california-fisherman-in-egregious-crabbing-case/.

Blackford, M. (2008). A tale of two fisheries: Fishing and overfishing in American waters. *Origins: Current events in historical perspective*. https://origins.osu.edu/article/tale-two-fisheries-fishing-and-over-fishing-american-waters.

Blanchard, Mills, C., Jennings, S., Fox, C.J., Rackham, B.D., Eastwood, P.D., & O'Brien, C.M. (2005). Distribution-abundance relationships for North Sea Atlantic cod (Gadus morhua): observation versus theory. *Canadian Journal of Fisheries and Aquatic Sciences, 62* (9), 2001–2009. https://doi.org/10.1139/f05-109.

Borquez, A. & Anand, A. (2022). News Sentiment Analysis: The Case of Chinese Vessels in the EEZs of Latin American Countries. *Pacific Focus, 37* (1), 183–212. https://doi.org/10.1111/pafo.12205.

Borrell, B. (2017). The last trial of the Codfather. *Hakai Magazine*. https://hakaimagazine.com/features/last-trial-codfather/.

British Sea Fishing (n.d.). Commercial fishing: From the earliest times to the present day. https://britishseafishing.co.uk/commercial-fishing/.

California Department of Fish and Wildlife (CDFW) (2022, March 1). Commercial crab fishing violations on the rise. https://wildlife.ca.gov/News/commercial-crab-fishing-vilations-on-the-rise.

Cushing, D.H. & Jenner, H. (1966). *The Arctic Cod: a study of research into the British trawl fisheries*. Pergamon Press: London, England. https://doi.org/10.1016/C2013-0-05445-X.

Davidson, P.C., Sydeman, W.J., & Thayer, J.A. (2017). Are there temporal or spatial gaps in recent estimates of anchovy off California? *California Cooperative Oceanic Fisheries Investigations (CalCOFI)* Rep., Vol. 58, 56–68. https://static1.squarespace.com/static/56a6b01dd8af105db2511b83/t/608064b7658e3b09e462018a/1619027156459/Davison+et+al+2017+CalCOFI+Rep.pdf.

Davies, R.W.D. & Rangeley, R. (2010). Banking on cod: Exploring economic incentives for recovering Grand Banks and North Sea cod fisheries. *Marine Policy, 34* (1), 92–98. https://doi.org/10.1016/j.marpol.2009.04.019.

Dulvy, N., Paucourea, N., Rigby, C., Hilton-Taylor, C., Fordham, S., & Simpfendorfer, C.A. (2021). Overfishing drives over one-third of all sharks and rays toward a global extinction crisis, *Current Biology*, 31 (21), 4773–4787. e8, https://doi.org/10.1016/j.cub.2021.08.062.

Dunlop, K. (2021, January 6). While seemingly still serving time, the Codfather is back to business in Dartmouth. *Standard Times/South Coast Today*. https://www.southcoasttoday.com/story/business/real-estate/2021/01/06/codfather-carlos-rafael-looking-buy-real-estate-dartmouth-fishing-smuggling-conspiracy-tax-evasion/6555163002/.

Einhorn, C. (2021, January 27). Shark populations are crashing, with a 'very small window' to avert disaster. *New York Times*. https://www.nytimes.com/2021/01/27/climate/sharks-population-study.html.

Ellis, E. (2020). Do Latin American waters continue to fall prey to China's fishing? *Center for Strategic and International Studies*. https://www.csis.org/analysis/do-latin-american-waters-continue-fall-prey-chinas-fishing.

Farzan, A. (2019, August 20). The 'Codfather' was a seafood kingpin, until fake Russian mobsters took him down. Now he'll never fish again. *Washington Post*. https://www.washingtonpost.com/nation/2019/08/20/codfather-fishing-russian-mobsters-carlos-rafael/.

Fernández, S., Arboleya, E., Dopico, E., Ardura, A., & Garcia-Vazquez, E. (2019). Non-indigenous fish in protected spaces: Trends in species distribution mediated by illegal stocking. *Aquatic Conservation, 29* (12), 2240–2252. https://doi.org/10.1002/aqc.3238.

Flores, J. (2022, May 29). S.F. D.A. wants a fisherman to pay nearly $1 million over 'largest,' 'most egregious' illegal Dungeness crabbing case. *San Francisco Chronicle*. https://www.sfchronicle.com/sf/article/S-F-D-A-wants-a-fisherman-to-pay-nearly-1-17206804.php.

Food and Agriculture Organization of the United Nations (FAO) (2020). The state of the world's fisheries and aquaculture, 2020. https://www.fao.org/state-of-fisheries-aquaculture.

Herzinger, B. (2020, November 20). China is fishing for trouble at sea. *Foreign Policy*. https://foreignpolicy.com/2020/11/20/china-illegal-catch-fishing-biden-trump/.

Ingimundarson, V. (2003) Fighting the cod wars in the Cold War: Iceland's challenge to the Western Alliance in the 1970s. *The RUSI Journal, 148* (3), 88–94, DOI: 10.1080/03071840308446895.

Jackson, J., Kirby, M., Berger, W., Bjorndal, K., Botsford, L., Bourque, B., Bradbury, R., Cooke, R., Erlandson, J., Estes, J., Hughes, T., Kidwell, S., Lange, C., Lenihan, H., Pandolfi, J., & Johannesson, G.T. (2004). How 'cod war' came: The origins of the Anglo-Icelandic fisheries dispute, 1958–61. *Historical Research: The Bulletin of the Institute of Historical Research, 77* (198), 543–574. https://doi.org/10.1111/j.1468-2281.2004.00222.x.

Johnson, M.D. (2022, June 2). Crabber faces nearly $1 million in fines in the 'most egregious case of unlawful crabbing activity in San Francisco history.' *Field and Stream*. https://www.fieldandstream.com/conservation/california-crabber-fined-illegally-activity/.

Kaufman, A. (2017). New England cod fishermen share coal miners' plight in this new documentary. *Huffington Post*. https://www.huffpost.com/entry/sacred-cod-documentary_n_58ed1547e4b0ca64d919d595.

Mair, H. (1997). North Sea cod stocks close to collapse. *Marine Pollution Bulletin, 34* (3), 144. https://doi.org/10.1016/S0025-326X(97)84989-2.

Murdock, E. & Villanueva, V.R. (2019). Unintentional partner: How the United States helps the illegal shark fin market. *National Resource Defense Council*. https://www.nrdc.org/sites/default/files/unintentional-partner-shark-fin-market-report_0.pdf

Myers, S.L., Chang, A., Watkins, D., & Fu, C. (2022, September 26). How China targets the global fish supply. *New York Times*. https://www.nytimes.com/interactive/2022/09/26/world/asia/china-fishing-south-america.html.

NOAA Fisheries (2022, March 29). Fisheries Economics Report of the United States, 2019. https://www.fisheries.noaa.gov/resource/document/fisheries-economics-united-states-report-2019.

NOAA Fisheries (2019a). Fisheries in the United States, 2019. http://media.fisheries.noaa.gov/2021-05/fus-2019-fact-sheet-v4.2-2-webready.pdf?null.

NOAA Fisheries (2019b, August 19). Details of the settlement of the government's civil case against Carlos Rafael and his fishing captains. https://www.fisheries.noaa.gov/new-england-mid-atlantic/enforcement/details-settlement-governments-civil-case-against-case-against-carlos.

NOAA Fisheries (2019c, August 2). Number of U.S. fish stocks at sustainable levels remains near record highs. https://www.fisheries.noaa.gov/media-release/number-us-fish-stocks-sustainable-levels-remains-near-record-high.

Pontecorvo, G. & Schrank, W.E. (2014). The continued decline of the world catch of marine fish. *Marine Policy*, 44, 117–119. https://doi.org/10.1016/j.marpol.2013.08.016.

Research and Markets (2019, February 7). Commercial fishing industry: Global market outlook (2016–2026). *PR Newswire*. https://www.prnewswire.com/news-releases/global-commercial-fishing-industry-market-to-2026---exhaustion-of-marine-resources-are-inhibiting-market-growth-300791788.html.

Rosenberg, A. (1996). Scientific review of definitions of overfishing in U.S. fishery management plans. *NOAA*. https://repository.library.noaa.gov/view/noaa/33512.

Schmalz, D. (2015, November 5). Chain reaction anchovies – a key food source for local marine ecosystem – might be in a state of collapse. *Monterey County Weekly*. http://www.montereycountyweekly.com/news/local_news/anchovies-a-key-food-source-for-local-marine-ecosystem-might/article_694d8eba-833-11e5-ab71-972eadd1888.html.

Simenstad, C.A., Estes, J.A., & Kenyon, K.W. (1978). Aleuts, sea otters, and alternate stable-state communities. *Science*, *200* (4340), 403–411. http://www.jstor.org/stable/1746443.

Smellie, S. (2021, April 18). It's more than just a fish: Scientists worry cod will never come back to N.L. [Newfoundland & Labrador]. *CTV News*. https://atlantic.ctvnews.ca/it-s-more-than-just-a-fish-scientists-worry-cod-will-never-come-back-in-n-l-1.5392101.

Steinsson, S, (2016) The cod wars: A re-analysis. *European Security*, *25* (2), 256–275, DOI: 10.1080/09662839.2016.1160376.

Urbina, I. (2020, August 17). How China's expanding fishing fleet is depleting the world's oceans. *Yale Environment 360*. https://e360.yale.edu/features/how-chinas-expanding-fishing-fleet-is-depleting-worlds-oceans.

United States Department of Justice (2016, October 6). Seven men plead guilty for illegally harvesting and selling American eels. https://www.justice.gov/opa/pr/seven-men-plead-guilty-illegally-harvesting-and-selling-american-eels.

United States Department of Justice (2013, October 28). Five Virginia charter fishing boat captains sentenced for Lacey Act violations. https://www.justice.gov/opa/pr/five-virginia-charter-fishing-boat-captains-sentenced-lacey-act-violations.

United States Department of Justice Office of Public Affairs (2015, January 21). Thirteen commercial fishermen charged in North Carolina with illegally harvesting and selling Atlantic striped bass. https://www.justice.gov/opa/pr/thirteen-cmmercial-fishermen-charged-north-carolina-illegally-harvesting-and-selling.

United States Department of Justice Office of Public Affairs (2009). Five Maryland commercial fishermen plead guilty to illegally overfishing striped bass. https://www.justice.gov/opa/pr/five-maryland-commercial-fishermen-plead-guilty-illegally-overfishing-striped-bass.

United States Geological Survey (USGS) (2016, May 1). What a drag: The global impact of bottom trawling. *Coastal and Marines Hazards and Resources Program*. https://www.usgs.gov/programs/cmhrp/news/what-drag-global-impact-bottom-trawling

U.S. Attorney's Office (2021, May 6). Operation targeting illegal fishing in the Bahamas nets conviction of Florida Keys man and vessel transfer. https://www.justice.gov/usao-sdfl/pr-operation-targeting-illegal-fishing-bahamas-nets-conviction-florida-keys-man-and-vessel.

U.S. Attorney's Office (2017, September 25). Owner of one of the nation's largest commercial fishing businesses sentenced for falsifying records and smuggling proceeds abroad. https://www.justice.gov/usao-ma/pr/owner-one-nation-s-largest-commercial-fishing-businesses-sentenced-falsifying-records.

U.S. Regional Fishery Management Councils (n.d.). Conserving and managing the fisheries of the United States. http://www.fisherycouncils.org/.

Valencia, M. (2017, April 17). Loss of 'Codfather' permits could hurt New Bedford. *Boston Globe*. https://www.bostonglobe.com/metro/2017/04/21/loss-codfather-permits-could-hurt-new-bedford/PpvcUf5L1Ak7MXCizuGsZO/story.html.

WBUR (2014, November 11). Fishermen protest cod fishing restrictions in Gulf of Maine. https://www.wbur.org/radioboston/2014/11/11/cod-fishing.

5 Wildlife Trade

Introduction

Wildlife trade is the focus of various multi-lateral and international agreements. Within the United States there are several laws that focus on the importation and export of animal species and products. There are older laws that govern domestic hunting practices and address the persistent problem of poaching. Hunting and poaching concerns are addressed by state conservation agencies. The control and oversight of wildlife trade is addressed at U.S. ports of entry through U.S. customs enforcement and through the U.S. Fish and Wildlife Service. This chapter will highlight the domestic laws and international agreements and demonstrate how wildlife trafficking operators impact both domestic security and U.S. businesses.

Wildlife trade is likely the most commonly thought of crime when people consider natural resource crimes. It represents a practice that has been around since the period of the antiquities and even then some species were traded to the point of extinction. "Ramses II was regularly seen with a tamed lion and Julius Caesar had allegedly received a giraffe from Cleopatra" (Van Uhm, 2016). People throughout the world have collected animals or their parts for medicine, decoration, pets, clothing, or food. Various demands on wildlife continue today to include private and unregulated zoos, tourist souvenirs that often come in the form of birds, sea horses, and reptiles, and activities such as recreation trophy hunting, and the poaching of high demand animals for profit. In many nations throughout the world there is weak enforcement of resource regulations, corrupt customs and conservation officers, and ineffectual punishment schemes with low cost fines and no imprisonment for poaching or wildlife crimes (Naylor, 2005). Poaching is distinguished from animal theft based on property rights. Poaching is theft of a public resource whereas animal theft is theft of private property. Poaching is defined generally as taking fish or game illegally or trespassing to take game and/or fish.

Animal protection activists and organizations have successfully drawn attention to the problem of diminishment of the elephant population due to poaching for the trade of ivory. While ivory can be collected from the tusks of narwhal (*Monodon monoceros*) and walrus (*Odobenus rosmarus*), it is most commonly harvested from the tusks of elephants. On January 18, 1990, an international ban on the trade of ivory went into effect. The ban had some effect in slowing trade in ivory but the

DOI: 10.4324/9781003241201-5

international ban did not make domestic trade in ivory illegal. China officially banned its ivory trade in 2017 and the United States created a near total ban on domestic trade in ivory with limited exceptions in 2016. The nation of Japan does not have a domestic ban on trade in ivory. This demonstrates that agreed upon international treaties do not necessarily drive domestic regulation. It is hard for an international agreement like the Convention on International Trade in Endangered Species of Wild Flora and Fauna (CITES) to reach its goals of a ban on ivory trade when there are open domestic markets for ivory and there is a high demand for a product that is becoming increasingly rare.

U.S. Fish and Wildlife (FWS) agents monitor wildlife shipments into and within the United States to ensure compliance with CITES and domestic laws. In addition to focusing on the ivory ban, the Fish and Wildlife Service focuses on export of American species and the import of other animals in addition to monitoring hunting at the 560 national wildlife refuges and fishing at the 340 national wildlife refuges, 35 wetland wildlife districts, and 20 national wildlife fisheries. All federal

Table 5.1 Global Illegal Wildlife Trade Values (US$)

	Year	*Value (billion $)*
UNEP, CITES, IUCN, TRAFFIC (Maguire & Haenlein, 2015)	2013	5–20
TRAFFIC (WWF International, 2012)	2014	5–20
Congressional Research Service (Pires, 2012)	2013	7–10
Kevin Xie, *Harvard International Review* (Wellsmith, 2011)	2015	7–10
Royal United Services Institute (African Wildlife Foundation, 2014)	2015	7–23
WWF and Dalberg Global Development Advisors (Wyatt and Cao, 2015)	2012	7.8–10
Stephen F. Pires, *Global Crime* (Morrison, 2014)	2012	8–10
Melanie Wellsmith, *European Journal on Criminal Policy and Research* (Southwick, 2013)	2011	9–11
African Wildlife Foundation (UNEP, 2013)	2014	10
U4 (The David Sheldrick Wildlife Trust, 2015)	2015	10–20
Sarah Morrison, *The Independent* (Office of the Director of National Intelligence, 2013)	2014	12
Natalie Southwick, *InSight Crime* (Ratchford, et al., 2013)	2013	15–20
UNEP and INTERPOL (Bergenas, 2013)	2013	15–20
David Sheldrick Wildlife Trust (Hastie & McCrea-Steele, 2014)	2015	15–20
Office of the Director for National Intelligence (Rossi, 2012)	2013	17
IFAW (Wilkins, 2014)	2013	19
Stimson Center (Vira, 2014)	2013	19
IFAW (UNEP, 2016)	2014	19
Victoria Rossi, *Insight Crime* (France-Presse, 2011)	2012	20
Hugh S. Wilkins, *Environmental Policy and Law* (Nat Geo Wild, 2011)	2014	20
C4ADS (Schearf, 2012)	2014	23
UNEP (Stiles, et al., 2013)	2016	23

Source: Originally published in May (2017). Creative Commons license.

laws that govern and provide authority to the U.S. Fish and Wildlife Service are under 16 United States Code Chapter 9.

Laws Most Commonly Enforced by Federal Law Enforcement

Aside from aforementioned laws such as the Lacey Act and the Endangered Species Act, there are a number of acts enforced by the U.S. Fish and Wildlife Service as they inspect shipments of animals and animal products that enter the U.S. at ports of entry such as seaport, airports, and land crossings. The Department of Homeland Security and the U.S. Department of Agriculture also have officers stationed at ports of entry to inspect suspicious shipments, particularly those which may have contraband to include the shipment of animal parts or animals that are endangered or prohibited from importation or export from the United States. Additionally, officers from public land agencies such as the National Park Service and Bureau of Land Management may report and investigate violations of these Acts. All agencies that investigate suspicions of violations of the following acts must coordinate with the U.S. Fish and Wildlife Service to enforce the Act. The full authority of the Acts is granted by Congress to the U.S. Fish and Wildlife Service, not to government agencies generally; therefore, when a federal agent uncovers violations, notifications are sent to the U.S. Fish and Wildlife Service which becomes the lead agency in both civil and criminal enforcement. The laws that are enforced include: the African Elephant and Conservation Act, The Bald and Golden Eagle Act, the Marine Mammal Protection Act, and the Migratory Bird Act.

African Elephant and Conservation Act

On October 7, 1988, the federal government enacted the African Elephant and Conservation Act (16 U.S.C. 4201). This act addresses the loss of African elephants (*Loxodonta Africana)* in the wild. African elephants are found in 37 African nations. There are approximately 415,000 elephants found in the wild (IUCN, 2021). The law permitted the U.S. government to fund and support foreign nations' actions against poachers. It also created restrictions in the importation and trade in ivory. The new law made it illegal for any person or vendor in the United States to export raw ivory or import ivory from a country that does not produce ivory, and it compels any importation of raw or worked ivory to have certification that verifies that the ivory is in compliance with CITES.

The Bald and Golden Eagle Act

On June 8, 1940, the federal government enacted the Bald and Golden Eagle Act (16 U.S.C. 668-668d). This act prevents any unpermitted take of a bald eagle (*Haliaeetus leucocephalus*) or a golden eagle (*Aquila chrysaetos*) alive or dead or in part, to include feathers and nest. If a person transports, attempts to sell or trade, exports or imports any protected eagle or part, the government can assess a civil penalty of

$12,000. If a person disturbs the nest, shoots, wounds, kills, or attempts to trap a protected eagle, disrupts its breeding, feeding, or sheltering behavior, or causes injury to a protected eagle, the government can impose a criminal penalty of $100,000 and one year imprisonment. The U.S. Fish and Wildlife Service provides permits to American Indian tribes for the purpose of limited collection of protected eagle feathers for the purpose of ritual or religious ceremony. The federal agency may also provide a permit for an eagle take for right-of-way permit holders such as those who construct or operate wind and/or solar farms (Bureau of Land Management, 2017).

Marine Mammal Protection Act

On October 21, 1972, U.S. Congress passed the Marine Mammal Protection Act (16 U.S.C. 1361–1407). This law was passed in conjunction with a series of environmental protection laws in the same year – the Federal Insecticide, Fungicide, and Rodenticide Act (FIFRA), the Clean Water Act (CWA), and the Marine Protections, Research, and Sanctuaries Act. The Marine Mammal Protection Act prohibited the sale, trade, import, and export of U.S. based marine mammals to include manatees (*Trichechus manatus*), dolphins (*Cetacea*), sea otter (*Enhydra lutris*), walrus (*Odobenus rosmarus*), dugong (*Sirenia*), and the polar bear (*Ursus maritimus*). The scientific consensus at the time was that human activities were disrupting populations of these species. The Marine Mammal Protection Act was intended to limit human activities within the species' habitats.

This act specifies under 16 U.S.C.1361 (2):

> such species and population stocks should not be permitted to diminish beyond the point at which they cease to be a significant functioning element in the ecosystem of which they are a part, and, consistent with this major objective, they should not be permitted to diminish below their optimum sustainable population.
>
> (Marine Mammal Commission, n.d.)

The civil penalty for a violation of the Marine Mammal Protection Act is a fine of $25,000.

Migratory Bird Act

One of the oldest conservation laws, the Migratory Bird Act was passed on July 3, 1918 (16 U.S.C. 703–712). This act prohibits the killing, capture, sale, and transportation of a protected bird species, in whole or in part to include feathers, nests, and eggs, which migrated between the United States and Canada. The act covered nearly 1,000 bird species. At the time the Act passed, the American public was reacting to the extinction of Labrador Ducks (*Camptorhynchus labradorius)*, Great Auks (*Pinguinus impennis)*, Passenger Pigeons (*Ectopistes migratorius*), Carolina Parakeets (*Conuropsis carolinensis*), and Heath Hens (*Tympanuchus cupido cupido)*.

To this day, the act is the most often used to protect non-endangered species. By the 1970s the federal government began to threaten prosecution against timber, mining, chemical, and oil and gas extraction companies for an unnecessary killing of birds. Until then, only hunters were prosecuted under the Migratory Bird Act. The U.S. Department of Justice warns companies that if they do not make infrastructure modifications to prevent bird deaths, the government can prosecute them for violations of the Act. The government induces voluntary compliance effectively through this recent application of the law.

In 2000, a federal appeals court found that private citizens can sue the U.S. government for violations of the Migratory Bird Act; however, a citizen cannot sue a private company for the same violations (Greenspan, 2015). The finding from the court differs from other environmental protection acts which permit citizens to sue corporations for violations of environmental laws: Resource Conservation and Recovery Act (42 U.S.C. §6872), Clean Water Act (33 U.S.C. §1365), Clean Air Act (42 U.S.C. §2604), and Endangered Species Act (16 U.S.C. §1540(g)).

By 2004, the list of bird species was amended to cover only birds that originate and migrate through the United States or its territories. The bird must have a biological or ecologic function on U.S. land. In 2020, the bird list was modified to include birds covered in treaties that are introduced to the United States or its territories via human activities. The list of protected birds can be found under the Code of Federal Regulations (CFR) Title 50 Part 10.13.

Rhinoceros and Tiger Act

On September 24, 1994, the Rhinoceros and Tiger Act was signed into law (16. U.S.C. 5306(a), 1538). This law permitted the U.S. Fish and Wildlife Service to provide funds to non-governmental organizations, the CITES Secretariat, and to foreign governments that participate in conservation of rhinoceros (*Rhinocerotidae*) and tigers (*Panthera tigris*). The law prohibits the sale, trade, import, and export of tigers and rhinoceros in whole or part. The civil penalty for violating this act is $17,403.

Wild Bird Conservation Act

On October 23, 1992, the Wild Bird Conservation Act was signed into law (16 U.S.C. 4901–4916). This act prohibits the importation of exotic birds to the United States when their importation is disruptive to the species or does not serve a biological function in the United States. The term "exotic" is used to include any live or dead bird (animal under species *Aves*) that is not indigenous to the fifty states or District of Colombia. It also includes protection for importation of birds which are primarily found in Africa, Madagascar, Australia, and South America in an attempt to preserve wild flocks. The civil penalty for violating 4910(a)(3) is $20,217 whereas any other violation of the Wild Bird Conservation Act has a penalty of $839 (Civil Procedures, 2016).

Biological and Ecological Conservation

For those who are focused on biological diversity, a main concern of wildlife trade is the impact on available wildlife populations. When one visits zoos or animal parks that are focused on conservation, signs usually appear that designate an animal species as "critically endangered," "vulnerable," or "not vulnerable in the wild," etc. The posted signs often reflect the status of an animal based on the International Union for the Conservation of Nature (IUCN). Founded in 1948, the IUCN is a European-based environmental organization which, along with the UN Environment Program and World Wildlife Fund, has promoted directives that endorse sustainable development, environmental assessments, and conservation areas. The IUCN is unlike the UN in that it does not create treaties or binding conventions. It fosters cooperation between non-governmental organizations, governments, and political entities throughout 160 nations. In 1963 the IUCN created an endangered or threatened species list, referred to as the IUCN Red List. This detailed list specifies a scale of how abundant or scarce an animal is in the wild. The range of the IUCN categories are: Extinct, Extinct in the Wild, Critically Endangered, Endangered, Vulnerable, Near Threatened, Least Concern, Data Deficient, and Not Evaluated (IUCN.org). Vulnerable, Endangered, and Critically Endangered species are considered to be threatened with extinction. The Red List reviews animal species as well as fungus and plants. The Red List is used by zoos, academics, and conservationists, along with data from the U.S. Endangered Species Act and Convention on Biological Diversity (CBD), a part of the United Nations Environment Program, to determine conservation policies, biodiversity assessments, and estimations of an ecological system.

The reliance on the IUCN data has not been without controversy. Several scientific assessments have challenged the data and thereby its use in determining biodiversity and species loss. In a paper published in *Diversity and Distributions*, authors C. Loehle and W. Eschenbach wrote,

> Only six continental birds and three continental mammals were in standard bases as going extinct since 1500 compared to 123 bird species and 58 mammal species on islands. Of the extinctions, 95% were on islands. In evaluating extinction data, it is useful to consider islands as a special case. It is well known that island biota are generally at a higher risk of extinction.
>
> (Loehle & Eschenbach, 2012)

Other publications indicate that the rate of extinction loss is less than commonly believed when the IUCN data is scrutinized. One key criticism is the calculation of risk to a species. Scientific evaluators assess elements, characteristics, and qualities that are often uncertain. A study funded by the National Science Foundation, the University of California, Santa Barbara, and the Australian Research Council tested the consistency of the classification schemes by having eighteen scientists conduct evaluations of thirteen species. All were provided the same data. They were tasked with assessing the classification of risk of extinction of each species. The researchers reported:

> We tested three widely used systematic classification protocols employed by the World Conservation Union, NatureServe, and the Florida Fish and Wildlife Conservation Commission. We provided 18 assessors with identical information for 13 different species to infer estimates for each of the required parameters for the three protocols. The threat classification of several of the species varied from low risk to high risk, depending on who did the assessment. This occurred across the three protocols investigated. Assessors tended to agree on their placement of species in the highest (50–70%) and lowest risk categories (20–40%), but there was poor agreement on which species should be placed in the intermediate categories.
>
> (Regan, et al., 2005)

Their study was published in the journal *Conservation Biology*. Other scientists have reached similar conclusions when examining specific species (Webb, 2008). Researcher Grahame Webb of the School of Environmental Research in Australia found that the protocols for classifications by the IUCN Red List were complicated due to the demands of scientists and advocates, the demand to accurately assess historical abundance, to develop biodiversity benchmarks and "to meet the often conflicting views and values of diverse IUCN members" while confronting the politics of conservation (Webb, 2008).

Despite concerns expressed by Professor Webb and others, the IUCN Red List continues to be relied upon for conservation policies. The argument of activists and conservation biologists appears to be a concern for wildlife trade impacts on species' populations. A quantitative meta- analysis of thirty-one studies, conducted by Oscar Morton and others at the University of Sheffield (United Kingdom), demonstrated that animal species declined when they were close to human settlements and were in areas where there were insufficient game wardens to enforce hunting quotas and enforce protected area boundaries. In the study published in *Nature Ecology and Evolution*, Morton and others researched wildlife populations in areas that allowed hunting and areas where no hunting occurred. The researchers examined 133 species – ninety-nine mammal species, twenty-four bird species, and ten reptile species – and determined that animals that were traded for food experienced a nearly 60% decline in population, when animals such as songbirds were being trapped for sale as pets, populations declined nearly 73%, and animal populations in protected areas dropped by 39% (Morton, et al., 2021). The research did not evaluate amphibians, invertebrates, or plants. Of the thirty-one studies evaluated, only four were in Asia which is a hot spot for wildlife trade. Yet, a review of the study published in *Science* quoted Steve Broad, executive director of TRAFFIC, a non-governmental organization based in Cambridge, England, focused on wildlife trafficking, biodiversity, and sustainable development, as concluding that the study's results could be from "habitat degradation or loss" rather than wildlife trade (Pennisi, 2021).

The divergence of conclusions and interpretations by NGOs, government agencies, and academic researchers makes it hard to know conclusively the specific amounts of species' population loss. Some species, such as those which produce ivory, are heavily traded on the black market and receive a great deal of attention by the media, governments, and NGOs due to the value of ivory and, therefore, the data is more robust. Other species, while receiving less focus, are susceptible to illegal markets. Media and conservation focus on elephant ivory, rhino horn, and pangolin scales, yet much of the illegal trade in animal parts involves reptiles, birds, and primates (Interpol, 2022). In a 2022 combined law enforcement operation, codenamed Thunder 2022, which took place for the month of October 2022, a combination of police, customs, conservation enforcement agencies, financial intelligence units, and forestry officers in 125 nations worked to arrest 934 suspects, identified 141 companies involved in illegal sales of species listed under CITES, and the seizures of 2,200 animals, animal parts, and plants. The seizures included 1,190 tortoises and turtles, 1,795 reptiles, and 750 birds (Interpol, 2022; Weerth, 2020). Despite these impressive numbers, one consideration to put the scale of animal trafficking versus plant trafficking in perspective, is of the 35,811 species listed on CITES, 24,484 species are orchids (Masters, et al., 2022). The overwhelming focus by researchers, the press, and NGOs is on animal trade, not plant trade.

Government Funding of Conservation and Enforcement

The United States was not a part of Operation Thunder 2022 but the United States government via the U.S. Agency for International Development (USAID) and the State Department has funded training and resources for conservation enforcement in multiple nations. The U.S. Fish and Wildlife Service established law enforcement attachés in U.S. embassies in Botswana, China, Gabon, Peru, Tanzania, and Thailand. In 2016, more than seventy prosecutors and judges in eleven African nations received training from the U.S. Department of Justice via USAID grants (U.S. State Department, 2017). USAID in conjunction with the State Department funded canine detection units situated in airports, sea ports, and other transit zones in Kenya, Tanzania, and Uganda which enabled the seizure of 1,000 live tortoises and more than two tons of ivory in a two month period in 2016 (U.S. State Department, 2017).

The U.S. Fish and Wildlife Service funded training and forensic capacity for the identification of species in forty-eight nations. The funding, which averages $54 million per year, is allotted through a grant program that is awarded to five species conservation funds: African Elephant Conservation Fund, Asian Elephant Conservation Fund, Rhino Tiger Conservation Fund, Great Ape Conservation Fund, and Marine Turtle Conservation Fund. The funding is awarded to non-governmental organizations, individuals, multi-national secretariats, foreign national and local government agencies, for-profit organizations, public and private institutions of higher education, and U.S. territorial or tribal governments. In Central America, the Office of the U.S. Trade Representative, under the Dominican Republic-Central America-United States Free Trade Agreement (CAFTA-DR) supported the Central

American Wildlife Enforcement Network (CAWEN) which promoted enforcement operations in Costa Rica, El Salvador, Honduras, and Panama. Additionally, the Office of the Director of National Intelligence created a Combating Wildlife Trafficking analytical group to assist in operations overseas (U.S. State Department, 2017).

Through funding and training, the U.S. government facilitates conservation operations throughout the world and works to develop stronger enforcement structures in areas which are known to be source countries for wildlife trade. The U.S. government has, through the passage of the Eliminate, Neutralize, and Disrupt Wildlife Trafficking Act of 2016 (P.L. 114–231, 16 U.S.C. §§7601–7644) and an executive order (Order 13773) signed by President Donald Trump on February 9, 2017, ordered an annual assessment of federal agencies' priorities and assessments of international efforts to prevent wildlife trafficking in the future. The Act established a task force co-chaired by the U.S. Department of the Interior, Secretary of State, and the Attorney General (U.S. State Department, 2021).

In a manner similar to allocation of funding that supports conservation efforts overseas, the United States federal government funds programs via grants to state conservation agencies. Since 2000, the U.S. Fish and Wildlife Service's Wildlife and Sport Fish Restoration Program has allocated $1 billion to all states and U.S. territories including the District of Colombia via the State Wildlife Grant Program. The money is used by state and territorial fish and wildlife agencies to create and operationalize programs that promote wildlife habitats. Grant funds are used to conduct research such as fish and wildlife surveys, complete species restoration, conduct habitat management, and to monitor of species populations. Traditionally, funds collected from fishing and hunting licenses paid for conservation efforts to state wildlife agencies to include enforcement by game wardens. Over the last twenty years many states experienced a significant decline in hunting participation. Funds for state conservation agencies were derived from hunting license sales and federal excise taxes on firearms, ammunition, and angling equipment provided additional funding via the Pittman-Robertson Wildlife Restoration Act and Dingell-Johnson Sport Fish Restoration Act.

The Pittman-Robertson Wildlife Restoration Act (16 U.S.C.A. 669 et seq.) was passed in 1937. This act took the excise tax on ammunition and firearms and diverted those funds to state wildlife agencies. This law prevents states from redirecting funds collected from hunting license fees and hunting equipment sales to other agencies. The excise tax is collected from importers and manufacturers of hunting and fishing equipment. Under 16 U.S.C. 669b(a) and 26 U.S.C. 4181, there is an 11% tax on firearms and ammunition, including shells and cartridges, 10% tax on revolvers and pistols, 11% tax on bows, attachable accessories, quivers, broadheads, or points. Commonly each year the breakdown of excise tax revenue is as follows: 34.7% from ammunition, 30.3% from firearms, 30.2% from pistols and revolvers, and 4.8% from archery equipment (Congressional Research Service, 2022).

Under the Pittman-Robertson Act the federal share for states is not to exceed 75% of the project cost (16 U.S.C. §§669e, 669g(b), and 669h-1). The federal share for territories is outlined in 16 U.S.C. §669g-1, which states, "the Secretary [of the Interior] shall in no event require any of said cooperating agencies [in the territories] to pay an amount which will exceed 25 per centum of the cost of any project" (Congressional Research Service, 2019). The federal allotment of funding is based on a two-part formula. The first calculation is the area of the state compared with the total area of all states. The second calculation is the number of paid hunting licenses sold in one state compared to the total number of paid hunting licenses in all states. Hunting licenses sold in U.S. territories and the District of Colombia are not calculated in the total number of hunting licenses sold.

The user-pay system created a public benefit. As hunting has fallen out of favor as an appealing activity, funding available to state conservation agencies have diminished. "Hunting participation peaked in 1982, when nearly seventeen million hunters purchased 28.3 million licenses. Today, however, only 11.5 million people in the United States actually hunt. That's less than 4% of the national population" (Moore, 2021). According to a 2016 National Survey of Fishing, Hunting, and Wildlife-Associated Recreation conducted by the U.S. Fish and Wildlife Service, the number of hunters in the United States declined by 16% (2.2 million individuals) compared to the similar survey in 2011 (from 13.7 million in 2011 to 11.5 million in 2016) (Congressional Research Service, 2019).

Similar to the Pittman-Robertson Wildlife Restoration Act, the Dingell-Johnson Sport Fish Restoration Act (16 U.S.C. §§777 et seq.) collects excise taxes to distribute to the states using a similar formula to the hunting act but applies it to fishing. The Dingell-Johnson Sport Fish Restoration Act, passed by Congress in 1950, collects taxes from motorboat fuel, fishing equipment, and electric outboard motors. The formula is a calculation of 60% derived from fishing license totals and 40% comes from the calculation of the state's geographic size. The funds are used to promote and protect fish habitat.

While there are federal funds and grants to support state wildlife agencies, 60% of all parks and wildlife agency revenues are derived from licenses and passes (Brown, 2020; Rott, 2018). The reduction in the number of hunting licenses has significantly reduced wildlife agencies' capacities. Law enforcement divisions of state wildlife agencies comprise on average 5% of the wildlife agency's budget. When the conservation agency's overall budget declines, so do the available funds for law enforcement operations that are tasked with enforcing state conservation laws. States have tried to compensate for fewer funds by lottery ticket sales, specialized license plate proceeds, motorized recreation vehicle registration fees, and fees from annual state park passes. The funds collected employing these methods have not successfully filled the gaps created by a reduction in hunting license fees (Moore, 2021).

The U.S. Fish and Wildlife Service

As of 2022, there are 208 criminal investigators in the Fish and Wildlife Service (U.S. Fish and Wildlife Service, 2022). There are an additional 135 fish and wildlife inspectors who check shipments that arrive throughout U.S. ports of entry. The U.S. Fish and Wildlife Service initiated a law enforcement service in response to the Lacey Act. In 1975, the U.S. Fish and Wildlife Service hired its first biological technician to work as an inspector at John F. Kennedy Airport in Queens, New York. Since then, the U.S. Fish and Wildlife Service has operated a Wildlife Inspection Program which is implemented in forty-five ports of entry. Since then, the law enforcement unit expanded to include: a Branch of Training and Inspection, International Operations Unit, Special Investigations Unit, Wildlife Intelligence Unit, the National Fish and Wildlife Forensics Laboratory, National Wildlife Repository and National Eagle Repository, Digital Evidence Recovery and Technical Support Unit, Professional Responsibility Unit (internal affairs), Investigations Unit, Branch of Planning and Analysis, and its Law Enforcement Management Information System (U.S. Fish and Wildlife Service, 2022). These units work to support wildlife case investigations with the intent of filing cases for criminal prosecution under the federal Department of Justice. The training and inspection units train foreign conservation agencies in support of investigation and the prosecution of wildlife trade cases overseas.

The U.S. Fish and Wildlife Service does not issue hunting and fishing licenses. Those are issued by state conservation agencies. The U.S. Fish and Wildlife Service issues permits for the importation and exportation of animals, animal parts, plants, or timber that are listed under CITES. The permits include the importation of wildlife hunting trophies which may include rhinoceros horn. While rhinoceros horn is not legal to trade in the United States, a hunter who lawfully obtained a permit from the governments of Namibia or South Africa – the two nations which allow limited, regulated rhinoceros hunting – to hunt a rhinoceros, its body or parts can be imported with the proper Fish and Wildlife Service permit. This permitted importation is considered a loophole in ivory trade bans. That loophole is exploited by criminal groups which illegally sell and trade banned ivory and ivory products.

As an example, the U.S. Fish and Wildlife Service initiated a wide-ranging multi-year enforcement action called Operation Crash. The intent was to find and prosecute those who illegally trade in ivory from elephants or rhinoceros. In 2011, a man who used the name John Sullivan contacted a taxidermist in Commerce City, Colorado and told the taxidermist that he wanted rhinoceros hunting trophies to decorate a building in Ireland. The taxidermist who was aware of the laws requiring permits to export a hunting trophy alerted the Fish and Wildlife Service. Soon thereafter two undercover agents sold a pair of rhinoceros horns to two men, Richard O'Brien and his brother-in-law, Michael Hegarty upon their arrival in Colorado (Fears, 2014; Higgenbotham, 2014). When Fish and Wildlife Special Agent Curtis Graves, acting as an undercover agent, asked the buyers if they were nervous about the purchase, they responded that their "organization made similar transactions all over the world" and that "their modus operandi was foolproof" (Fears, 2014). They handed Agent Graves $12,850 in cash and were promptly arrested (Higginbotham 2014).

The undercover agents discovered that the purchasers had criminal histories and were members of an international crime syndicate known as the Rathkeale Rovers – a criminal organization named for their base: Rathkeale, Ireland. O'Brien and Hegarty were sentenced to six months imprisonment and two years of supervised release. Not long after, in 2012, Michael Slattery, a member of the Rathkeale Rovers, purchased a rhinoceros horn trophy at an auction outside of

Dallas, Texas with forged documents. Under U.S. law any person who lawfully imports a rhinoceros or elephant ivory as a hunting trophy is allowed to sell the trophy so long as the buyer is a resident of the same state. The trophy cannot be sold for profit, meaning the seller must not sell the hunting trophy for more money than was spent on the hunt and the lawful permitting process. In the 2012 crime, Mr. Slattery possessed forged documents to show he was a resident of Texas. He was sentenced to one year in prison in 2014.

The value of the rhinoceros horn and ivory trade greatly exceeds the risk of punishment. A pound of rhinoceros horn sells for as much as $45,000 and the punishment for wildlife trafficking tends more toward fines than imprisonment (Fears, 2014). In an interview with *Bloomberg Business*, then Deputy Assistant Director Edward Grace stated that a first time offender who attempted to import a kilogram of heroin into the United States would receive a ten year prison sentence; whereas, the same person would be ordered to less than a year, if any prison sentence was ordered, and more likely only a fine, if he was to import a kilogram of rhinoceros horn. Deputy Assistant Director Grace stated, "It's a high profit, low risk crime" (Higginbotham, 2014). As exemplified by Mr. Hegarty's criminal behavior, the prison terms tend to be a minor cost of doing business. In 2017, Mr. Hegarty was tried in a federal court in Miami, Florida for attempting to smuggle a drinking cup carved from a rhinoceros horn from the United States to England. He was sentenced to eighteen months in prison (Willsher & Carroll, 2021).

In September 2021, eight men were convicted in a court in Rennes, France, for trafficking in rhinoceros horn and elephant ivory between East Asia and Europe. Four of the men were members of the Rathkeale Rovers. The Rovers had been stopped in a random traffic inspection in September 2015 and were found to have four non-certified elephant trunks and €32,800 ($34,918) in cash (Willsher & Carroll, 2021). French police discovered that the Rovers converted the ivory into powder in two workshops they operated in France. With the assistance of two Chinese citizens who were defendants at the same trial, the Rovers then shipped the rhino horn and ivory tusk powder to Vietnam and China where the powder is used in traditional medicine. The workshops held an additional thirty-two raw ivory tusks and an additional eleven processed tusks (O'Connor, 2021).

> Unknown in the United States, the Rovers were infamous in Europe for their snatch-and-grab thefts at museums in Britain and other nations, yanking rhinoceros horn from exhibits, police said. Thanks to gangs such as the Rovers, replicas are used in place of real rhino horns in museums throughout Europe.
>
> (Fears, 2014)

Members of the Rathkeale Rovers were fined €316,000 ($336,405) by the French court.

The Rathkeale Rovers were known to engage in illicit trade of antiques which led to their foray into wildlife trade. They already had an established international network having committed such crimes as selling counterfeit electronics, money laundering, drug trafficking, tarmacking fraud (a common scam in which criminals sell inferior and/or inappropriate asphalt for the surfacing of roads and driveways), and robbery. The crime syndicate is believed to operate in sixteen countries (Embuscado, 2016). Reports from Europol indicate that the criminal organization had been operating in wildlife trade since 2009. In January of 2010, customs inspectors in Ireland's Shannon Airport confiscated eight rhinoceros horns that were in two passengers' luggage (Higginbotham, 2014). One of the passengers was Michael O'Brien, the brother of Richard O'Brien who was arrested for attempting to purchase the rhinoceros horn in Colorado in 2011. Due to the tightknit group of smugglers and criminals within the syndicate, the Irish police have not been able to arrest them. While the Rathkeale Rovers are known to Dublin's Criminal Assets Bureau, which is responsible for investigating organized crime, the Rovers tend not to commit their crimes in Ireland. Thus the Irish police have been able to provide criminal intelligence to Europol but have not been able to curtail the Rovers' criminal actions. Since these arrests were made, Michael O'Brien has sued *Bloomberg Business* for defamation for referring to him as a "criminal mastermind" (O'Connor, 2021).

By the end of 2017, Operation Crash concluded with fifty individuals criminally charged, thirty-nine convictions of illegal trafficking in rhinoceros horns, $2.1 million in fines, $5.6 million in restitution, and a combined 438 months' imprisonment (36.5 years) for all offenders (Eisele, 2017). The operation was focused on smuggling, unlawful rhinoceros hunting by American hunters, and sale of raw and carved rhinoceros horns. Defendants were charged with violations of the Lacey Act and Endangered Species Act, as well as mail fraud and conspiracy. Some of the recovered illegal funds seized during Operation Crash were used to purchase land in Kenya in hopes of enhancing conservation efforts to preserve the rhinoceros (Eisele, 2017).

Online Wildlife Sales

International smugglers who commit taxidermy larceny in museums or purchase hunting trophies under false pretenses are only one part of illegal transnational wildlife trade. The American company Facebook, and its online subsidiary Instagram, often advertise wildlife for sale. The sites are protected by the First Amendment right of free speech. Even though Facebook declared in 2016 that it was committed to stopping illegal wildlife trade by joining the Coalition to End Wildlife Trafficking Online with thirty other technology companies, various webpages depict vulnerable or endangered animals such as cheetahs for sale (World Wildlife Fund, 2021). The Coalition agreement compelled the technology firms to remove 80% of their online wildlife sale sites by 2020. The Alliance to Counter Crime Online, a program within the Center on Illicit Networks and Organized Crime, conducted a study to determine how effective the Facebook pledge was. In 2020, 473 Facebook webpages were identified as sites that promoted the sale of wildlife (Paul, et al., 2020). More than half were created after Facebook joined the coalition. While the site reduced English language pages, sites in Arabic, Vietnamese and Indonesian languages did not decrease (Paul, et al., 2020). Not all wildlife listed for sale are endangered or threatened but the impact of permitted animal sales encourages a global market in wildlife trade.

Companies like Facebook create opportunities for small and medium size vendors to reach consumers far beyond their local market. Studies have been conducted to determine how many orchids were sold on the website, eBay. Researchers from the Netherlands analyzed purchases of orchids or items listed as orchids. Throughout 2019 and the first six months of 2020 a total of 1,942 items were purchased with a value of $37,742.62 (Masters, et al., 2022). The plants and plant materials had their DNA tested at Kew Gardens in England and other laboratories. Some of the plants were mislabeled and others contained adulterants which represented items that were of lesser value than those sold. This demonstrates the need for greater oversight and regulations for online plant and animal sales.

Social media can provide intelligence and indicators of illegal markets to investigators. It can also provide evidence of illegal hunting. On February 5, 2021, a federal court in Oregon ordered Adrian D. Wood to six months of confinement and five years of probation for hunting in Crater Lake National Park. The defendant pled guilty to violating the Lacey Act for shooting a bull elk. The hunter posted images of his kills on social media and sent images of his kills via texts to other hunters who alerted the U.S. Fish and Wildlife Service (FWS). FWS investigators seized GPS equipment which showed that Mr. Wood hunted within the boundaries of the national park. In addition to his probation and confinement, Mr. Wood was ordered to pay $42,500 in restitution to the park and forfeit his hunting equipment which included several firearms and assorted ammunition (Department of Justice, 2021).

Another case demonstrates how wildlife traffickers use online sites to locate buyers. On August 24, 2022, Jose Manuel Perez pled guilty to Lacey Act violations of trafficking and smuggling wildlife. Mr. Perez, along with his sister Stephany Perez who has been indicted for conspiracy to violate the Lacey Act, imported more than 1,700 reptiles into the United States across the Mexico border. The defendants used social media to sell the animals they smuggled into the U.S. They posted images and videos of the animals in the wild in Mexico as advertisements for buyers in the United States. Animals imported from Mexico include Mexican box turtles (*Terrapene Mexicana*), Yucatan box turtles (*Terrapene yucatana*), immature crocodiles (*Crocodylus acutus*), and Mexican beaded lizards (*Heloderma horridum*). Animals were often smuggled via car across the border at El Paso, Texas. The defendants sometimes paid individuals as transports to cross the border with smuggled animals. On February 25, 2022, Mr. Perez entered the United States with sixty reptiles concealed in his clothing. He had animals hidden in his pants both in the pockets and in the groin area, in his jacket pockets, and in his pant legs. Three of the animals died in this smuggling attempt. The total value of the sixty reptiles was $740,000 (Department of Justice, 2022). The U.S. Fish and Wildlife Service investigators worked with the Department of Homeland Security to facilitate the federal investigation that was prosecuted in the Central District of California Federal Court.

While there are opportunists such as Jose and Stephany Perez who pursue smuggling animals as a low-risk high-reward business, others who would otherwise know better can easily cross the line into illegality with the presumption that online sales are not monitored. Dr. Richard Kazmaier, a professor of biology at West Texas A&M University was indicted in January of 2022 for illegally smuggling animal parts into the United States. Dr. Kazmaier pled guilty to violating the Lacey Act after he admitted to importing

> wildlife items from Bulgaria, Canada, China, Czech Republic, Indonesia, Latvia, Norway, Russia, South Africa, Spain, the United Kingdom, and Uruguay into Texas without declaring them. Kazmaier admitted he purchased and imported approximately 358 wildlife items with a total market value of $14,423 from eBay and other online sales websites.
>
> (Department of Justice, 2023b)

The biologist admitted to importing fourteen protected species without the appropriate and required permits for: caracal (*Caracal caracal*), the greater naked-tailed armadillo (*Cabassous tatouay*), Eurasian otter (*Lutra lutra*), lynx (L. lynx), king bird-of-paradise (*Cicinnurus regius*), and vervet monkey (*Chlorocebus pygerythrus*). Dr. Kazmaier did not import live animals. His imports included taxidermy, skulls, and skeletons. The professor was discovered by law enforcement as part of Operation Global Reach which the U.S. Fish and Wildlife Service launched to target wildlife being exported from Indonesia. Dr. Kazmaier resigned from his position as faculty in October 2022. These cases demonstrate the utility of searching for evidence of illegal hunts and trades using information posted on the internet via social media sites.

Wildlife Trade and Organized Crime

Wildlife trade is often related to organized crime (Anagnostou & Doberstein, 2022; Felbab-Brown, 2022; Moreto & Van Uhm, 2021; Nurse & Wyatt, 2020; Van Uhm & Wong, 2021). The data to support the role of transnational organized crime is inconsistent. Like many crimes, illegal trafficking of wildlife can be an opportunistic crime. When compared to the international drug trade, which has robust long-term data, wildlife trade estimates vary between $5 billion and $40 billion, whereas the global drug trade is estimated to have a value of $94 billion at the wholesale level and $332 billion at the retail level (South & Wyatt, 2011). While there is sufficient data to determine the volume and value of narcotics, the difficulty with estimating the cost of the illicit trade of wildlife is that the value is based often on customs declarations, not the retail value which can vary widely. The nature of the products is that they come from remote areas and are often mislabeled intentionally. The difference between some of the better studied illicit networks like narcotics trafficking compared to wildlife trade is that there are just over 200 federal wildlife agents in the U.S. whereas there are 5,000 narcotics law enforcement officers (Elliot, 2009). The data therefore is weaker in wildlife crimes. The conservation agencies that drive the data are capturing a small part of the wildlife trade. Even though this is likely true with narcotics trade, the amount of data is more robust due to the number of seizures, arrests, and intelligence gathering operations. While drugs are often smuggled, wildlife trade tends to be shipped with forged documents which serve to make the shipment appear legal. This along with the small number of fish and game officers make the wildlife trade data less reliable. A table created by Global Financial Integrity demonstrates the cost range as produced by various entities seeking to determine the global value of illicit wildlife trafficking (Table 5.1).

Parallel trafficking is more likely to happen with criminal organizations rather than opportunistic offenders. Parallel trafficking can be defined as one organization involved in multiple criminal activities. This is distinguished from shared smuggling route crimes where the same pattern and route for smuggling contraband takes place (Anagnostou & Doberstein, 2022). Illicit markets, whether for weapons, drugs, or wildlife trade, involve concealed profits and financial transactions. Since organized crime networks are entrepreneurial, they frequently will participate in multiple criminal trades and activities at once and maximize opportunities as demand exceeds supply for illicit products.

> Criminal organizations actively analyze opportunities to enter new black markets, balancing the potential rewards, with the existing penalties to diversify the range of their illicit activities accordingly. The business models for traffickers seek to develop economic synergies by leveraging their networks in transportation and money laundering, which equips them to deal in everything from counterfeit automobile parts to human parts.
>
> (Office of Economic Cooperation and Development, 2016)

Inspectors in Miami, Florida, found condoms filled with cocaine sewn into 312 boa constrictors. The weight of the cocaine was eighty pounds (Rosenberg, 2009). Other cases have been uncovered where drugs and wildlife products were combined to be part of a parallel trafficking case.

The strongest links between organized crime and wildlife trafficking are associated with China and Mexico. While much focus of illicit wildlife trade is on ivory, which often involves small and diffuse networks in Africa, there is a robust trade in reptiles and fish that comingle with narcotics smuggling and money laundering (Felbab-Brown, 2022; Moreto & Van Uhm, 2021).

> The legal trade in wildlife also increasingly facilitates the money laundering activities of Mexican criminal groups, with various wildlife products used by Mexican criminal groups as a value transfer mechanism to Chinese traders in exchange for precursor chemicals for illegal drugs as such fentanyl and methamphetamine, which are then produced in Mexico from the precursors. Indeed, in Mexico, far more so than in other parts of the world, poaching and wildlife trafficking for Chinese markets is increasingly thickly intermeshed with drug trafficking, money laundering, and value transfer in illicit economies.
>
> (Felbab-Brown, 2022)

Organized crime groups in Mexico, particularly the Sinaloa Cartel, have taken over various licit markets in agriculture and fishing. The takeover of some fisheries has put the cartel in direct contact with Chinese traders (Sumaila, et al., 2020; Witbooi, et al., 2020). The relationship between Mexico and China is unique in that neither nation's governments appear to be sincere in attempting to enforce environmental laws or restrict poaching, illegal wildlife trade, or mitigate illicit markets.

While much can be written about direct connections between Chinese and Mexican organized crime, the United States can operate as an intermediary between smaller operators who do not appear to be connected to organized crime but function in a black market that is created by the larger parallel traffickers. In Operation Apex, the U.S. Fish and Wildlife Service along with the Drug Enforcement Administration (DEA), U.S. Marshals Service, and Homeland Security Investigations (HSI) pursued a case where two businesses and twelve individuals were targeted for illegal wildlife trade, trafficking in marijuana, and money laundering (Drug Enforcement Administration, 2020). The case involved bulk cash deposits that derived from illegal activities. The cash was deposited and laundered through the purchase of diamonds and precious metals. Federal investigators seized $3.9 million from multiple bank accounts and approximately $1 million in diamonds and $3 million worth of gold, silver, and other precious metals (Department of Justice, 2020). In addition, federal agents seized 34.5 pounds of marijuana, 18,000 marijuana plants, eighteen totoaba (*Totoaba macdonaldi*) fish bladders, and documentary evidence of trade of six tons of shark fins (Drug Enforcement Administration, 2020; Ortiz, 2020). The totoaba is an endangered fish and its bladder is considered a delicacy in the Asian market (Carrington, 2017). The shark fins were shipped through Phoenix Fisheries, LLC, a Florida-based business which created false commercial invoices to ship the shark fins to Hong Kong. The sharks and fish were harvested in Mexico and arranged for shipment to Hong Kong via the United States and Canada (Department of Justice, 2020). The twelve defendants were arrested in Arizona, California, Florida, Georgia, and Michigan. This case demonstrates the value of wildlife trade, the opportunities to comingle multiple illicit smuggling operations, and parallel trafficking crimes. Those arrested in this case were charged with mail and wire fraud conspiracy, conspiracy to possess with intent to distribute controlled substances, and money laundering conspiracy (18 U.S.C. §§1349, 1956 (h)) and 21 U.S.C. §846). These charges vary from the environmental laws such as the Lacey Act and have larger criminal penalties in both fines and prison sentencing.

Conclusion

Wildlife trafficking is a topic well known to the public through media exposure. The buying and selling of protected or managed species has escalated globally. The demand has been accelerated due to the increase in wealth across the population in China which drives two of the largest illegal traded products: ivory and pangolin. The United States acts both as a pass-through nation and a consumer nation of illegally harvested animal products. Owning or consuming rare and endangered species promotes a wealthy status. Traders in wildlife species or parts are able to transact in large sums of cash which causes wildlife trafficking to be associated with money laundering, corruption, and fraudulent documentation.

The prior mention of the links between cartels, organized crime, and wildlife trafficking has been established by U.S. researchers, the federal government, various international non-governmental organizations, and third-party risk managers who assess risk in global supply chains (Bernal, 2023). Mexican cartels can trade in wildlife products to the Chinese to avoid money laundering sanctions. The trade in wildlife shows us that there are variations in the types of traffickers from the large scale international crime syndicate to the local poacher. This range does not impede investigations or enforcement. In some ways, the detection and adjudication of wildlife crimes is easier in that the criminals who engage in narcotics trafficking also engage in wildlife trafficking. The law enforcement resources that are applied to trafficking routes can be used to track various illicit products, not just one.

United States law enforcement has been most productive at the ports of entry and through detection from the use of social media websites. Preventing illegal wildlife products from entering the country is the most effective tool to address this crime. The penalties that are already in place to address wildlife trafficking are effectively applied from both state and federal governments. The greatest threats to wildlife via illegal trade often occur outside the borders and grasp of U.S. law.

Discussion Questions

1. What are the characteristics of the most trafficked species? Who is the largest consumer of trafficked wildlife?
2. What is the appeal of consuming or owning a trafficked species?
3. Why are trafficked plants and plant products not covered by the press as often as animal species?
4. How do the regulations of wildlife trafficking affect art and antique dealers in the United States?
5. How do investigators use social media to assist in identifying criminals who engage in wildlife trafficking?

Further Reading Recommendations

1. Ashe, D. (2020). Wildlife trafficking. Association of Zoos and Aquariums. http://aza.org/connect-stories/stories/wildlife-trafficking.
2. Financial Times. Big game, big money: Inside the illegal wildlife trade [Video]. https://youtu.be/lzYrtRkGcuo?si=j2Bb6hL_Y2kcAJMl.
3. Rademeyer, J. (2012). *Killing for profit: Exposing the illegal rhino horn trade*. Zebra Press.
4. United States Customs and Border Protection. Wildlife trafficking. http://cbp.gov/trade/programs-administration/natural-resources-protection/wildlife-trafficking.
5. U.S. Department of Homeland Security. Help make wildlife traffickers an endangered species. http://ice.gov/features/wildlife.

References

African Wildlife Foundation (2014). Tackling poaching & illegal wildlife trafficking in Africa. https://www.awf.org/sites/default/files/media/Re-sources/Facts%20%26amp%3B%20Brochures/Wildlife%20trafficking%20booklet_lower-res.pdf.

Agence France-Presse (2011, July 28). Uganda frees smuggled parrots back into the wild. *Modern Ghana*. http://www.modernghana.com/news/342420/uganda-frees-smuggled-parrots-back-into-the-wild.html.

Anagnostou, M. & Doberstein, B. (2022). Illegal wildlife trade and other organized crime: A scoping review. *Ambio*, *51* (7), 1615–1631. https://doi.org/10.1007/s13280-021-01675-y.

Bergenas, J. (2013). Killing animals, buying arms: Setting the stage for collaborative solutions to poaching + wildlife crime. *Stimson Center*. http://www.stimson.org/sites/default/files/file-attachments/killing_animals_buying_arms_WEB_1.pdf.

Bernal, R. (2023). Global wildlife trafficking on the rise, aided by cartels. *The Hill*. http://news.yahoo.com/news/global-wildlife-trafficking-rise-aided-100000660.html?guccunter=1.

Brown, A. (2020, December 14). The pandemic created new hunters. States need to keep them. *Pew Trusts*. https://www.pewtrusts.org/en/research-and-analysis/blogs/stateline/2020/12/14/the-pandemic-created-new-hunters-states-need-to-keep-them.

Bureau of Land Management (2017). Bald and Golden Eagle Protection Act: Eagle accidental take permit guidance for renewable energy development. Instruction Memorandum IM2017–040. https://www.blm.gov/policy/im-2017-040.

Carrington, D. (2017, May 16). Chinese appetite for tortoaba fish bladder kills off rare porpoise. *The Guardian*. https://www.theguardian.com/environment/2017/may/16/chinese-appetite-totoaba-fish-bladder-threatens-rare-vaquita.

Civil Procedures (2016). Adjustments to penalties. 50 CFR Part 11.33. https://www.govinfo.gov/content/pkg/FR-2016-06-28/pdf/2016-15268.pdf.

Congressional Research Service (2022, October 12). The Pittman-Robertson Wildlife Restoration Act. *In Focus*. https://crsreports.congress.gov/product/pdf/IF/IF12229.

Congressional Research Service (2019, April 5). Pittman-Restoration Act. Understanding apportionments for states and territories. (Report R45667). https://crsreports.congress.gov/product/pdf/R/R45667.

David Sheldrick Wildlife Trust (2015). Dead or alive? Valuing an elephant. http://iworry.org/wp-con- tent/uploads/2013/09/Dead-or-Alive-Final-LR.pdf.

Department of Justice (2023b, January). Texas biologist sentenced for wildlife trafficking. https://www.justice.gov/opa/pr/texas-biologist-sentenced-wildlife-trafficking.

Department of Justice (2022, February). Environmental Crimes Section monthly bulletin. https://www.justice.gov/enrd/page/file/1542701/download.

Department of Justice (2021, March). Environmental Crimes Section monthly bulletin. Sentencing. https://www.justice.gov/enrd/page/file/1396081/download.

Department of Justice (2020, October). Environmental Crimes Section monthly bulletin. https://www.justice.gov/enrd/page/file/1357456/download.

Drug Enforcement Administration (2020). International money laundering, drug trafficking and illegal wildlife trade operation dismantled. http://www.dea.gov/press-releases/2020/09/04/international-money-laundering-drug-trafficking-and-illegal-wildlife.

Eisele, T. (2017, October 11). Operation Crash: Stopping a network of illegal wildlife traffickers in United States. *National Association of Conservation Law Enforcement Chiefs*. https://www.naclec.org/press-pages/2017/10/11/operation-crash-stopping-a-network-of-illegal-wildife-traffickers-in-united-states.

Elliot, L. (2009). Combating transnational environmental crime: "Joined up" thinking about transnational networks. In K. Kangaspunta & I.H. Marshal (Eds.), *Eco-crime and justice: Essays on environmental crime.* United Nations Interregional Crime and Justice Research Center.

Embuscado, R. (2016, March 1). Irish syndicate found guilty of plot to steal museum artifacts worth 79 million. *Art Net News*. https://news.artnet.com/art-world/rathkeale-rovers-convicted-of-museum-raids-438080

Fears, D. (2014, October 17). Overwhelmed U.S. port inspectors unable to keep up with illegal wildlife trade. *Washington Post.* https://www.washingtonpost.com/national/health-science/overwhelmed-us-port-inspectors-unable-to-keep-up-with-illegal-wildlife-trade/2014/10/17/2fc72086-fe42-11e3-b1f4-8e77c632c07b_story.html.

Felbab-Brown, V. (2022, March 8). China-linked wildlife poaching and trafficking in Mexico. *Brookings Institution.* https://www.brookings.edu/research/china-linked-wildlife-poaching-and-trafficking-in-mexico/.

Greenspan, J. (2015, May 22). The history and the evolution of the Migratory Bird Act. *Audubon.* https://www.audubon.org/news/the-history-and-evolution-migratory-bird-treaty-act.

Hastie, J., & McCrea-Steele, T. (2014). Wanted – dead or alive: Exposing online wildlife trade. *International Fund for Animal Welfare.* http://www.ifaw.org/united-states/resource-centre/wanted-dead-or-alive-exposing-online-wildlife-trade.

Higginbotham, A. (2014, January 6). The rhino racket: Who is stealing all of Europe's horns? *Bloomberg Businessweek, 436*, 52–57.

International Union for the Conservation of Nature (IUCN) (2021, March 25). African elephant species now endangered and critically endangered – IUCN red list. https://www.iucn.org/news/species/202103/african-elephant-species-now-endangered-and-critically-endangered-iucn-red-list.

Interpol (2022, December 6). Global crackdown on illegal wildlife and timber trade: Interpol and World Customs Organization join forces. https://Interpol.int/News-and-Events/News/2022/Gobal-crackdown-on-illegal-wildlife-and-timber-INTERPOL-and-World-Customs-Organization-join-forces.

Loehle, C. & Eschenbach, W. (2012). Historical bird and terrestrial mammal extinction rates and causes. *Diversity and Distributions, 18* (1/2), 84–91. http://www.jstor.org/stable/41420097.

Maguire, T. & Haenlein, C. (2015). An illusion of complicity: Terrorism and the illegal ivory trade in East Africa. *Royal United Services Institute*. https://rusi.org/sites/default/files/201509_an_illusion_of_complicity_0.pdf.

Marine Mammal Commission (n.d.). Marine Mammal Protection Act. https://www.mmc.gov/about-the-commission/our-mission/marine-mammal-protection-act/.

Masters, S., Anthoons, B., Madesis, P., Saroja, S., Schermer, M., Gerritsen, W., Karahan, A., Verdoes, R., Schwallier, R, Van Andel, T., De Boer, H., & Gravendeel, B. (2022). Quantifying an online wildlife trade using a web crawler. *Biodiversity and Conservation, 31*, 855–869. https://doi.org/10.1007/s10531-022-02367-z.

May, C. (2017, March). Transnational crime and the developing world. *Global Financial Integrity*. https://www.gfintegrity.org/wp-content/uploads/2017/03/Transnational_Crime-final.pdf.

Moore, A. (2021). Decline in hunting threatens conservation funding. *College of Natural Resource News*. https://cnr.ncsu.edu/news/2021/01/decline-in-hunting-threatens-conservation-funding/.

Moreto, W.D. & Van Uhm, D.P. (2021). Nested complex crime: Assessing the convergence of wildlife trafficking, Organized crime and loose criminal networks. *British Journal of Criminology, 61* (5), 1334–1353. https://doi.org/10.1093/bjc/azab005.

Morrison, S. (2014, February 6). Time to hunt down the 'kingpins' of wildlife crime. *The Independent*. http://www.independent.co.uk/voices/ comment/time-to-hunt-down-the-kingpins-of-wildlife-crime-9113150.html.

Morton, O., Scheffers, B.R., Haugaasen Torbjørn, & Edwards, D.P. (2021). Impacts of wildlife trade on terrestrial biodiversity. *Nature Ecology & Evolution, 5* (4), 540–548. https://doi.org/10.1038/s41559-021-01399-y.

Nat Geo Wild (2011). Exotics, crimes against nature. https://www.youtube.com/watch?v=KzgTAbp-Fyo.

Naylor, R.T. (2005). The underworld of ivory. *Crime, Law and Social Change, 42* (4–5), 261–295. https://doi.org/10.1007/s10611-005-2143-7.

Nurse, A. & Wyatt, T. (2020). *Wildlife criminology*. Bristol University Press. https://doi.org/10.2307/j.ctv10kmc42.

O'Connor, R. (2021, September 10). Notorious Irish Traveller gang convicted in France of trafficking in rhino horns, elephant tusks. *The Irish Post*. https://www.irishpost.com/news/notorious-irish-traveller-gang-convicted-in-france-of-trafficking-rhino-horns-elephant-tusks-219741.

Office of Economic Cooperation and Development (2016). Illicit trade converging criminal networks. OECD Publishing. https://doi.org/10.1787/9789264251847-enUR.

Office of the Director of National Intelligence (2013, September 6). Wildlife poaching threatens economic, security priorities in Africa. https://www.dni.gov/files/documents/Wildlife_Poaching_White_Paper_2013.pdf.

Ortiz, A. (2020, September 4). International crime ring that trafficked in shark fins dismantled, U.S. Says. *New York Times*. https://www.nytimes.com/2020/09/04/us/shark-fin-ring-georgia.html.

Paul, K., Miles, K., & Huffer, D. (2020). Two clicks away: Wildlife sales on Facebook. *Center on Illicit Networks and Organized Crime*. https://www.counteringcrime.org/wildlife-sales-on-facebook.

Pennisi, E. (2021, February 15). Wildlife trade imperils species, even in protected areas. *Science*. https://www.science.org/content/article/wildlife-trade-imperils-species-even-protected-areas.

Pires, S.F. (2012). The illegal parrot trade: A literature review. *Global Crime, 13* (3).

Ratchford, M., Allgood, B., & Todd, P. (2013). Criminal nature: The global security implications of the illegal wildlife trade. International Fund for Animal Welfare. http://www.ifaw.org/united-states/resource-centre/criminal-nature-global-security-implications-illegal-wildlife-tra-0.

Regan, T.J., Burgman, M.A., McCarthy, M.A., Master, L.L., Keith, D.A., Mace, G.M., & Andelman, S.J. (2005), The consistency of extinction risk classification protocols. *Conservation Biology, 19*, 1969–1977. https://doi.org/10.1111/j.1523-1739.2005.00235.x.

Rosenberg, M. (2009, February 6). Exotic animals trapped in net of drug trade. *Reuters*. https://www.reuters.com/article/us-drugs-animals-odd-idUSTRE5154PM20090206.

Rossi, V. (2012, September 4). Colombia police rescued over 46,000 illegally trafficked animals in 2012. *InSight Crime*. http://www.insight-crime.org/news-briefs/colombia-46000-illegally-trafficked-animals-2012.

Rott, N. (2018, March 22). Decline in hunters threatens how U.S. pays for conservation. *National Public Radio*. https://www.npr.org/2018/03/20/593001800/decline-in-hunters-threatens-how-u-s-pays-for-conservation.

Schearf, D. (2012, February 21). Thai wildlife group raided for criticizing elephant poaching. *Voice of America.* http://www.voanews.com/ content/thai-wildlife-group-raided-for-criticizing-elephant-poaching-139978243/169726.html.

South, N. & Wyatt, T. (2011). Comparing illicit trades in wildlife and drugs: An exploratory study. *Deviant Behavior, 32* (4), 538–561. https://doi.org/ 10.1080/01639625.2010.483162.

Southwick, N. (2013, November 28). 58,000 trafficked animals seized annually in Colombia. *InSight Crime*. http://www.insightcrime.org/ news-briefs/58000-trafficked-animals-seized-annually-in-colombia.

Stiles, D., et al. (Eds.) (2013). Stolen apes: The illicit trade in Chimpanzees, Gorillas, Bonobos and Orangutans, a rapid response assessment. *United Nations Environment Program*. http://www.grida.no/publications/rr/apes/.

Sumaila, U.R., Zeller, D., Hood, L., Palomares, M.L.D., Li, Y., & Pauly, D. (2020). Illicit trade in marine fish catch and its effects on ecosystems and people worldwide. *Science Advances, 6* (9). https://doi: 10.1126/sciadv.aaz3801.

United Nations Environment Program (2016, September 29). Apes seizure database reveals true extent of illegal trade. http://web.unep.org/newscentre/apes-seizure-database-reveals-true-extent-illegal-trade.

United Nations Environment Program (2013, November 6). UNEP and INTERPOL assess impacts of environmental crime on security and development. Press Release. http://www.unep.org/newscentre/Default.aspx?DocumentID=2755&ArticleID=9686&l=en.

U.S. Fish and Wildlife Service (2022). Law enforcement at a glance. https://www.fws.gov/sites/default/files/documents/LE-at-a-Glance_0.pdf.

U.S. State Department (2021, November 4). 2021 END wildlife trafficking strategic review. https://state.gov/2021-end-wildlife-trafficiking-strategic-review/.

U.S. State Department (2017, March 3). U.S. task force on wildlife trafficking: Efforts to combat wildlife trafficking: Fact sheet. https://2017-2021.state.gov/u-s-task-force-on-wildlife-trafficking-efforts-to-combat-wildlife-trafficking/index.html.

Van Uhm, D. (2016). Wildlife trade through the ages. In *The illegal wildlife trade. Studies of organized crime*, vol. 15. Springer, Cham. https://doi.org/10.1007/978-3-319-42129-2_1.

Van Uhm, D. & Wong, R.W. (2021). Chinese organized crime and the illegal wildlife trade: Diversification and outsourcing in the Golden Triangle. *Trends in Organized Crime*, *24* (4), 486–505. https://doi.org/10.1007/s12117-021-09408-z.

Vira, V., Ewing, T., & Miller, J. (2014). Out of Africa: Mapping the global trade in illicit elephant ivory. *C4ADS*. https://static1.squarespace.com/static/566ef8b4d8af107232d5358a/t/56af83ee1f40390e88337743/1454343151910/Out+of+Africa.pdf.

Webb, G.J.W. (2008) The dilemma of accuracy in IUCN Red List categories, as exemplified by hawksbill turtles *Eretmochelys imbricata. Endangered Species Research*, *6*, 161–172. https://doi.org/10.3354/esr00124.

Weerth, C. (2020). WCO and INTERPOL on wildlife crime 2020: Results of the Joint Thunder Operation 2020. DOI:10.13140/RG.2.2.11385.49762.

Wellsmith, M. (2011). Wildlife crime: The problems of enforcement. *European Journal on Criminal Policy and Research*, *17* (1).

Wilkins, H.S. (2014). Linking environment with peace and security: Decisions on sanctions on illicit wildlife trafficking. *Environmental Policy and Law*, *44* (3).

Willsher, K., & Carroll, R. (2021, September 8). Eight men convicted in French court for trafficking rhino horn and ivory. *The Guardian*. https://www.theguardian.com/world/2021/sep/08/eight-men-convicted-in-french-court-for-trafficking-rhino-horn-and-ivory.

Witbooi, E., Ali, K., Santosa, M.A., Hurley, G., Husein, Y., Maharaj, S., Okafor-Yarwood, I., Quiroz, I.A., & Salas, O. (2020). Organized crime in the fisheries sector threatens a sustainable ocean economy. *Nature, 588* (7836), 48–56. https://doi.org/10.1038/s41586-020-2913-5.

World Wildlife Fund (2021, March 1). New Facebook user alert. *Coalition to End Wildlife Trafficking Online*. https://www.endwildlifetraffickingonline.org/news/2021/3/1/new-facebook-alert-informs-users-about-wildlife-trafficking.

World Wildlife Fund & Dalberg Global Development Advisors (2012). Fighting illicit wildlife trafficking: A consultation with governments. http://d2ouvy59p0dg6k.cloudfront.net/downloads/wwffightingillicitwildlifetrafficking_lr_1.pdf.

Wyatt, T. & Cao, A.N. (2015). Corruption and wildlife trafficking, U4 Issue, No. 11. *U4 Anti-Corruption Resource Center*. http://www.u4.no/publications/corruption-and-wildlife-trafficking/.

6 Mining

U.S. Mining Laws

Most of the mining laws within the United States were passed more than a century ago. Some were modified and updated in the late twentieth century. Multiple attempts have been made by various Congressional senators to introduce or update mining laws after well-publicized events took place, such as the Upper Big Branch Mine explosion in West Virginia or the Gold King Mine spill in Colorado. When these reactionary measures have been introduced, they have failed to pass Congress. In contrast various executive orders were passed by both President Donald J. Trump and President Joseph R. Biden, Jr. The impacts of those executive orders which will be discussed toward the end of the chapter are unlikely to have a long-term impact on mining. This chapter will highlight persistent problems that have affected the Appalachian region. Legal remedies and court cases will be covered to show how the government can promote redress for these issues.

The basic laws which govern mining are those which were designed to address the management of public lands. The agency responsible for overseeing mining on public lands is the Bureau of Land Management (BLM). This agency manages 24 million acres of federal land, of which 90% is authorized to permit mining. When oil, gas, or coal is extracted on public lands, the lands are held under lease by the extraction company and the company pays a royalty fee to the federal government.

The General Mining Law of 1872, also known as the Mining Law, as it is the foundational mining law that is still in effect, was passed by Congress to encourage exploration of federal lands in the American West. The law permitted citizens to stake claims on lands in order for them to extract minerals such as gold, silver, and copper and gain legal title to the land for a nominal cost. The law did not compel the miner and land owner to quantify the amount of minerals extracted from the land. Based on the Mining Law, miners who file for claims for hardrock mineral exploration on public lands are not required to pay royalty fees to the federal government. The miner is only required to pay a one-time initiation fee and for annual maintenance fees. In the year 2020, BLM collected $65 million in fees from 391,000 mining claims on federal lands yet collected $550 million in royalties from solid minerals, such as copper and phosphate, extracted from public lands that were leased (GAO, 2020).

DOI: 10.4324/9781003241201-6

In 1920, Congress passed the Mineral Leasing Act (30 U.S.C. § 181 et seq.). This law established qualifications for leases, set out maximum limits on the number of acres of containing a mineral that can be held by a lessee, and prohibits leasing by a foreign person or entity (Bureau of Land Management, 2007). The Mineral Leasing Act addressed coal, phosphate, oil, oil shale, gas, and sodium on the public lands by requiring leases for extraction. Sand, gravel, pumice, stone, clay, or other substances used in road construction or building construction, fall under the Materials Act of 1947 (30 U.S. Code § 601). These materials require a sales contract or a free-use permit (43 CFR Part 3600).

In 1981, Congress passed the Federal Land Policy and Management Act (FLMPA) (Public Law 94–579) which requires BLM to record and adjudicate mining claims, collect location and annual maintenance fees, as well as track authorized mining claims. As of April 2022, BLM is overseeing 578 active mining plans and 867 active mining notices on federal lands (Office of Congressional and Legislative Affairs, 2022). The U.S. Department of Agriculture also permits mining on forestry lands. The FLMPA was revised in 2001 to require that permits for mining require reclamation plans so that the property is recovered by the mining company in order to prevent undue degradation of public lands. The mining lessee is required to have funds sufficient to reclaim lands once mining is completed on site. Currently, the government holds $3.3 billion in reclamation funds. Mining lease requirements subject lessees to the Clean Water Act, Clean Air Act, Endangered Species Act, Wilderness Act, and the National Historic Preservation Act.

There is a plethora of laws that address mining safety under the Mining Safety and Health Administration (MSHA). They are under the U.S. Department of Labor rather than under a public lands agency. As such, those laws will not be included in this text; however, often when there are workplace safety violations, there is also disregard for environmental safeguards. In cases where both MHSA and EPA violations were found, the cases are covered in this text.

Mining History

The mining industry by its essence compels workers and working conditions to be in challenging geological and physical conditions. By its nature mining has always required extensive and advanced engineering (McAteer, et al., 2011). Throughout mining history, miners were exposed to air pollutants including: dust particulates, silica, methane, diesel exhaust, and ambient mercury vapor. Lax environmental enforcement in the mines and the surrounding communities has been a persistent problem, not just in the United States but throughout the world and throughout mining history.

Mining has consistently had a reputation of being disruptive to local economies, societies, and environments. From the historic mines of the Old West, in gold camps across nineteenth-century California and South Dakota where adventurers sought to strike it rich with gold, or the continuous mining of coal in Appalachia, miners have left scars on the land, poisoned water systems, and generated social unrest. Notable events such as the riots, strikes, and shootouts between private detectives and miners, demonstrated the volatility of mine labor and tough working conditions. One of the most epic events was the Battle of Blair Mountain, which became the largest armed uprising in the United States after the Civil War, involving labor struggles where miners were under pressure to produce large volumes of a valuable commodity under hazardous working conditions with meager pay (Savage, 1990; Shogan, 2006).

On January 24, 1848, gold was discovered at Sutter's Creek which led to a substantial gold rush in the region. Even though myths persist of the California gold miner being representative of the rugged individualist, within two years of the initial gold strike, New York investors had taken over the California mines (Brands, 2002). The most unfortunate aspect of this undying myth is that it obscures the realities confronted by miners over the last 150 years. Miners frequently worked in unsafe conditions, made more precarious by corporate investors who demand large returns regardless of the commodities' fluctuating market value. Investor demand consistently resulted in compromise to worker safety regulations and lax enforcement of environmental provisions already in place. Inconsequential fines and government support of mine owners and their corporations inevitably meant that workers were left with few protections, low wages, and under-compensated or uncompensated injuries. This pattern of indifference by government and mine operators to human labor and the environment has persisted to the present day.

In the area of Sutter's Creek, California, corporate owned mines accessed substantial capital to employ hydraulicking methods of mining that ravaged the landscape (Brands, 2002). Companies built mountain reservoirs and dug one hundred-mile ditch systems in order to have a constant supply of water to power the hydraulic hoses (Richards, 2007). As a result, two water companies controlled the water in the Sutter Creek region (north central valley of California). Ultimately this meant that the smaller communities of independent miners were quickly denied water or experienced their diggings washing away. Towns and communities often experienced flooding and several were destroyed by torrents of water due to elimination or diversion of natural riparian systems (Brands, 2002).

Enclaves surrounding mining sites developed under lawless conditions and often unlawful encampments. True tales of the Old West proliferate with scenes of gunfights, brothels, corrupt lawmen, and an atmosphere where norms of accepted social behavior were not expected (Boessenecker, 2018; Morgan, 2011; Slaughter, 2002). These tales reflect a laissez-faire federal policy and underdeveloped state or local government structures and processes. The extraction of highly sought after metals, such as gold, copper, and silver, meant more taxes could be collected. Short-term thinking permeated both the thoughts of the miners as well as government officials. Partly, this thinking was due to neither the government nor the miner having long-term attachment or residence in the mining areas. New York City investors would never bear the consequences of landslides and flooding in California. Physically, legally, and financially the far-away investors only considered immediate gains and their capital ensured that government representatives would be in agreement with this narrowly focused perspective. Then and now, miners "were people of means who employed others to do the mining for them" (Richards, 2007).

This development was not unlike what took place in West Virginia and the mining of its coal. Initially settlers in West Virginia were pleased for the coal mining companies to develop large scale extraction operations because this meant a significant stimulus to the local economy and the proliferation of well-paid jobs. Residents of West Virginia had been largely isolated due to geography, and they were subsisting on small farms. The land was not suitable for industrial agriculture and even livestock production would be limited due the proximity of steep hills that blocked sunlight in areas known as hollows. The native landscape in Appalachia includes expansive broad leaf forests that shade the narrow hollows resulting in limited use for these lands. The hollows receive an average of forty inches of rain per year. Ultimately, this geographic feature left the residents of West Virginia with restricted economic potential and imperfect resources with which they could expand their own fortunes beyond subsistence living.

Blair Mountain, West Virginia

Miners in Logan County, West Virginia, in the early 20th century began to engage in conflict with the mine operators. Many of the miners were veterans who recently returned from service in Europe in World War I. While working at the mines of Mingo and Logan Counties, they were subject to rules of the mining companies as the miners resided in company provided housing. They paid rent to the company whose houses were on company land. The miners purchased food and sundry items at the company store. When miners became disgruntled with business practices, they started to agitate toward unionizing their labor. In the United States at that time, there were many workers in manufacturing who had started to unionize as part of the Progressive Era which occurred in the first two decades of the 20th century. By World War I, 10% of American labor was unionized (Klein, 2021). The relatively new United Mine Workers of America prompted 400,000 miners to strike in 1919 (Klein, 2021). This work stoppage was met with replacement of the union workers with non-union miners. The mining companies then evicted the miners who unionized from company housing causing the miners to demand that Congress intervene as they claimed they were dispossessed from shelter without due process (Shogan, 2006). Congressional representatives did not respond.

Union organizers traveled into West Virginia to push mine labor into joining the unions so that they could collectively and forcefully fight back against the mine operators. The organizers, Mary Harris "Mother" Jones and William H. Blizzard, were particularly adept at labor organizing and turning people against the mine owners. For their efforts, Mother Jones endured the label as "the most dangerous woman in America," and Blizzard was charged with treason (Gorn, 2002).

The local police were reluctant to take the side of the miners as they understood the political connections between mine owners and members of the judiciary and state government. Also, the local police did not have authority on the mine property as the mine operators had private detectives police their lands. As unionization expanded, the mine operators hired many more detectives from the Baldwin-Felts Detective Agency to push out union workers and assist in the placement of non-union labor. Many of the detectives were military veterans who had been expert marksmen and arrived heavily armed to Logan County.

> The Baldwin-Felts agents performed a variety of chores for the mine operators. Deputized by obliging sheriffs under West Virginia's permissive laws, they maintained order in the mining camps, collected rents, guarded the payroll and also kept out 'undesirables,' a broad category that included known criminals, professional gamblers, prostitutes, moonshiners and, certainly not of least importance, union organizers.
>
> (Shogan, 2006)

Common tactics used by lawmen and private detectives working on behalf of the mine owners included harassment, intimidation, espionage, and homicide (Blizzard, 2010). Workers who attempted to organize into unions were targeted for killing so that they could be examples to other miners.

Miners who had been evicted from company housing enjoined union miners to fight back against the Baldwin-Flats detectives using their own weaponry. The result was an armed revolt which became known as the Battle of Blair Mountain.

By August of 1921, violence erupted. It was one of the largest civil uprisings in the United States and the largest armed rebellion since the American Civil War. For five days in late August and early September, in Logan County, West Virginia, nearly 10,000 armed coal miners fought against 3,000 lawmen and hired gunmen, who worked at the behest of mining companies. The battle ended after approximately one million rounds were fired, and the United States Army intervened under a presidential order (Shogan, 2006).

> Over 12 miles and five days, the sheriff fought the miners, strafing the hillsides with machine gun fire and dropping homemade bombs from planes. There were at least 16 confirmed deaths in battle though no one knows exactly how many were killed.
>
> (Robertson, 2021)

The result of the Battle of Blair Mountain was the mass unionization of mine labor. It also led to restricted use of private armed security presence off mine property. Technical advancements would lessen the impact of Blair Mountain as the need for tens of thousands of miners would disappear.

Modern Mining

By the late 1940s, coal extraction became mechanized. According to data compiled by the National Mining Association, the number of individuals working in U.S. based coal mines went from 415,000 in 1950 to just fewer than 89,000 in 2012. As coal reserves decline in areas like central Appalachia, the number of those working for mining companies will continue to drop. Mountaintop removal methods in West Virginia indicate that the easiest coal seams that could be reached underground have become depleted. The removal of a mountain top deposits allows coal companies to attain a lower grade coal nearer the surface of the mountain. This method of coal extraction has created its own challenges to the environment. Since the 1990s, mountaintop removal mining (MTR) has become the most common form of mining in West Virginia, particularly in the southern portion of the state. There are few underground mines remaining in the United States as surface mining expanded in New Mexico and Wyoming. The reduction in the need for coal miners created opportunity for the few underground mines remaining to exploit miners and environmental protection.

Massey Energy

In the 1980s, Massey Energy, as it was managed by Donald Blankenship, employed severe tactics to bust the union. In 1984 Blankenship became prominent when the United Mine Workers of America (UMWA) engaged in a strike against a Massey subsidiary he operated. This strike led to conflict which lasted nearly a year and a half. This struggle included violence on both sides and was notable as the coal company brought in strikebreakers with armed guards (New York Times, 1985). By 1992, Donald Blankenship became the CEO of Massey Energy which operated coal mines throughout Kentucky, Virginia, and West Virginia.

In 1992, Massey Energy operated 35 underground coal mines. Most famously, the Upper Big Branch Mine was an underground mine operated in Boone and Raleigh counties, West Virginia. Between 2000 and 2010, Massey Energy had been cited for tens of thousands of safety violations to include many which were designated as "significant and substantial," a demarcation under federal regulations, across its mine portfolio (McAteer, et al., 2011). In the year 2007, Massey Energy was cited for violating the Clean Water Act 4,000 times (Young, 2010). On April 5, 2010, 29 miners were killed in the Upper Big Branch mine located within Boone and Raleigh Counties when it exploded. The explosion was caused by a spark from equipment that ignited an accumulation of methane. The ensuing fireball ignited coal dust that had accumulated well past legally permitted limits. The coal dust carried the explosion for more than two miles within the mine (McAteer, et al., 2011). Of the 29 victims, only ten died as a result of injuries from the explosion, the other 19 died of carbon monoxide asphyxiation (Kerley & Murray, 2011). Prior to the explosion, the miners had complained repeatedly of a failed ventilation system. Of the 22 miners whose remains were autopsied, 17 had evidence of coal workers' pneumoconiosis (CWP), also known as black lung disease (Go, et al., 2022). According to the (West Virginia) Governor's Independent Investigation Panel issued in May 2011, Massey Energy had developed a culture which "normalized deviance" and "placed profits before people" (McAteer, et al., 2011).

Massey had a history of citations and violations of federal laws. In 2000, a Massey owned mine accidentally released 250 million gallons of coal mining sludge in Martin County, Kentucky. In comparison, the coal slurry spill, which contains traces of heavy metals, rock, dirt, and clay, was twenty times the Exxon Valdez oil spill which involved a spill of 11 million gallons of crude spilled into Alaska's Prince William

Sound on March 24, 1989 (DARRP, 1989; Kilborn, 2000). The company paid for the cleanup costs then later entered an agreement with the Environmental Protection Agency for wastewater discharge violations, as part of the Clean Water Act, in which it paid $20 million in fines (EPA, n.d.). The violations included Sections 301 and 402 of the Federal Water Pollution Control Act as amended by the Clean Water Act of 1977 and the Water Quality Act of 1987 33 USC §§ 1311 and 1342.

In 2008, Massey Energy pled guilty to ten counts of criminal violations and was fined $2.5 million for a fire in its Aracoma Alma No. 1 Mine, located in Stollings, West Virginia, which killed two miners in 2006 (Hjalmarson & Johnson, 2012). Four foremen from the mine were charged with failing to conduct required mine evacuation drills. The company agreed to pay an additional $1.7 million in civil penalties to the U.S. Mine Safety and Health Administration for violating the Federal Mine Safety and Health Act (Huffington Post, 2010).

A fire in the mine started due to poor ventilation. Twelve miners were trapped in the main underground passageway and two died while trying to find an alternate escape route (Reuters, 2008). The continued failures by regulators to engage the authority provided to them by federal law led to the explosion at the Upper Big Branch mines and the death of two miners due to insufficient ventilation in the mines. For that failure, Massey CEO Blankenship was sentenced to one year in prison and ordered to pay a $250,000 fine (Department of Justice, 2016). The Massey Energy chief of security, Hughie Stover, was sentenced to three years in prison for lying to federal investigators and attempting to destroy evidence (Berkes, 2012). The security chief's punishment for lying to federal investigators exceeded the punishment of the executive of an energy company with an established history of death due to negligence on company property. This difference shows the muted punishments for environmental and safety violations at mines within the United States.

The public focus on the tragedy of the Upper Big Branch mine had limited impact on laws and regulations. After the explosion of the Upper Big Branch mine, Alpha Energy purchased Massey Energy's assets including its mines. In its negotiations with Alpha Energy, newly appointed Massey Energy CEO Baxter Phillips demonstrated that the penalties and scrutiny by federal agencies of mining companies was not a reason to alter the habits of the mining industry.

> But in a conference call with Alpha on January 31 [2011], [Massey CEO Baxter] Phillips said he would work with Alpha 'to reduce regulatory impediments,' a statement that suggests the new company well may continue past campaigns against the agencies that regulate coal, particularly MSHA and the EPA.
>
> (McAteer, et al., 2011)

The lack of enforcement despite a consistent record of safety and environmental violations led to other public concerns, such as a resurgence of coal workers' pneumoconiosis (CWP). A 2015 report by the National Institute for Occupational Safety and Health (NIOSH) revealed a dramatic increase in an advanced strain of coal workers' pneumoconiosis called progressive massive fibrosis (PMF). PMF is considered the most severe form of black lung. The shift in disease pattern is the result of increased mechanization which pulverizes particles in a manner that would not be accomplished with manual labor. The finer pulverized material leads to increased inhalation of fine particles which impacts the few miners working in these environments. The rates of PMF increased substantively between 2000 and 2012. Today's levels of PMF are equal to those witnessed in the early 1970s, the period before dust control measures were implemented as the Coal Act had only recently passed and mine operators were afforded time to meet the standards of the new law (CDC, 2018).

In 1969 the Federal Coal Mine Health and Safety Act, also known as the Coal Act, was passed. It specified the amount of dust that would be permitted within a mine and required that the mine be inspected four times per year. The law's impacts were substantial at first as a dramatic decrease of black lung occurred. The decline was sustained until the late 1990s. By 2000 the trends of CWP and PMF radically shifted. Today coal miners in the United States have higher rates of lung diseases than their predecessors as indicated by studies that started in the 1920s (Almberg & Cohen, 2023). Part of the reason is due to the mechanics of how coal is currently mined and the other part is that mining regulations aren't appropriately enforced. In the case of the Upper Big Branch Mine, federal inspectors who are supposed to conduct surprise inspections provided advance notice of inspections.

Terry Lilly, a miner in Fayette County, West Virginia told NIOSH investigators:

> We knew when the mine inspectors were coming before they even set foot below ground. They'd call us and let us know we had a visitor, and we'd get to work. We'd place dust monitors below vents, where they'd constantly get fresh air. We'd throw up curtains … And when the dust got too thick, [the] choice was to continue working or lose his job.
>
> (Arnold, 2016)

While there was media scrutiny of the Upper Big Branch Mine explosion, West Virginia Senator Joe Manchin III proposed new federal legislation. On January 25, 2011, Senator Manchin along with West Virginia Senator Jay Rockefeller proposed the Robert C. Byrd Mine and Workplace Safety and Health Act (S. 153). On April 15, 2011, a similar bill (H.R. 1579 – 112th Congress) was introduced to the House of Representatives by California Representative George Miller. The House bill had seven co-sponsors, including West Virginia Representative Nick J. Rahall II. The bills would have updated the Federal Mine and Safety Act of 1977 to ensure, in part, mandatory third party investigations of accidents at mines, refer criminal violations to the Attorney General's Office, and allow the Department of Health and Human Services' attorneys to question private parties as part of an investigation. Neither of the bills were approved or adopted. Both bills failed to make it past their respective committees (Actions - H.R. 1579, 2011; S.153, 2011).

The history of coal mining in West Virginia demonstrates a pattern whereby the government has had an ineffective approach to enforcing mining regulations.

History shows that environmental impacts of mining are often ignored as demonstrated by the scant amount of media focus on the coal slurry spill in Kentucky. Also, the pattern of hiring private security to protect mines and the exploitation of labor continues in mines in other parts of the world.

Conflict Minerals

Nature provides a set of free resources that are acquired and sadly sometimes misused in a global economy that prizes limited access to supplies and hard to acquire commodities.

> The nexus between the illegal mining of diamonds and armed conflict has been a concern for the international community for several decades. The extraction and sale of so-called "blood diamonds" and, more recently, "blood gold" is known to have sponsored non-state armed groups in different parts of the world ... The term "conflict mineral" (also known as "conflict resource") was used to describe the financing of violent rebel forces in Angola and Sierra Leone in the late 1990s. The concept was officially endorsed by the United Nations General Assembly (UNGA) in the context of conflict diamonds and has been referred to as such in several UNSC resolutions (e.g., Resolution 1173 [1998] and Resolution 1176 [1998]).
>
> (Zabyelina & Van Uhm, 2020)

Armed groups in Africa have become enriched and funded through extortion of mine operators, and the higher prices of minerals due to demand from China and India (Berman, et al., 2017; Humphreys, 2005). Spikes in the international prices of gold and copper stimulated criminal organizations to get involved the mineral trade. In Colombia, it is estimated that drug trafficking organizations have been involved in illicit gold mining since 2007 (Rettberg & Oritz–Riomalo, 2016). Some of the most pernicious conflict minerals are coming from Africa in the form of cobalt and diamonds. In 2018, Interpol released a report indicating the illegal extraction and taxation on gold, oil, and natural resources exceeds the profits from narcotics or financial schemes for transnational crime groups (Interpol, 2018). The World Atlas of Illicit Flows, composed of data from Interpol, RHIPTO – a Norwegian-based UN-collaborating rapid response center on environment, development, peace, and security, and the Global Initiative Against Transnational Organized Crime, found that 36% of funds that go toward arming and financing non-state actor driven conflicts come from natural resource crimes such as oil, diamond, gas, and mineral extraction (Interpol, 2018). Crime groups' collaboration with terrorist groups is not fully known yet the United Nations recognizes that criminal networks promote conflicts through the funding of terrorist groups and militias (de Boer & Bosetti, 2015).

The Federal Bureau of Investigation (FBI) discovered a conspiracy between a gold refinery in Florida and illicit gold vendors in Chile who were responsible for the importation of over $3.5 billion dollars of gold originating from various illegal activities, including drug smuggling, illegal gold mining, foreign bribery, forgery, and U.S. customs violations. These activities were conducted on behalf of several transnational crime groups in Latin America.

In January 2016, the FBI along with police in the nation of Chile started Operation Diez Condores. Criminal offenders in Chile obtained gold from illicit suppliers and collected the amassed gold in Santiago, Chile. In Santiago, the criminals would solicit forged papers by legitimate businesses dealing in gold. The criminal network would then hire couriers to travel with the amassed gold to the United States. The couriers would fly into Miami, Florida where the forged documents would be provided to U.S. Customs officials. The couriers would then take the gold to a refinery called NTR Metals Miami (NTR). NTR then paid for the gold via electronic fund transfer to the suppliers in Chile. Operation Diez Condores concluded with seven individuals being prosecuted for money laundering, customs fraud, racketeering, and smuggling in Chile and restitution of $16 million in the United States and $25 million in Chile. This operation stimulated the investigation of a similar pattern of gold smuggling by criminal organizations in Peru. The Drug Enforcement Administration criminally charged four men for illegally engaging in money laundering narcotics proceeds and unlawfully importing illicitly derived gold.

> In Case No. 17-cr-20215, from January 2013 through March 2017, Barrage, Rodriguez, Granda, and others conspired to purchase billions of dollars of criminally derived gold from Latin America and the Caribbean, which they believed to be or which in fact were the proceeds of unlawful criminal activities (including illegal mining, foreign bribery, foreign smuggling, foreign narcotics trafficking, and the entry of goods into the United States by false means and statements), through Elemetal LLC, a dealer in precious metals operating in the Southern District of Florida and "financial institution," as defined in Title 18, United States Code, Section 1956(c)(6)(A), in violation of Title 18, United States Code, Section Sections 1956(h) and 1957.
>
> In addition, Barrage, Rodriguez, Granda, and others conspired to promote criminal activities (including illegal mining, foreign bribery, foreign smuggling, foreign narcotics trafficking, and the entry of goods into the United States by false means and statements) by transmitting billions of dollars of wire payments from the United States to Latin America and the Caribbean to promote the delivery of additional criminally derived gold, in violation of Title 18, United States Code, Section Sections 1956(h) and 1956(a)(2)(A).
>
> (United States Attorney's Office, 2018)

Testimony by Regina Thompson, Deputy Assistant Director of the Criminal Investigation Division of the Federal Bureau of Investigation to the Senate Foreign Relations Committee on December 5, 2019, stated that transnational criminal organizations are using established criminal infrastructure – smuggling routes, access to corrupt officials, and smuggling techniques – to traffic in illegally obtained minerals and metals. The lawful trade in metals can provide venues for criminal organizations to obscure their involvement in an unlawful activity (Thompson, 2019).

> TCOs [transnational criminal organizations] use often-witting U.S. businesses to exploit U.S. regulations and export illegally extracted gold to the United States to launder billions of dollars of illicit proceeds from criminal operations in Latin America. Because gold bullion is classified as a commodity rather than a monetary instrument, the imported gold is not subject to Treasury Department reporting requirements; nor is it subject to customs duties, which limits law enforcement visibility into this money laundering method and increases profitability for TCO [the transnational organized crime].
>
> (Thompson, 2019)

The international market value and the fungibility of metals and minerals on the global marketplace make extracted resources an easy target for organized crime to launder money and to trade on the black market. Gold and minerals can easily enter the licit market with ease as the trade market for these commodities is so large throughout the world. Even the United Nations admits that there is no formulation to grasp how much of the world's illegal trade in lawful commodities like gold is occurring or how many criminal organizations are involved (de Boer & Bosetti, 2016).

On December 20, 2017, President Donald J. Trump signed Executive Order 137817 which compels the Secretary of the Interior to identify critical minerals that have vulnerabilities in their supply chain that are critical for the "economic and national security" of the United States (Office of the White House, 2020). The purpose of the act was to prioritize and expand the protection of the domestic supply chain for minerals and establish a secure critical minerals supply chain. It also fast-tracked the permitting process for extraction leases on federal lands (Whitefoot, 2020).

The impetus for the executive order was to diminish dependency on foreign mineral production and to vastly expand domestic production to meet the demands for metals and minerals due to an expansion of electric vehicles, solar and wind power systems, and large capacity batteries. These items require substantial amounts of lithium, cobalt, graphite, nickel, and manganese.

> The transition to clean energy is projected to create a 400 to 600 percent increase in global demand for key critical minerals like lithium, graphite, cobalt, and nickel to meet our climate goals, and for some minerals the increase in demand will be many times higher. Currently, the United States is reliant on Chinese imports for many of these minerals in processed form.
>
> (Office of Congressional and Legislative Affairs, 2022)

Conclusion

Aside from the trade of illicitly extracted metals and minerals which disrupt governments abroad, the U.S. dependency on foreign based mineral supply is a threat to the United States. Rare earth elements are a group of seventeen minerals essential to the manufacturing of hypersonic weapons, missiles such as the Javelin Missile, munitions, aircraft such as the F-25 fighter jet, and radiation-hardened electronics as well as consumer electronics like computers, cellular phones, hospital equipment and solar panels. Currently the United States imports 80% of the rare earth minerals it uses from China (Gould & Mehta, 2020) In 2018, 98% of the processed rare earth elements that the United States used in manufacturing was imported from China while the U.S. produced just over 9% of the world's raw supply of rare earth elements the same year (Cohen & Grant, 2021). The current status of mining in the United States involves lengthy permitting processes that take as much as eleven years due to the involved environmental reviews and public engagement requirements (GAO, 2016). The burdensome requirements indicate that the dependency between the U.S. and China will not shift in the near future.

President Joseph R. Biden, Jr., as part of the $2 trillion infrastructure plan, implemented a mandatory review of critical minerals within the United States by the United States Geological Survey. It is unlikely this law will stimulate greater development of mineral extraction within the United States as President Biden has also paused leases for mineral extraction on federal lands and has made identifying methods of recycling and reusing critical elements a priority (Friedman, 2022; Office of Congressional and Legislative Affairs, 2022). The mineral and metal industry is not prone to crimes of illicit extraction within the United States as the Mining Law permits a wide range of mining activity on public lands without much oversight. Unfortunately, large scale demand cannot be sufficiently met through domestic supply as environmental regulations limit domestic production. As a result, there is an expansive market for metals and minerals importation. This legal market is subject to infiltration by illicitly extracted metals and minerals. With the introduction of those metals, the United States is inviting and expanding the reach of organized crime.

Discussion Questions

1. For those who are concerned about environmental harms, such as environmental activists and environmental non-governmental organizations, why hasn't there been any outcry for the West Virginia miner who suffers from environmental exposure?
2. As environmental organizations and various members of Congress and state legislators, in addition to the Executive Branch under President Biden, demand more electric vehicles, there doesn't appear to be a plan to obtain sufficient metals and minerals required to achieve their targets. Why is the discussion of mining and its impacts not included in the discussion of the production of electric vehicles?
3. Why are some members of the U.S. government unwilling to discuss opening more federal lands to mining, given their commitment to reducing fossil fuels which compels more non-fuel sources of energy?
4. President Joseph R. Biden, Jr., stopped fossil fuel extraction on federal lands. This suspended mining on tribal lands which netted the tribes $1.4 billion

annually in revenue. Why shouldn't the tribes be able to mine their own lands without federal interference?

5. As technology improves and is implemented in more environments, demand for metals will continue to increase. Is it a risk to national security to procure metals from unstable countries like the Democratic Republic of the Congo and the People's Republic of China?

Further Reading Recommendations

1. American Geosciences Institute (n.d.). Interactive map of mineral resources and mines across the United States. http://americangeosciences.org/critical-issues/maps/mineral-resources-data-system-map-viewer.
2. Bureau of Land Management (n.d.). About mining and minerals. http://blm.gov/programs/energ-and-minerals/mining-and-minerals/about.
3. McNeill, J.R. & Vrtis, G. (2017). *Mining North America: An environmental history since 1522.* University of California Press.
4. United States Department of Labor (n.d.). Coal fatalities for 1900 to 2022. http://arlweb.msha.gov/stats/centurystats/coalstats.asp.
5. United States Geological Survey (2021). USMIN mineral deposit database. http://usgs.gov/centers/gggsc/science/usmin-mineral-deposit-database.

References

Actions - H.R. 1579-112th Congress (2011–2012): Robert C. Byrd Mine Safety Protection Act of 2011. (2011, May 20). https://www.congress.gov/bill/112th-congress/house-bill/1579/all-actions.

Almberg, K. & Cohen, R. (2023). Modern coal miners have higher death rates from lung diseases than their predecessors. *Center for Disease Control.* https://blogs.cdc.gov/niosh-science-blog/2023/02/27/mining-lung-disease/.

Arnold, C. (2016). A scourge returns: Black lung in Appalachia. *Environmental Health Perspectives, 124* (1), A13. https://link-gale-com.ezproxy4.library.arizona.edu/apps/doc/A440635910/AONE?u=uarizona_main&sid=bookmark-AONE&xid=ba99e7cb.

Berkes, H. (2012, February 29). Ex-mine security chief sentenced to three years. *National Public Radio (NPR).* https://www.npr.org/sections/thetwo-way/2012/02/29/147627956/feds-seek-tough-message-in-mine-disaster-sentence.

Berman, N., Couttenier, M., Rohner, D., & Thoenig, M. (2017). This mine is mine! How minerals fuel conflicts in Africa. *The American Economic Review, 107* (6), 1564–1610. http://www.jstor.org/stable/44251607.

Blizzard, W. (2010). *When miners march.* PM Press.

Boessenecker, J. (2018). *Shotguns and stagecoaches: The brave men who rode for Wells Fargo in the Wild West.* St. Marten's Publishing.

Brands, H.W. (2002). *The Age of gold: The California gold rush and the new American Dream.* Doubleday Books.

Bureau of Land Management (2007). Mineral Leasing Act of 1920 as amended. https://www.blm.gov/sites/blm.gov/files/MineralLeasingAct1920.pdf

Center for Disease Control (CDC) (2018, July 20). Prevalence of black lung continues to increase among coal miners. https://www.cdc.gov/niosh/updates/upd-07-20-18.html.

Cohen, A. & Grant, J.C. (2021, June 22) America's critical strategic vulnerability: Rare earth elements. *Foreign Policy Research Institute*. https://www.fpri.org/article/2021/06/americas-critical-strategic-vulnerability-rare-earth-elements/.

Damage Assessment, Remediation and Restoration Program (DARRP) (1989). Exxon Valdez. *National Oceanic and Atmospheric Administration*. https://darrp.noaa.gov/oil-spills/exxon-valdez.

de Boer, J. & Bosetti, L. (2016). Crime-conflict nexus: Identifying gaps and opportunities for policy research. http://cpr.unu.edu/research/projects/the-crime-conflict-nexus-identifying-gaps-and-opportunities-for-policy-research.html.

Department of Justice (2016, April 6). Blankenship sentenced to a year in federal prison. http://www.justice.gov/usao-dswv/pr/blankenship-sentenced-year-federal-prison.

Environmental Protection Agency (EPA) (n.d.). Massey Energy Company Inc. Clean Water Act Settlement. http://www.epa.gov/enforcement/massey-energy-company-inc-clean-water-act-settlement.

Friedman, L. (2022, February 20). Biden halts new drilling in legal fight over climate costs. *New York Times*. http://www.nytimes.com/2022/02/20/climate/carbon-biden-drilling-climate.html?searchResultPosition=4.

Go, L.H.T., Green, F.H.Y., Abraham J.L., Churg, A., Petsonk, E.L., & Cohen, R.A. (2022). Coal mine dust lung disease in miners killed in the Upper Big Branch disaster: A review of lung pathology and contemporary respirable dust levels in underground US coal mines. *Occupational and Environmental Medicine*, *79* (5), 319–325. DOI: 10.1136/oemed-2021–107694.

Gorn, E. (2002). *Mother Jones: The most dangerous woman in America*. Hill and Wang.

Gould, J. & Mehta, A. (2020, October 1). Trump Executive Order targets rare earths minerals and China. *Defense News*. http://www.defensenews.com/congress/2020/10/01/trump-executive-order-on-rare-earths-puts-material-risk-in-spotlight/.

Government Accountability Office (GAO) (2020, June 25). Mining on federal lands: More than 800 operations authorized to mine and total mineral production is unknown: Report GAO-20–461R. http://www.gao.gov/products/gao-20-461r.

Government Accountability Office (GAO) (2016, January) Hardrock mining: BLM and Forest Service have taken some actions to expedite the mine plan process but could do more. Report GAO-16–165. http://www.gao.gov/assets/gao-16-165.pdf.

Hjalmarson, D. & Johnson, L.J. (2012, February 13). Massey Energy's history of violations. *Lexington Herald-Leader*. http://www.kentucky.com/news/state/kentucky/article44028255.html.

Huffington Post (2010, July 2). Massey Energy foremen slapped with criminal charges for 2006 fire, mine worker dies in accident at another mine. https://www.huffpost.com/entry/massey-energy-foremen-sla_n_634132.

Humphreys, M. (2005). Natural resources, conflict, and conflict resolution: Uncovering the mechanisms. *Journal of Conflict Resolution*, *49* (4), 508–537.

Interpol (2018, September 26). Organized crime underpins major conflicts and terrorism globally. http://www.interpol.int/en/News-and-Events/News/2018/Organized-crime-underpins-major-conflicts-and-terrorism-globally.

Kerley, D. & Murray, M. (2011). Government agency faults Massey Energy in West Virginia mine disaster. *ABC News*. http://abcnews.go.com/US/massey-energy-fault-upper-big-branch-west-virginia/story?id=13639984.

Kilborn, P.T. (2000). A torrent of sludge muddies a town's future. *New York Times*. http://www.nytimes.com/2000/12/25/us/a-torrent-of-sludge-muddies-a-town-s-future.html?searchResultPosition=2.

Klein, C. (2021, February 18). Why labor unions declined in the 1920s: Stripped of wartime protections and branded as anti-American, labor unions languished in the Roaring Twenties. http://www.history.com/news/american-labor-unions-decline-1920s.

McAteer, J.D, Beal, K., Beck, Jr., J., McGinley, P., Monforton, C., Roberts, D., Spence, B., & Weise, S. (2011). Upper Big Branch: The April 5, 2010, explosion: A failure of basic coal mine practices. Report to the Governor: Governor's Independent Investigation Panel. http://media.npr.org/documents/2011/may/giip-massey-report.pdf

Morgan, L. (2011). *Wanton West: Madams, money, murder, and the wild women of Montana's frontier*. Chicago Review Press.

New York Times (1985, April 2) Six month old coal miners' strike grows bitter. *New York Times*. Section A, p. 10. http://www.nytimes.com/1985/04/02/us/six-month-old-coal-miners-strike-grows-bitter.html?searchResultPosition=1.

Office of Congressional and Legislative Affairs (2022). Mineral Law Reform. *Department of the Interior*. http://www.doi.gov/ocl/mining-law-reform.

Office of the White House (2020). Executive Order on addressing threats to the domestic supply chain from reliance on critical minerals from foreign adversaries. https://trump-whitehouse.archives.gov/presidential-actions/executive-order-addressing-threat-domestic-supply-chain-reliance-critical-minerals-foreign-adversaries/.

Rettberg, A. & Ortiz-Riomalo, J.F. (2016). Golden opportunity, or a new twist on the resource–conflict relationship: Links between the drug trade and illegal gold mining in Colombia. *World Development*, *84*, 82–96. https://doi.org/10.1016/j.worlddev.2016.03.02.

Reuters (2008, December 23). Massey to pay $4.2 million after mine deaths. http://www.reuters.com/article/massey-mine-doj-idUSN2354062720081223.

Richards, L.L. (2007). *The California Gold Rush and the coming of the Civil War*. Random House.

Robertson, C. (2021, September 6). A century ago, miners fought in a bloody uprising. Few know about it today. *New York Times*. https://www.nytimes.com/2021/09/06/us/coal-miners-blair-mountain.html?searchResultPosition=1.

S.153-112th Congress (2011–2012): Robert C. Byrd Mine and Workplace Safety and Health Act of 2011. (2011, January 25). https://www.congress.gov/bill/112th-congress/senate-bill/153.

Savage, L. (1990). *Thunder in the mountains: The West Virginia mine war, 1920–1921* (5th ed.). University of Pittsburgh Press.

Shogan, R. (2006). *The battle of Blair Mountain: The story of America's largest labor uprising*. Basic Books.

Slaughter, B.L. (2002). *Horse thieves, hoodlums, and hanging judges: Crime and punishment on the Nevada frontier, 1859–1878* (Order No. 3071458). Available from ProQuest Dissertations & Theses Global; Social Science Premium Collection. (276379799). https://ezproxy.library.arizona.edu/login?url=https://www.proquest.com/dissertations-theses/horse-thieves-hoodlums-hanging-judges-crime/docview/276379799/se-2.

Thompson, R. (2019). Illicit mining: Threats to U.S. National Security and International Human Rights. *Federal Bureau of Investigation*. https://www.fbi.gov/news/testimony/illicit-mining-threats-to-us-national-security-and-international-human-rights-120519.

United States Attorney's Office (2018). Four Peruvian members of multi-billion dollar, international gold money laundering scheme indicted. *U.S. Department of Justice*. https://www.justice.gov/usao-sdfl/pr/four-peruvian-members-multi-billion-dollar-international-gold-money-laundering-scheme.

Whitefoot, A. (2020, September 30). Trump signs executive order to fast-track federal mining permits. *Duluth News Tribune*. https://www.duluthnewstribune.com/business/trump-signs-executive-order-to-fast-track-federal-mining-permits.

Young, J. (2010, April 9). A history of safety and environmental violations. *Living on Earth*. https://loe.org/shows/segments.html?programID=10-P13-00015&segmentID=1.

Zabyelina, Y. & Van Uhm, D. (2020). The new El Dorado: Organized crime, informal mining, and the global scarcity of metals and minerals. In Y. Zabyelina & D. Van Uhm (Eds.), *Illegal mining: Organized crime, corruption and ecocide in a resource-scarce world* (pp. 3–30). Palgrave-Macmillan, https://doi.org/10.1007/978-3-030-46327-4.

7 Whaling

Introduction

Commercial whaling was at its peak in the United States between 1812 and 1852. Nearly all commercial whaling ended in the United States in the 1920s. As noted in Chapter 4, with the wide-ranging passage of environmentally focused laws in the 1970s, an effective ban on whaling was established within all U.S. territories. As there is no specific whaling law, the Endangered Species Act is used to prevent whaling within U.S. waters. There have been exemptions made to permit American Indian tribes to harvest whales. These events have been met with controversy as they permit unnecessary whaling to occur off American littoral waters.

People often think of whaling within the context of the novel, *Moby Dick*, written by Herman Melville in 1851. Commercial whaling began approximately 1000 years ago by the Basques in Spain. The modern whaling industry many consider was started in the 1600s by Dutch and British sailors in the Artic region. The whaling trade enabled much of the development of manufacturing and domestic items by being both the petroleum and plastic industry of its time. Whale was a valuable commodity for a multitude of reasons as many parts of the whale were used in the manufacturing of commercial products including the use of whale baleen for combs, fishing line, roofing material, corsets, buggy whips, piano keys, chess pieces, hoops that were used in hoop skirts, and toys (Marrero & Thornton, 2011; McNamara, 2019). Whale oil, derived from boiling down the fat and skin of the whale, was used to illuminate streetlights and housing and business lamps, in addition to being used for making ropes, paint, soaps, varnish, textiles, and candles, as well as a lubricant in machinery (Marrero & Thornton, 2011; McNamara, 2019).

Not long after the release of the novel, *Moby Dick*, petroleum in the United States was discovered in Pennsylvania in 1859. The development of oil extraction and distillation, initially into the production of kerosene, drove the reduction in demand for whale oil. When *Moby Dick* was written, whaling was already in decline due to the destruction of whaling ships preceding and during the Civil War. The Confederates cruisers, such as the *Alabama* and the *Shenandoah*, destroyed more than fifty whaling ships from New England (New Bedford Whaling Museum, n.d.). For a short period, whaling was revived due to new inventions. The three inventions of the steam engine, explosive harpoons, and compressed air helped

DOI: 10.4324/9781003241201-7

revitalize the American whaling industry temporarily. These inventions, adapted by whalers, enabled the industry to bring in the largest whales that had been elusive for capture in the past. Whalers could bring in larger whales with fewer ships. By the end of the Civil War, the American whaling industry failed to adapt to new technologies for mechanized whaling that were developed in Norway; thus, the American whale industry was outcompeted by a cheaper, higher quality product available on the market. Norwegians ships employed mechanized chaser boats equipped with high-powered deck cannons firing heavy-caliber, explosive harpoons which significantly increased the volume and efficiency of whale harvest off all continents except Africa: hence, the economics shifted away from an American dominated whale trade to a European dominated whale trade.

Whaling, like many natural resource commodities, operated within an economic market that was subject to speculation and expansively varied economic outcomes. The volatile economics of natural resource and commodity markets attracted risk taking investors and business enterprises. After the Civil War, the value of whale oil decreased. Fewer U.S. based ships engaged in whaling, a decline of investments in whaling expeditions took place, and the profits of these expeditions diminished (New Bedford Whaling Museum, n.d.). Speculative high-risk business entrepreneurs that engaged in the whaling industry when it was a lawful industry would become the model for the business interests involved in illegal whaling. The trade of a large scale commodity, such as whale harvesting, required skilled labor, investment in infrastructure and transportation costs, and a labor force willing to risk danger and long periods away from home while enduring physically taxing and perilous work. The whaling industry of the past is mirrored in many natural resource extraction enterprises today, such as fishing, mining, and timber harvesting which continue to demand high risk investment, precarious work environments, and dependence on volatile markets.

There is a consistent parallel throughout the trade of wildlife and natural resource commodities: there are high risk, high reward trade schemes whether the trade of the product is lawful or illicit. The cost of the raw material fluctuates widely within short periods of time so those who would invest in harvesting or collection of the commodity tend to be speculators, gamblers, and those who seek financial windfalls. It is thereby not surprising that those who engage in poaching and in lawful harvest are risk takers who are operationalizing what was in economics terms a renewable resource but is now under the regulatory schemes as a finite, limited resource. The illegality increases both the risks and the costs. Restrictions on trade increase the value of a product which has limited availability on the market. Whaling is a commodity exchange with significant restrictions imposed through international regulatory schemes, making the potential economic reward that much higher for those who engage in illegal whaling.

While there are many accounts of the number and type of whales caught, there is scant scrutiny of the consumers who created demand for whale products. To ignore the consumer demand and the role whaling played in industrial development is to ignore its impacts on municipal development where whale products were primarily used. As industrialization expanded in the 1800s, the demand for whales increased with an estimation that more whales were captured in the 19th century than in the prior four centuries (Marrero & Thornton, 2011).

Laws and Regulations

While the whaling industry reduced significantly and was no longer operationalized by U.S. based companies, whaling continued by nations such as Norway, Russia, Japan, and Iceland. In 1946, the International Whaling Convention (IWC) was created to globally regulate the whaling industry by addressing commercial whaling of twelve whale species: bowhead (*Balaena mysticetus*), sperm (*Physeter macrocephalus*), humpback (*Megaptera novaeangliae)*, pygmy right (*Caperea marginata*), right (*Eubalaena australis*), minke (*Balaenoptera acutorostrata*), sei (*Rudolphius laticeps*), Antarctic bottlenose a.k.a. Southern bottlenose (*Hyperoodon planifrons*), Arctic bottlenose a.k.a. Northern bottlenose (*Hyperoodon ampullatus*), Byrde's (*Balaenoptera brydei*), blue (*Balaenoptera musculus*), and fin (*Balaenoptera physalus*). The Convention was a reaction to a broadened public awareness and demand to mitigate the decline of whale populations worldwide. Initially fifteen nations signed the treaty including the Norway, Japan, United States, the United Kingdom, and the U.S.S.R (International Whaling Commission, n.d.-a). While the international convention professed reduction in whale hunts, there was limited enforcement initially due to the persistence of high quotas (catch limits) of whale harvest in place that resulted in the continuation of many commercial whaling companies' operations. The continued commercial whaling under the high-level quotas established in the IWC led to significant reduction in various whale species populations. This prompted United States' officials to propose a ten-year moratorium on all commercial whaling starting in 1972. This proposal failed in 1972 and again in 1973 (Aron & Burke, 1999). As the whale populations declined precipitously around the world, legislators in Australia took notice and created a new management proposal which was strongly endorsed by officials from the United States (Aron & Burke, 1999). In October 1972, the United States Congress passed the Marine Mammal Protection Act, 16 U.S.C. 1361.

In an attempt to reduce the impacts of whaling, oceanic sanctuaries were established. In 1979, the Convention established whaling-free sanctuaries in the Indian Ocean and in 1994, within the Southern Ocean surrounding Antarctica (Marrero & Thornton, 2011). One of the successes of the Convention was the gathering and assessment of data on whale populations throughout the world. By the 1980s whale products were being primarily used to manufacture margarine and pet foods. By that time, the general public perceived whaling as unnecessary. This sentiment coincided with an increased expansion of animal protection laws which left limited support for the continuation of whaling for commercial purposes. In 1986, forty years after its initial passage, the International Whaling Convention was modified to impose an indeterminate ban on commercial whale trading. The ban stopped all commercial trade of whales globally without a time limit. The United States government along with 88 other nations' representatives observe the ban with few exceptions. The public exhibited tolerance of whaling for what was considered non-commercial exploitation; thereby, the public supported exceptions for whaling granted to nine Alaskan indigenous groups and for the purpose of research (International Whaling Commission, n.d.-b). Not long after, the U.S. federal government extended its exceptions to other American Indian groups.

In 1997, the United States government via the National Marine Fisheries Service of the National Oceanic and Atmospheric Administration (NOAA-NMFS) granted the Makah tribe of the Olympic Peninsula of Washington state an exception permit of the Marine Mammal Protection Act (MMPA) to harvest four gray whales (*Eschrichtius robustus*) each year for five years. The agreement was based on the tribe's initial agreement with the United States government: the 1855 Treaty of Neah Bay (Governor's Office of Indian Affairs, n.d.). The treaty permitted continued whaling by members of the Makah tribe. The Makah's whale harvests were stopped via the formation and enforcement of animal protection laws in the early part of the 20th century as all states had animal anti-cruelty laws by 1907 (Oldham, 2003). Immediately following this exception, the Makah tribe demanded a higher catch limit as the tribal members had reignited their habits and interests in whale hunting in addition to using federal funds to establish a whale processing plant.

The actual purpose of the Makah whale harvest was for the operation of a whale processing plant to market whale products outside of the United States. Initially, the Makah tribe argued that they would engage in whale harvesting for cultural and ceremonial purposes. As soon as government officials granted the exception, the Makah tribe engaged in processing the whales for commercial use. The Makah tribe members employed power boats, a.50 caliber weapon, an ice truck, and a $335,000 federal grant to initiate their whale hunting practice (Associated Press, 2007). Given the modern tools and federal funding it is challenging to accept as sincere the tribe's argument that they reestablished their hunting traditions for cultural reasons as given traditional methods of whale hunting were not employed. After the United States government granted this exception, the nations which did not sign on to the international treaty (IWC) and continued to engage in commercial harvesting followed the Makah tribe by demanding an increase in their annual catch allotment. The nations of Iceland, Norway, Japan, Greenland, Canada, Russia, South Korea, Saint Vincent and the Grenadines, as well as the Faroe Islands all engage in commercial harvest of whales. While these nations have received criticism by environmental groups for their whaling practice the Makah tribe has not.

By granting exception to the Makah tribe, which did not require whales for sustenance as they had not engaged in whaling for more than 70 years prior to the government exception, the government expanded a demand and a legitimate market for whale products. A mechanism for bypassing the political consensus for animal rights and environmental conservation is to promote commercial exploitation as an indigenous right based on historical customs and identities. The exception was based on the assumption that the Makah tribe would strictly abide by a four-whale limit per year for five years and an academic researcher who reported to the court that a 20-whale take would not impact the overall population of gray whales. After a successful hunt in 1999, continued hunts were delayed due to litigation filed with the courts that the environmental impact statement was not completed correctly (National Oceanic and Atmospheric Administration, 2012). While the court was processing a hearing, members of the Makah tribe conducted an illegal hunt and killed a gray whale after a court ordered all hunts to cease. Despite the illegal hunt, the courts eventually granted the Makah tribe an exception permit under the Marine Mammal Protection Act.

While there was local opposition in Seattle as noted via publications in the local paper against whale hunting as well as opposition by the ant-whaling non-profit group, the Sea Shepherd, major environmental and animal rights groups did not oppose the whale hunt (Oldham, 2003). The Sierra Club, Greenpeace, the Humane Society of the United States, and the Progressive Animal Welfare Society (PAWS) did not oppose the permitting of the whale hunting by the Makah on the basis that they supported indigenous hunts (Oldham, 2003). The Makah hunting of the gray whales was not controversial to animal rights groups despite the hunt of a species that was only recently taken off the endangered species list. The gray whale was taken off the endangered species list in 1994 and the first Makah hunt took place on 1999.

St. Vincent and the Grenadines did not have a population that was dependent upon whaling prior to 1875. Whaling started in the area when a settler family started to hunt whales in 1875. The current allotment of whale hunts for St. Vincent and the Grenadines is four humpback whales each year for a population of 10,000 people. Members of the IWC confronted the argument that whale hunting in the region was for indigenous reasons and likely could not be valid based on archeological records which failed to show up any evidence of historic whale hunts. The position that the arrival of settlers in the late 19th century could not be considered "aboriginal" was called out as "racist" (Black, 2012). This persuaded the IWC to grant the permits for whale hunting.

Other arguments made at the IWC against the granting of whale hunting by St. Vincent and the Grenadines residents included observations that the whales captured and killed included pregnant females and sexually immature whales. The IWC permit restricts the whale hunt to older whales that cannot reproduce. Despite the violations of the whale hunt permits, the IWC did not take actions against the member state, St. Vincent and the Grenadines, who argued the Bequians, people who live on Grenadine's second largest island, learned to hunt whales by the Yankee whalers in the 19th century (Black, 2012).

South Korean delegates argued before the IWC that they should be able to engage in an expansive whale harvest as they have a much longer history of whale hunting than the Bequians.

> Korea's history of whaling dates back 8,000 to 9,000 years ago. The Koreans have the oldest documented whale hunt anywhere on the planet – with ancient rock art showing the unmistakable coming together of harpoon and whale, and piles of bones testifying to their consumption. But Koreans, unlike Bequians, aren't allowed to hunt anymore.
>
> (Black, 2012)

This is a recurring theme in environmental issues that are promoted through political and popular speech and disseminated through non-governmental organizations like Greenpeace and the Sea Shepherd. Demands that a corporation or organized formal economic activity operated by a wealthy nation like South Korea should be curtailed due to animal rights or environmental concerns are quickly subverted by those making the demands if/when they perceive the beneficiary of the activity is an indigenous or an impoverished group. Officials from New Zealand supported giving whale hunting permits by groups claiming to be indigenous despite having openly rejected any whaling through a prohibition that was formalized in 1991 when government officials declared New Zealand a "committed conservation country" (Museum of New Zealand, n.d.; Oldham, 2003).

Soon after the Makah's right to hunt whales was affirmed by a federal court, the International Whaling Convention declared that it would consider permitting indigenous populations in Greenland to hunt humpback whales. In 2010, the IWC granted the indigenous in Greenland to hunt nine humpback whales in addition to minke and fin whales (Pfeiffer, 2010). Soon after Greenland was permitted to kill a quota of whales, IWC member officials noted that whale meat was being sold to tourists in Greenland. In addition to these quotas, Russian indigenous peoples in Chukotka in eastern Siberia have a quota of 350 gray and ten bowhead whales each year, while Alaskan Inupiat have a quota of 56 bowhead whales each year (International Whaling Commission, n.d.-c; International Whaling Commission, n.d.-a).

One of the primary criticisms of the International Whaling Convention is that the nations that engaged in whaling controlled the whaling trade through the convention. This discouraged competition and eradication of the whaling industry. The nations of Norway, Iceland, South Korea, and Japan subsidize their respective whaling ships as well as whale processing and storage of whale products. Their participation in the whaling trade while engaging in the Convention appeared duplicitous. The complaint that the largest nations with the strongest economic interests in controlling the whale trade enhanced their control of the whale stocks through their participation in Convention meetings appears to have gone unheeded initially. It wasn't until the 1990s that nations such as the United States, the United Kingdom, and Australia tried to strengthen the impact of the Convention by lowering quotas and restricting them to research purposes only. Nations such as South Korea and Japan claim to conduct research on whales they hunt while the nations of Norway, Russia, and Iceland, while party to the IWC, simply ignore the rules and hunt whales.

As whale catches were permitted for the purpose of research under the IWC, South Korea and Japan claimed that they were gathering whales for scientific research one year after the 1986 international ban on commercial whaling. Japan did not engage in commercial whale hunting after 1988 yet many believed that Japan's whale hunts for research were indeed for commercial purposes as whale meat was found in public school lunches (Faiola, 2005). In 2014, officials from the Australian government sued Japan in the International Court of Justice under the United Nations. The court ruled that Japan was not engaging in scientific research of the killed whales and was actually using the whales for sale in a commercial market. The result was that Japan was banned by the international court from engaging in future scientific expeditions to gather whales.

Arguments made by officials from these countries include the recognition that indigenous populations and those who claim to be indigenous are granted exceptions despite evidence that these groups engage in commercial enterprises promoting the sale of whale meat and whale products. Thus, the ban on commercial hunting depends on the demographic regardless of history, anthropological, or other considerations.

This duplicitous and political process spurred Japanese officials to challenge the IWC in 2018 by asking the international group for a permit to conduct a limited commercial harvest of whales. The IWC immediately declined the right of the Japanese to gather whales for commercial markets where whale meat and products are traded within Japan's domestic market. The following year, in 2019, Japanese government officials declared that Japan would withdraw from the IWC (Kolmas, 2020). Japanese whaling is taking place within the Exclusive Economic Zone (EEZ) of the littoral waters of Japan. As the first 12 miles off the Japanese coast are exclusively under the jurisdiction of the Japanese government, antagonistic moves by groups like the Sea Shepherd would be prohibited.

Data on how many whales were harvested is available but there is not good census data of the whale populations across the world given the whales' elusiveness and large migration patterns. Even today, the primary whale species that are hunted either by Japan or indigenous groups are listed under the International Union for Conservation of Nature (IUCN) as "unknown" or insufficient data. This fact is often overlooked even though it is critical in understanding the impacts of whaling either by the indigenous groups or nations like South Korea or Japan.

Greenpeace and the Sea Shepherd

In 1975, a popular "Save the Whales" campaign sponsored by Greenpeace USA and joined by other environmental groups including the World Wildlife Fund was actively promoted and disseminated information about the impacts of commercial whale harvest worldwide. While the environmental groups applaud themselves in changing the legislative landscape, it is unclear that their public campaigns have had any effect. Whaling is still conducted by Japan, Iceland, Norway, and other nations, harvesting approximately 1,700 to 2,000 whales per year (compared to the estimated 10,000 whales that were captured annually during the heyday of whaling). As to how effectively the campaign has helped the whales, the populations of the whales most often hunted can be assessed. Of the aforementioned species listed in the ICW, the humpback whale has increased in numbers while all the other whale populations are listed as "unknown" or "data deficient" by the International Union for Conservation of Nature (IUCN). Currently the minke is the most commonly hunted whale and it is listed as data deficient in its assessment of vulnerability toward population collapse.

Despite the data challenges and the low level of modern whaling, Paul Watson, a militant environmental activist, formed the Sea Shepherd organization and referred to his fleet of ships as the Neptune Navy. Sea Shepherd was created when Mr. Watson was kicked out of Greenpeace in 1977. He was considered too willing to violate laws to advance his environmental agenda. By 1978 Mr. Watson was fundraising to purchase vessels that could be deployed to target whaling vessels under observer status via the IWC. The Sea Shepherd organization, which bills itself as a conservation society, often employs tactics which are extralegal.

In 1979, Mr. Watson, a Canadian citizen, captained a vessel which rammed a whaling vessel, *Sierra.* While the vessel survived the collision, it was docked in Lisbon, Portugal in 1980 when it was sunk through the use of limpet mines: the Sea Shepherd claimed responsibility. The following year, two whaling vessels, *Isba I* and *Isba II*, were sunk at a harbor in Spain. The Sea Shepherd again claimed responsibility. In 1986, the Sea Shepherd sunk two whaling vessels in Reykjavik, Iceland, even though at the time Iceland fishermen were in compliance with the IWC and had desisted from whaling. For this action, Paul Watson was banned from entering Iceland or its waters.

From this point, Paul Watson, who is emboldened as he and his crew often attack other vessels at sea or flee jurisdiction of nations where they commit sabotage, continued to escalate his actions. Members of his crew carry rifles and throw petroleum on vessels they attack then throw signal flares containing phosphorous at law enforcement officers who attempt to respond in rubber dinghies, threatening the lives of the responders. As the Sea Shepherd traveled across the world targeting whaling vessels, its increased use of violence caused the United Nations to revoke the Sea Shepherd's status as an observer under the IWC.

> Paul Watson claims in an open letter to the people of Norway that Sea Shepherd has sunk eight ships and rammed and damaged a further six vessels. In the same letter, he states: "The Sea Shepherd Conservation Society is a law abiding organization. We rigidly adhere to and respect the laws of nature or lex natura. We hold the position that the laws of ecology take precedence over the laws designed by nation states to protect corporate interests … the smell of guilt is already a stench in the nostrils of God."
>
> (Institute of Cetacean Research, n.d.)

Throughout Mr. Watson's and his crews' harassment and deliberate sabotage of other vessels, their actions were in violation of the United Nations Convention on the Laws of the Seas. This Convention, of which the U.S. is a signatory, prohibits non-state actors from engaging in any enforcement on the high-seas and specifically prohibits vigilantism. The response of Mr. Watson and his organization was always to declare that he has followed the United Nations World Charter for Nature signed in 1982. It is a non-binding agreement that permits citizens to "safeguard and conserve" nature. Yet, this UN charter is also clear that it prohibits vigilantism. Throughout the actions taken by Mr. Watson and his crew, his vessels were unflagged – effectively not registered with any nation – making it an unlawful vessel. Mr. Watson by many accounts took pride in commanding a fleet of "pirate vessels" (Khatchadourian, 2007).

By 1994, after a myriad of other violent acts involving vessels at various ports and under no flags, all members of the IWC declared that the Sea Shepherd was a terrorist organization. IWC Commissioner for the United States James Baker declared: "Acts of violence against fishermen of any nation cannot be tolerated. Their safety and livelihood could be threatened unless US officials vigorously condemn violence on the high seas" (Institute for Cetacean Research, n.d.). In 1997, Paul

Watson was arrested in Holland for the 1992 attempted scuttling of the Norwegian fishing and whaling vessel, *Nybrœna*. The Dutch police, serving an arrest warrant issued by Interpol, imprison Mr. Watson for eighty days. This did nothing to deter Mr. Watson or his organization. At an animal rights conference in the United States in 2002, Mr. Watson stated that if someone is killed in one of his actions, he would consider it "collateral damage."

The Sea Shepherd claims to have saved 6,000 whales with its fleet of 40 vessels (Kennedy, 2017). Mr. Watson remains in his private residence in Vermont as he has been placed on Interpol's Red Notice list which means he has to be detained in any country where he arrives for extradition to Japan. Additionally, he has been banned from Canada, Costa Rica, Denmark, and Iceland due to his willingness to engage in violent action as a non-state actor under no authority. Japanese officials have charged him with causing damage to several Japanese vessels, including the *Nisshin Maru*, which Mr. Watson blockaded and prevented from making contact with a refueling ship (Maritime Executive, 2013). Mr. Watson had also used his crews to entangle ship propellers as they sailed in the Southern Ocean causing damage to their ships and causing them to collide with the Sea Shepherd's vessels (Khatchadourian, 2007). Despite the illegal actions taken by this radical environmental group, Mr. Watson benefits from tolerance of terrorism affected by those claiming to be environmentalists and ambiguities in law. As his actions often take place in international waters, he relies on nations which could prosecute such as New Zealand and Australia to act in support of his missions. In fact, those nations' Green Party politicians have been vocally in support of the Sea Shepherd. Mr. Watson has used media to attract supporters and funding to his cause despite its overt violations of international laws. Ironically, Mr. Watson engages in illegal behavior as a mechanism in his mind to stop others from committing illegal behavior.

It's unclear why the United States does not extradite Mr. Watson to Japan since the international community has declared him to be a terrorist and he meets the US legal definition of a terrorist. This history of the Sea Shepherd exemplifies why international agreements are so complicated. For the Sea Shepherd to claim legitimacy, it requires the IWC, yet all members of the IWC have declared Sea Shepherd as a terrorist organization and Paul Watson a terrorist. Despite this he lives freely and enjoys tremendous public support as he was depicted on the Discovery Channel via a program with the name, *Whale Wars*. This program aired from 2008 to 2015. During the airing of this program, which depicted Paul Watson as a heroic adventurous figure, he was able to solicit funds from famous Hollywood actors including fellow Canadian Pamela Anderson, Tommy Lee, Anthony Kiedis (the lead singer of the rock band the Red Hot Chili Peppers), and Sam Simon, co-creator of *The Simpsons* (Darby, 2012).

In an interview with *New Yorker* magazine, Paul Watson referred to himself as a "coercive conservationist." In detailing his own early exploits, he referred to the first vessel he captained, the *Farley Mowat*, a trawler built in Norway in 1958 thus:

> The ship, black with yellow trim, featured a skull and crossbones painted across its superstructure and, on the forward deck, a customized device called "the can opener": a sharpened steel I-beam that is propelled outward

> from the ship's starboard side and is used to scrape the hulls of adversaries. Watson's plan was to transfer as much furniture, equipment, and crew as he could from the Farley to the Hunter, in part because the Farley was old and barely seaworthy, in part because it was operating illegally and could be confiscated upon entry into port, and in part to ready it for a procedure that he called Operation Asshole – so named because it involved ramming one vessel into another's stern.
>
> (Khatchadourian, 2007)

The case of whaling demonstrates the weaknesses of international agreements, their inconsistencies and the inability of a coordinated effective response by the international community. As the United States has some of the strongest anti-terrorist laws in the world, it is incoherent that federal officials haven't seized the assets of the Sea Shepherd and extradited Paul Watson for trial in Japan. The Sea Shepherd's flagrant violations of various maritime laws, indifference to human life and property, and its self-appointed guardianship of the ocean creates distrust amongst mariners who witness violent actions by organizations that supplant government sponsored navies. Fishermen who observe the violent activities and crimes by the Sea Shepherd have complained repeatedly throughout the world that ambiguous and non-committal actions by nations against organizations like the Sea Shepherd creates a lawless environment across the seas. Governmental inaction by a multitude of nations creates a climate whereby various crimes occur. The ocean environment is very difficult to police but inconsistent governmental actions and imperfect and missing data elicit more complexities and opportunities for vigilante activity and opportunities for crime.

Mr. Watson's and the Sea Shepherd's positions reflect a radical form of environmental organizations. The mainstream environmental organizations, such as the Sierra Club, Audubon Society, Nature Conservancy, and Arbor Day Foundation, neither espouse nor promote this form of vigilantism. Mr. Watson appears to follow a pattern of radicalization noted by an environmental group known as Earth First. As noted by Martha Lee, "the radicalization of environmental groups, has been caused by the growing fear of irreversible anthropogenic environmental degradations, and such fears have taken on millenarian or apocalyptic tones" (Bondaroff, 2008; Lee, 1995). While mainstream environmental organizations pursue advocacy, community engagement, and education as well as legal filings against polluters or those who violate environmental laws, radical environmental organizations such as Earth First and the Sea Shepherd while drawing some supporters also create a backlash due to their violent behavior and lack of accountability. Iceland had joined the International Whaling Commission's moratorium on whaling in 1989 but by 2006 Icelandic officials announced that the nation would restart commercial whaling (Bondaroff, 2008). The radical actions by groups like the Sea Shepherd are not accepted by law abiding societies such as the Icelandic community. The Icelandic people generally reject tactics of sabotage, property destruction, and threats to people's lives or livelihoods, particularly fishermen.

The actions of radical environmental groups match a framework of terrorism in that they take action which is contrary to law or regulations, believe that laws protecting their cause (in this case the environment) will not be enforced, serious damage will be conducted, legal means were attempted and proven unsuccessful, and appeals to the community have failed (Vanderheiden, 2005). Under this framework, the radical environmental organizations justify their actions and motivations yet claim that they aren't terrorists as they intend to conduct property damage, not create physical harm to people. Yet, their actions have a history of causing harm to both people and property. The radical environmental groups mirror terrorists in their strict adherence to ideology and sense of moral standing (Vanderheiden, 2005). Mr. Watson's position as a well-funded individual with a television program and lack of legal accountability reflects the uneven application of environmental laws, international agreements, and response by promoters of conservation. While Mr. Watson and his organization have been rebuked by several nations, he has not been rebuked or admonished by the American press, academic researchers, mainstream environmental organizations, or American politicians.

Conclusion

Laws addressing whaling are limited to international agreements. Even when a nation like Norway enters the agreement, there are no actions taken against the Norwegian national government when it does not abide by international agreed upon standards. The restrictions of the International Whaling Commission drove Japan to withdraw from it. Despite withdrawing from the agreement, commercial whaling in Japan resumed in a manner that significantly impacted the whale population. Japanese communities relied on whaling for sustenance and commerce for more than 400 years, yet nations like Japan and Korea, with an even longer tradition, were prohibited from continuing traditional practices. Other communities such as those in St. Vincent and the Grenadines without a long history of whaling have been permitted to whale hunt. The Makah in the U.S. Northwest hunted using modern equipment which would not reflect a traditional hunt. The rules and restrictions from the International Whaling Commission appear arbitrary.

As Beccaria's crime theory posits, if the crimes are not addressed swiftly with certain punishment, there is an increase in crime. In the case of whaling, not only is the refusal to abide by the terms of the International Whaling Commission by Norway and Japan relevant but so is the acquiescence to Mr. Watson's illegal activities. By his own admissions he knowingly engages in violent acts at sea and at port without recourse due to laissez-faire attitudes of the states who would want Japan and Norway restricted. The inconsistent if not biased response by the international community enables states to act voluntarily and without worry about global censure.

The shift in whaling patterns has more to do with economics than international treaties. Even when Japan departed from the treaty, there was no resurgence of commercial investment in whaling. Cultural shifts in Japan led to fewer Japanese citizens with an appetite for whale meat. There appears to be a paucity of fishing crews willing to engage in whaling. Without government subsidy, whaling is an economic loss for entrepreneurs. In this way, whaling affirms trade in wildlife. When there is demand, supply will reach the target – lawfully or unlawfully.

In whaling, there does not appear to be significant demand. As some whale populations globally rebound, it is clear that even where whaling is practiced, the scale of the harvest is insufficiently impactful to reduce population numbers. According to the International Whaling Commission, humpback, sei, Bryde's, and fin whales appear to be increasing. Too little is known to accurately assess the populations of the blue, sperm, and gray whales. The Southern right and right whales continue to experience reduced populations (International Whaling Commission, n.d.-d).

Discussion Questions

1. Do you think that rules regarding whaling are evenly applied and does this matter?
2. Why do you think that Paul Watson and the Sea Shepherd have been protected by the international community rather than sent for prosecution in Iceland or Japan? What does this tell you about the relationship between nations that share in international agreements?
3. Why do you think groups that claim to be indigenous receive permits for whale hunting whereas other groups do not? Is this a fair approach to species conservation?
4. Why do you think the United States has no domestic laws directly relating to whaling?

Further Reading Recommendations

1. Estes, J., DeMaster, D., Doak, D., Williams, T., & Brownell, R. (Eds.) (2007). *Whales, whaling, and ocean ecosystems*. University of California Press.
2. Hall, E. (n.d.). The story of the stashed whale baleen. Smithsonian Institution. http://ocean.si.edu/museum/story-stashed-whale-baleen.
3. McMurry, J. (2021). Japan's whaling town struggles to keep 400 years of tradition alive. *The Guardian*. http://theguardian.com/world/2021/dec-26/japans-whaling-town-struggles-to-keep-400-years-of-tradition-alive.
4. Meynecke, O. (2021). Humpback whales may have bounced back from near-extinction, but it's too soon to declare them safe. *The Conversation*. http://theconversation.com/humpack-whales-may-have-bounced-back-from-near-extinction-but-its-too-soon-to-declare-them-safe-157232,
5. NOAA Fisheries (2021). Track whale detections with this interactive map. http://fisheries.noaa/gov/feature-story/track-whale-detections-interactive-map.

References

Aron, W. & Burke, W. (1999). Flouting the convention. *Atlantic*, *283* (5), 22–29.

Associated Press (2007, September 9). A.50 caliber gun for whale hunting? *CBS News*. http://www.cbsnews.com/news/a-50-caliber-gun-for-whale-hunting/.

Black, R. (2012, July 3). Indigenous whaling granted after 'racism' claim. *BBC*. http://www.bbc.com/news/science-environment-18693753.

Bondaroff, T.P. (2008). Throwing a wrench into things: The strategy of radical environmentalism. *Journal of Military and Strategic Studies, 10* (4). http://jmss.org/article/view/57662/43332.

Darby, A. (2012, January 12). The stars who are forking out for the campaign to save the whales. *Sydney Morning Herald.* https://www.smh.com.au/environment/conservation/the-stars-who-are-forking-out-for-the-campaign-to-save-the-whales-20120110-1ptm6.html.

Faiola, J. (2005, June 19). In Japan, cultivating a taste for whales. *Washington Post.* http://www.washingtonpost.com/archive/politics/2005/06/19/in-japan-cultivating-a-taste-for-whale/f971a0c0-ba0b-425c-a29d-05ed0e80c38f/.

Governor's Office of Indian Affairs (n.d.). Treaty of Neah Bay, 1855. *State of Washington.* http://goia.wa.gov/tribal-government/treaty-neah-bay-1855.

Institute of Cetacean Research (n.d.). Sea Shepherd's violent history. https://www.icrwhale.org/eng/history.pdf.

International Whaling Commission (n.d.-a). Description of the USA Aboriginal subsistence hunt: Alaska. http://iwc.int/management-and-conservation/whaling/aboriginal/usa/alaska.

International Whaling Commission (n.d.-b). History and purpose. http://iwc.int/commission/history-and-purpose.

International Whaling Commission (n.d.-c). Description of Aboriginal subsistence hunt in Chukotka, Russia Federation. http://iwc.int/management-and-conservation/whaling/aboriginal/russian-federation.

International Whaling Commission (n.d.-d). Introduction to population status. http://iwc.int/about-whales/population-status.

Kennedy, M. (2017, August 29). Sea Shepherd says this year it won't send ships to disrupt Japanese whalers. *National Public Radio.* https://www.npr.org/sections/thetwo-way/2017/08/29/547015438/sea-shepherd-says-this-year-it-wont-send-ships-to-disrupt-japanese-whalers.

Khatchadourian, R. (2007, November 5). Neptune's Navy. *New Yorker.* http://www.newyorker.com/magazine/2007/11/05/neptunes-navy.

Kolmas, M. (2020, November 18). When shaming fails: Japanese withdrawal from the International Whaling Commission. *Australian Institute of International Affairs.* http://www.internationalaffairs.org.au/australianoutlook/when-shaming-fails-japanese-withdrawal-from-the-international-whaling-commission/.

Lee, M. (1995). *Earth First! Environmental apocalypse.* Syracuse University Press.

Maritime Executive (2013, February 7). Sea Shepherd severs fuel supply to Japanese whaling fleet. https://maritime-executive.com/article/Sea-Shepherd-Severs-Fuel-Supply-to-Japanese-Whaling-Fleet/.

Marrero, M. & Thornton, S. (2011). Big fish: A brief history of whaling. *National Geographic.* https//www.nationalgeographic.org/article/big-fish-history-whaling/.

McNamara, R. (2019). Objects made from the whaling industry: Oil, candles and household tools. *Thoughtco.* https://www.thoughtco.com/products-produced-from-whales-1774070.

Museum of New Zealand (n.d.). Whaling, then and now. http://www.tepapa.govt.nz/about/touring-exhibitions/whales-tohora/whale-people/whaling-then-and-now.

National Oceanic and Atmospheric Administration (2012, May 21). Notice of intent to terminate the existing draft environmental impact statement and prepare a new environmental impact statement. *Federal Register.* http://www.federalregister.gov/documents/2012/05/21/2012-12262/notice-of-intent-to-terminate-the-existing-draft-environmental-impact-statement-and-prepare-a-new.

New Bedford Whaling Museum (n.d.). Yankee whaling. http://www.whalingmuseum.org/learn/research-topics/whaling-history/yankee-whaling/.

Oldham, K. (2003, February 26). Makah whale hunt succeeds on May 17, 1999. *History Link*. http://www.historylink.org/File/5310.
Pfeiffer, T. (2010, June 25). Greenland wins back right to kill humpback whales. *Reuters*. http://www.reuters.com/article/us-whaling-greenland-idUSTRE65O35720100625.
Vanderheiden, S. (2005). Eco-terrorism or justified resistance? Radical environmentalism and the "War on Terror." *Politics and Society, 33* (3), 425–447.

8 Forestry

Introduction

This chapter will cover federal laws that are imposed upon national forests. There are both federal and state forests within the United States. As state conservation laws vary and are enforced by state forestry agencies, this chapter will focus on the national forest policy as set forth through the United States Department of Agriculture. Law enforcement is challenged through large-scale illegal marijuana grows on federal forest lands. Additionally, the United States government oversees the importation of timber products throughout the world. This chapter will cover cases of U.S. law violations that occur through mislabeled and illegally harvested trees and timber.

Illegal timber harvests are the most profitable environmental crime globally. Illegally harvested timber is embedded in the lawful global timber trade. The crimes aren't just the illegal harvest, but also fraudulent labeling of timber to avoid customs duties and tariffs, fraudulent declaration to obscure the origin of the wood product, and these are often accompanied by corruption of local officials where the timber is harvested. When trees are illegally logged in conflict areas around the world, the sale of the timber often is used by illegal actors to finance conflict and violence. The United States has a highly regulated timber industry. This prevents illegal harvesting on a commercial scale. The greatest forestry-related crimes in the United States are the importation of illegally harvested or willfully mislabeled timber and the destruction and alteration of forest lands which are used to illegally cultivate marijuana. The scale of marijuana grows on U.S. public lands is creating environmental damage in multiple states. In California, 80–90% of all marijuana sales are linked to illegal grows (NPR, 2021). The long-term consequences of large-scale grows, which are run by organized crime enterprises, involve the destruction of public lands. Tons of trash, construction material, banned pesticides, and propane tanks litter various state and federal forests in addition to miles of PVC pipes that divert streams and rivers. The land is denuded and terraced and the wildlife deliberately poisoned. The movement toward expanding marijuana legalization across the U.S. will expand this threat to American forests.

DOI: 10.4324/9781003241201-8

Initial Laws Aimed at Protecting Forests

The first U.S. law to protect the nation's forests was passed in 1897 as the Organic Act of the Forest Service. It was written by Gifford Pinchot. Pinchot was the first chief of the newly created U.S. Forest Service, established by President Theodore Roosevelt in 1905. Prior to the creation of the U.S. Forest Service, the Department of the Interior oversaw the national forests which were considered abundant and inexhaustible. When Pinchot was appointed by President Roosevelt, there were no national policies or university studies on forest management. Pinchot studied forestry in France.

In 1905 President Roosevelt and Chief Forester Pinchot identified 60 forests encompassing 56 million acres that took the new label as national forests. By 1910, they selected 150 national forests covering 172 million acres. Today they number 154 national forests that cover 190 million acres of land. The remainder of forest lands in the United States either belongs to the individual states as state park land or is under private ownership. When Pinchot took control of the new agency he differed from many of his contemporaries, such as John Muir. Pinchot was not a romanticist and did not view the forests through the lens of a "spiritual nature." He was a pragmatist who sought to reconcile benefits the forests provided to citizens while seeking to balance demands on the forests in a manner that promoted the greatest social good while sustaining the forest ecosystem. From this perspective the modern national forest service's mission began fulfilling the demands of a growing population through considered conservation.

It is remarkable that a man such as Pinchot was able to promote successfully the ideas of both social good through forest use and conservation simultaneously. The transcendentalist period (1830–1860) strongly influenced social perceptions of nature. With writings by Margaret Fuller, Henry David Thoreau, and Ralph Waldo Emerson, nature was perceived as a spiritual place that should not be disturbed and that human knowledge should come from intuition and imagination as much as it does from scientific methods or observation. The transcendentalists' fundamental idea was that there must be conservation of undisturbed nature, unspoiled by man. Pinchot, born in 1861, was educated after the transcendentalists' publications became widespread and confronted the foundational transcendentalists' arguments as they persisted in influencing public sentiment. Yet Pinchot was clear eyed in his approach to forest management. He insisted that the forests were to be used for public benefit – via scientific and controlled, profitable applications to timber harvesting, water and animal collection. He invented the concept of a conservation ethic. His intent was to manage the forests professionally through advanced scientific methods in order to maximize social good while minimizing waste and the generation of deleterious effects to the ecosystems. Pinchot ordered the creation of a national policy rather than a private or regional one.

Unfortunately, the forests weren't always managed well. In part, this was due to scientific beliefs in the mid-twentieth century that promoted massive clearcutting policies. Clearcutting, also known as clear felling, is a term used in logging that denotes an area where most or all trees are uniformly cut down: an entire stand of trees is removed. The term clearcutting refers to tree harvesting for timber. It is not a term used to denote tree removal for the purpose of clearing land for another purpose such as construction of a mine or a housing development.

These policies not only created stark views of cleared lands, but instigated landslides and mud slides during periods of heavy rains and had observable impacts on wild animal populations – in particular to the bird populations. As a result, in 1976, Senator Hubert Humphrey declared,

> The days have ended when the forest may be viewed only as trees and trees viewed only as timber. The soil and the water, the grasses and the shrubs, the fish and the wildlife, and the beauty of the forest must become integral parts of the resource manager's thinking and actions.
>
> (United States Forest Service, n.d.)

Senator Humphrey's views were written into the National Forest Management Act of 1976 (NMFA).

This law was passed when there were serious national debates about clearcutting practices in the northwestern United States. At the time, the northwest states of Oregon and Washington were experiencing significant alteration to wide swaths of national forests due to clearcutting practices. The NMFA requires the Secretary of Agriculture to assess forest lands, develop a management program based on combined use, assess conservation principles, and apply a resource management plan for each unit of the National Forest System. NMFA is the leading and most fundamental regulation governing national forests.

This led Congressional officials such as Humphreys, Senator Frank Church, and Congressman Harley Staggers to develop regulations that limit the size of clearcut areas, protect streams from logging effects, restrict annual rates of cutting, and demand reforestation of affected areas. While these provisions are interpreted as promoting conservation, the U.S. Forest Service is still a federal agency that relies on Congressional appropriation. This means that the agency has to show that it is using Congressional funds effectively while demonstrating that the forests are also of beneficial use via recreational use and timber harvest. The Forest Service, under the Department of Agriculture, still has to validate its economic role in the national production of natural resource commodities. Consequently, the Forest Service is in a constant balance of regulatory restraint, public demand, activist pressure, bureaucratic burden, and conservation. This very real complication is rarely recognized by those who seek to influence policy on national forests.

The Multiple Use Sustained Yield Act of 1960 (16 U.S.C. 528–531) was passed by Congress to limit deforestation through logging activities and water reclamation projects. This law ordered the management of national forests to "best meet the needs of the American people." U.S. forests were no longer to be exploited primarily for economic gain. Instead, the forests would be utilized through a mix of "outdoor recreation, range, timber, watershed, and wildlife and fish purposes" (Multiple Use Sustained Yield Act of 1960). This law was the clarification of Gifford Pinchot's intent and, in fact, is a rewording of the original Organic Act of

1897. The Multiple Use Sustained Yield Act was not a re-prioritization as water use and timber harvesting are still the primary uses of the forests.

The law does distinguish what the Forest Service must confront: the difference between market demand and land demand. Market demands dictate the timber harvest and water usage whereas the conservation of the forest for non-commodity applications reflects land demand. While the law did not resolve this conflict, it was important in bringing legal status and social awareness to the preservation and access to this natural resource.

The Water Source Protection Program, enacted as 16 U.S.C. §6542, provided clarification of the purpose of using the forest lands for water use. The law posits that forest management activities are "necessary to protect, maintain, or enhance water quality" through the Department of Agriculture Secretary who was required to engage "forest management activities as part of watershed protection and restoration projects carried out on National Forest System land, with the primary purpose of – (A) protecting a municipal water supply system; (B) restoring forest health from insect infestations and disease" (16 U.S.C. §6542).

As a continuation of the transcendentalist movement, the Wilderness Act of 1964 (16 U.S.C. §§1131–1136) was passed. The Act recognized the value of preserving "an area where the earth and its community of life are untrammeled by man, where man himself is a visitor who does not remain" (Id. at §1131(c)). The Wilderness Act of 1964 was written with intent to designate more land as wilderness in order for preservation of natural environments for future generations (Environment and Natural Resource Division, n.d.). A total of 9.1 million acres of land were preserved under this Act. The law states that:

> designated wilderness areas shall be administered for the use and enjoyment of the American people in such manner as will leave them unimpaired for future use and enjoyment as wilderness, and so as to provide for the protection of these areas, the preservation of their wilderness character, and for the gathering and dissemination of information regarding their use and enjoyment as wilderness.
>
> (Id. at §1131(a))

The law prevents commercial enterprises and the establishment of permanent roads, water and grazing rights are prohibited, construction of permanent structures are prohibited, and flyover limits are imposed with the exception of insect or fire suppression. These restrictions are created to limit human activity on protected lands.

This law has been invoked as justification by radical environmentalists to commit crimes in the national forests. Often the impetus for their actions involves a subjective interpretation of wilderness. In environmental studies texts there are differences in the concepts of natural and wilderness. The arguments employed by the activists frequently reflect a position that the designated wilderness areas should be free of all activities except for hiking or other low impact and limited activities.

Conflict arises when government officials attempt to designate parcels of lands as wilderness that previously did not have the designation. Rural communities that are adjacent to the identified lands routinely decry that they are being economically repressed. Rural residents often use these public lands as hunting areas, and to conduct timber harvest, fishing, and engage in other recreational activities such as snowmobile excursions. These residents also often express their desires for development in their area as they have often experience limited economic opportunities where they live. They feel their livelihoods are usurped by ideologies of people who live far from the impacted areas.

The cost of preserving wilderness is hard to measure while the rural communities are able to quantify benefits of not restricting development of these areas. The restrictions that a land parcel experiences under the Wilderness Act are a significant impediment for the long term. Rural communities' positions have become antagonistic to environmental activists. Rather than tempting to ameliorate the realities confronted by rural communities that inhabit the lands adjacent to targeted potential wilderness areas, environmental activists tend to deride rural citizens as anti-science or antagonistic to environmental ethos. This disparate view prevents cooperative resolutions and frequently stimulates more fevered reactions by environmental activists who are willing to take radical action to advance their agenda and perspective.

Illegal Activities in Forests

In the United States, illegal activities took place in national, state, and private forests by environmental activists who have been radicalized into becoming eco-terrorists. Starting in the 1980s, a surge in criminal activities occurred through direct actions by impassioned environmentalists who believed that mainstream environmentalism was ineffective and too incremental in its approach to change. Mainstream environmentalists traditionally have been concerned with increased sustainability and mitigating environmental harms through pollution controls and enforcement of environmental protections such as the Endangered Species Act. Radical environmental activists began forming organizations because their members wanted to engage in direct action against corporations and the United States government. The activists believed that they needed to create media attention through provocative action and criminal activity as necessary to stop ecological harms. While traditional activists engaged in relatively benign activities such as letter writing campaigns, protests, and sit-ins, radicalized activists began engaging in more serious behavior that included destruction of property, criminal trespass, sabotage, road blockages, and extreme violence such as arson and homicide (Woodhouse, 2018). The radical environmentalists formed groups that became renowned for their demands and actions. Some of the most infamous radical environmental groups were Earth First, Greenpeace, Sea Shepherd, Earth Liberation Front, Animal Liberation Front, and Extinction Rebellion.[1]

At the beginning of Earth First activities in 1980, members occupied trees by installing platforms and refusing to climb down. They chained themselves to trees, laid down in front of bulldozers, and dismantled heavy equipment such as tractors to prevent logging. Later Earth First members began spiking trees. This involved hammering in metal rods or spikes into tree trunks so that if a logger attempted to cut the tree, his blade would shatter. The effect is injury or death to the logger. Also, the spike may have the same effect if the timber makes it to the mill. The saw blades at the mill will collide with the spikes causing similar effects to mill operators. Firefighters who have had to cut trees to create fire breaks have confronted spiked trees causing disruption to fire control. The stated slogan of Earth First is "No Compromise in Defense of Mother Earth." Earth First members and sympathetic allies from other environmental organizations such as Greenpeace have had significant impact in creating delays of lawful forestry activities such as timber felling.

In 1990 there were social protests: a sudden surge of tree sitters – people who camped in trees – and those who blocked logging roads in an attempt to stop clearcutting of old growth forests in Oregon and Washington. The protests became very disruptive to logging operations and compromised U.S. Forest Service functions and ability to control activities in the forests. The environmentalists focused on the northern spotted owl (*Strix occidentalis caurina*), which had just been listed as a threatened species under the Endangered Species Act, as justification of their activities. It was through the NMFA that orders were given to stop timber harvests in spotted owl habitats. The conflict was not limited to disagreement between the environmentalists and the government. Conflicts spilled into the communities where loggers lived. Their economic livelihoods were being threatened. The conflict elevated to a struggle between environmentalists who primarily lived in cities against loggers who lived in rural communities. In 1994, the Northwest Forest Plan was created to resolve the political impasse. The plan sought to balance the timber industry, local community demands, and federal forest management practices. The resolution was to stop logging in selected old growth forests for a specified period of time. Logging never reached the agreed upon levels leaving many of the forest adjacent communities impoverished.

Other Environmental Organizations and Their Links to Criminal Acts on Forest Lands

Members of Greenpeace engage in other activities such as illegally mounting oil rigs in the waters of Russia and Norway, parachuting through no-fly zones and into stadiums, and seizing the keys to more than 1,000 Volkswagen cars after illegally entering the German port of Emden. The purpose of the key seizure was to prevent the cars from being exported. Greenpeace's overriding intent is to create spectacle to draw attention to their cause and to provoke government and corporations into more restrictive environmental policy changes.

The Sea Shepherd is an organization that spun off from Greenpeace because members of the original Greenpeace didn't think the organization was engaging in actions radical enough to stop whaling. The Sea Shepherd anointed itself as a "self-appointed policing agency" whose mission was to stop all forms of whaling. The Sea Shepherd was responsible for ramming and sinking several whaling and fishing ships in the waters of Iceland, Mexico, the Faroe Islands (territory of Denmark), Canada, Spain, Costa Rica, and Portugal. In these incidents, Paul

Watson, the head of the organization, proudly proclaimed that loss of human life is part of the collateral damage of the work he feels compelled to do.

After decades of intense media attention including a television program, *Whale Wars*, on Animal Planet, the Sea Shepherd garnered the ire of several governments including Iceland, the United States, Australia, and New Zealand. When activists were confronted with government action they didn't approve of, including the permitting of whaling, they retaliated with criminal behavior. In one instance they damaged a Department of Fisheries and Oceans building in Quebec, Canada, threw signal flares containing phosphorous at police, used iron spikes to puncture police dinghies, and shot at police.

While organizations such as Greenpeace and the Sea Shepherd may seem disparate from organizations such as Earth First that spiked trees and illegally trespassed into logging areas, members of these organizations often participate in more than one organization's efforts. Rodney A. Coronado was an early participant in the Sea Shepherd, actively taking part in the sinking of two vessels near Iceland. He later participated in the Animal Liberation Front (ALF) organization. In that organization Coronado participated in several criminal events including the firebombing of a research laboratory at Michigan State University (MSU). The ALF broke into the animal disease laboratory of the USDA, exploded laboratories such as the one at MSU, and damaged private mink farms. Coronado was criminally charged with arson, theft, destruction of government property, and receiving stolen property (Hawkins, 2017).

Individuals who worked with Greenpeace assisted individuals who sat in trees to stop logging and facilitated tree sit-ins by famous celebrities such as Joan Baez, Bonnie Raitt, and Woody Harrelson. The overlap in key players who play pivotal roles in radical environmentalist organizations are like career criminals who make their living by violating the laws. Multiple individuals from these organizations have been criminally charged with serious violations including piracy, attempted murder, destruction of property, larceny, arson, and illegal use of explosives (Hwang, 2021). The law enforcement resources that are used to capture them are extensive including the coordination of the FBI and Interpol. These radical environmental organizations share tactics for recruitment and training of environmentalists. They teach individuals how to engage in sabotage, how to contact friendly media sources, how to engage sympathetic members of the public through savvy social media postings and how to negotiate with corporations whose land they trespass or whose activities are illegally disrupted (Woodhouse, 2018).

Like other organized crime groups, radical environmentalist organizations expertly use media to promote themselves as vulnerable victims who are unfairly pursued by government actors. They project images of wanting to be lawful while they earnestly engage in non-profit activities such as public awareness campaigns and fund raising. In reality, they not only pose risk to human life, property, and ecosystems they are claiming to protect, they engage and train others to commit serious criminal offenses (Trujillo, et al., 2005). Also, both organized crime and radical environmental organizations create unfair disadvantages for legitimate enterprises such as those engaged in lawful logging.

By spiking trees and otherwise sabotaging logging activities, radicalized environmentalists prevent safe forest management and drive up costs of domestic timber products. They negatively impact rural communities that depend upon logging. The radical environmentalists are not local residents of the logging communities where their activities occur. The environmentalists are interlopers exploiting natural resources for their own political agenda. Disruption to U.S. based logging and the multitude of lawsuits by environmental groups to further restrict logging in the United States creates a vacuum filled by cheap, illegally harvested timber imported from forests in other nations (Bisschop, 2012).

Illegal Timber Harvesting

Illegal timber harvests in Africa and Asia threaten national security of the United States. It is estimated that between 60% and 70% of all tropical timber imported into the European Union is from trees that are harvested illegally (Odura, 2016; Price, 2022). In the west coast Central African nation of Gabon, 70% of the timber exported is harvested illegally. This is problematic for Gabon's national economy, its wildlife and ecosystem integrity, as well as for its ability to control its natural resources. The value of the forests is used to profit transnational criminal groups that have infiltrated nations like Gabon across Africa.

> In Africa, authoritarian governments, ungoverned spaces and conflicts have created the perfect storm for criminals and terrorist groups to expand their illicit trafficking and smuggling operations. The lucrative business of illicit trade has also been militarized in some areas, bribing complicit government officials to shield illicit enterprises from scrutiny and coercing soldiers to protect the illicit markets.
>
> (Luna, 2021)

The illegal harvesting of timber on scales this large indicates that organized crime groups are transferring natural resource assets via the illicit global marketplace. Illegal trade of bulk commodities such as oil and timber require a specialized labor force with industrial scale equipment. It demands a brokerage system of dishonest port authorities and other public officials who permit the passage of timber shipments. For the United States and other western nations, the illicit harvests are problematic because this level of commodity transfers strengthens illicit criminal organizations that increasingly do business with terrorist organizations on the African continent.

Forests in Central America, far eastern Russia, the Amazon basin, and Africa have been grossly impacted via illegally logging. Large swaths of forests have been harvested for illegal timber that has been sold on the illicit market or purposely mislabeled to obscure national origin. Other crimes associated with illegal timber harvesting include fraudulent documentation, incursions onto protected lands – either protected via conservation specifications or through protection of indigenous land holdings, violation of property rights – private or public, and stimulating the corruption of public officials. Communities that are dependent upon these lands or resources struggle as incursions on the land and its resources deprive native people of potential economic opportunities (African Press Organization, 2012; Balliett, 2010).

It is estimated that 25% of each sale of illegally harvested timber fills the coffers of corrupt officials and criminal enterprises that run these consignments (Bisschop, 2012). This level of illegality not only induces more criminal consignments, it provides a consistent funding source that reinforces the power and structure of the criminal group within the region. The criminal group is further strengthened when it operates within a nation that is deprived of tax revenues. The illegal harvests deny financial inputs to state treasuries thus increasing the level of corruption within public offices. A cycle of deprivation and corruption is created, in part, through illegal harvesting of timber in forest rich nations.

In Africa, illegal transfers of commodities such as gold, diamonds, and timber products, along with illegal harvesting of ivory, have become a sustained economic engine for terrorist and militia groups that sell or trade these commodities for the purchase of guns and munitions. While the United States and Europe import furniture cheaply made from illegally harvested timber and China imports significant amounts of illegal timber, the motive for the criminal group is to fortify its position through violence and control of illicit markets.

These activities, while not directly impacting the United States, create criminality within the U.S.' domestic criminal markets. The interplay between the criminal organizations that move illegally garnered natural resources from Africa to the markets of China often use the U.S. and Europe as a transfer point or money laundering location which serve the expansion of illicit markets worldwide.

> The lucrative criminal activities enabling and fueling the multitrillion-dollar illicit economies include the smuggling and trafficking of narcotics, opioids, weapons, humans, counterfeit and pirated goods; illegal tobacco and alcohol products; illegally harvested timber, wildlife and fish; pillaged oil, diamonds, gold, natural resources and precious minerals; and other contraband commodities. Such contraband and illicit goods are sold on our main streets, on social media, in online marketplaces and on the dark web every minute of every day. The United Nations has estimated that the dirty money laundered annually from such criminal activities constitutes up to 5 percent of global gross domestic product, or $4 trillion.
>
> (Luna, 2021)

United States' companies often conceal illegal logging through supply chain transfers. Once a tree is felled and modified into timber, it is difficult to ascertain if the harvest was legal or illegal. Unlawfully harvested timber is co-mingled with legally harvested timber in large shipments. In the United States, much of the illegally harvested timber arrives in the form of completed products such as furniture. Ikea, a Swedish based furniture company, has been identified as a purchaser of large amounts of illegal timber that originates in Far East Russia (Chaudhuri, 2015).

The company claims that it has foresters on the ground to ensure that the timber is harvested within the constraints of legality and sustainability.

These claims are used to "greenwash" its image – a marketing maneuver conducted by companies to create an image of environmental sustainability. Ikea stores proliferate within the United States as purveyors of inexpensive furniture that is made with ecologically sound timber products. Yet, those who scrutinize Ikea's business practices show that the company employs only three foresters in Russia and two in China (Liddick, 2011). This is a grossly insufficient number of overseers in a region that is plagued by illegal timber harvesting. According to the World Bank, nearly 50% of the timber harvested in Far East Russia is harvested illegally. This means that U.S. consumers are facilitating environmental crimes through their purchases.

Illegal Narcotics Grows in U.S. National Forests

Illicit marijuana (*Cannabis sativa*) grows were found in forest lands in the 1960s. The grows were small scale and located in remote areas. They were considered individual scale grows. In the 1980s state, local, and federal law enforcement agents noted that the grows in the forests were becoming larger, indicating that they were not simply for individual use. The grows were in less remote areas and were not as dispersed as they had once been. In 1995, land managers in the national forests of California noted that the grows were becoming industrial in scale (Milestone, et al., 2012; Warren, 2021). It became clear to the U.S. Forest Service that the grows were being managed and operated by drug-trafficking organizations, i.e. organized crime. The marijuana grows were now guarded by armed personnel with guns and often semi-automatic weapons, there were sophisticated logistics and cultivation methods including construction of water pipelines which siphoned water from streams into a catchment area near the grow site (Felbab-Brown, 2021).

Grow sites have expanded their environmental footprint. It is customary to locate grow sites that take up fifty acres of land and some have been found on public forests that extend across more than a mile of land. The land use often includes miles of plastic or PVC tubing for the water delivery as well as plastic tarps to conceal the grows, propane tanks, and hundreds of plastic planters (Carah, et al., 2015). This does not include the amount of human waste which includes trash from food, clothing, tents, camping equipment, and human excrement on the site (Bauer, et al., 2015; Sullivan, 2017; Westervelt, 2019). All of these create deleterious effects on the environment.

Illegal marijuana grows have accelerated greatly since marijuana has become legalized. California legalized medical marijuana in 1996. Ten years later, California voters passed Proposition 64 to legalize recreational use of marijuana. The first legalization for recreational use occurred in Colorado and Washington in 2012. Since then, one-quarter of the country including the states of Alaska, Arizona, California, Illinois, Maine, Massachusetts, Michigan, Montana, New Jersey, Nevada, Oregon, South Dakota, Vermont, Virginia, and the District of Columbia has legalized the purchase and use of marijuana. Shifting an illegal activity into the legal market does not eliminate the illicit market. Paradoxically legalization has the opposite effect. Legalizing marijuana has vastly accelerated illegal marijuana grows (Boehm, 2014). This is because the cost of the legitimate market is expensive. It requires business permits, insurance, taxation, compliance with regulatory schemes, and employee payments and benefits. Conversely the illegal market only requires some form of payment to employees without any additional costs beyond operational expenses, many of which are free since the land and water used tend to be public resources or stolen resources. Since the illegal market is operating outside of regulatory schemes often illegal products are used in lieu of required or restricted components.

In the case of marijuana grows, banned pesticides and rodenticides are brought from Mexico into the United States. Many of the pesticides and herbicides needed to grow these large-scale marijuana gardens require large amounts of administrative effort to acquire commercial or industrial permits. The illegal grow bypasses costs through importation of inexpensive and toxic chemicals as well as the absence of any permitting. Data from California indicates that the licit market of marijuana generates $3 billion annually whereas the illicit market generates $9 billion annually (Conway, 2022). Seventy percent of the illicit market gets its marijuana from illegal grows on public lands.

The demand for vice outstrips supply leading to illegal marijuana grows. The legalization of the vice expands the amount of users. There are those who would not engage in illegal activity. Approximately 20–30% of the population would not participate in an activity if it were illegal but would try it if it became legal. The remainder of the population remains steadfast in either opposition or involvement in an activity regardless of legal status (Quinney, 1965). As a result, legalizing marijuana sales and purchases leads to an increase in the demand for the product. In marijuana sales, the cost of the illegal marijuana is lower than the cost of the legal marijuana which has higher overhead and input costs. Since the buyers and sellers now have legal cover, they do not fear being a part of the illegal market. Current estimates are that the sellers of illegal marijuana outnumber legal sales 50 to 1 (Los Angeles County Sheriff, 2022).

The legal market serves as a cover for the illegal growers and traders. Growers, distributors, and sellers experience reduced deterrence when the product becomes legalized with minimal regulatory oversight. Regardless of which state passed laws relating to marijuana legalization, no state has substantially provided resources to ensure enforcement of the limited regulations which often include restricted amounts – usually one ounce – and prohibitions of sales to those under the age of 21.

In the case of marijuana grows, the substantive increases in demand has led to massive upticks in illegal marijuana grows. Many of these illegal grows take place on public lands such as those under the jurisdiction of the United States Forest Service or the Bureau of Land Management in addition to state public lands such as state forests or ecological preserves whose aims are to maintain and foster conservation for rare and endangered species. In 2020, in Los Angeles County, California, 150 illegal grows were uncovered. Between January 2021 and June 2021, 500 illegal grows were discovered by the Los Angeles County Sheriff's Office

(KCAL News, 2021). These illegal marijuana grows have had significant detrimental impacts on the environment. In one police operation, known as the Antelope Valley Marijuana Eradication Operation, 131 arrests were made with 19 of them for water theft. Two bears were found dead near the grow sites. They expired from ingesting pesticides used at the marijuana grows according to California Fish and Wildlife (Cain, 2021).

Marijuana grows often employ illegal pesticides that were banned due to their persistent toxicity in the environment. The amount of animals and native plants that are destroyed has been extensive. In addition, streams have been diverted or contaminated and cleared lands are often illegally graded or terraced causing soil erosion. Areas that experience a significant amount of human activity become compacted causing further environmental damage. This is because rain percolation cannot occur in these arid ecosystems once the soils are compacted. Thus, the forests become more strained even when rain arrives.

The United States Forest Service estimates that illegal marijuana grows are operating in 72 forests in 22 states (Boehm, 2014). Native trees and other vegetation are cut down or otherwise killed to make room for the marijuana plants. The soil is tilled, and fertilizers and pesticides, including Fosfuro de Zinc, a common Mexican rat poison containing zinc phosphide, are spread throughout grow sites. This rodenticide requires a license to acquire and employ under agricultural regulations. In one site in the Lassen National Forest, forest service rangers hauled out 6,000 pounds of trash, most of it hazardous chemicals, from a 60-acre grow site. The chemicals were dumped in a water drainage area causing significant environmental damage to a riparian area in an arid landscape. Law enforcement officers who are tasked with addressing illegal grows report many cases of wildlife poaching by those who work at the illegal grow sites. There are substantial amounts of poison associated with the illicit grow sites. The pesticides either impact wildlife at the site or are carried away by animals that consume it and die elsewhere.

Three illegal grow sites in Lassen National Forest included 11,360 pounds of trash, 1,250 pounds of fertilizer, and 18 miles of pipes that siphoned water from a creek to the grow site (Quinton, 2016). This is far more damaging than it may appear. In California, a state that experiences successive and extreme drought, this is intensely problematic for water managers as 60% of the total water supply for Californians originates on national forest lands (Carah, et al., 2015). Thus, the illicit marijuana grows are a water intensive crop that vastly impacts wildlife in the national forests. Several scientific studies have been conducted on watersheds within California. Their conclusions are that multiple species of fish, amphibians, and other wildlife face considerable negative impacts just based on water depletion. One study conducted by California Department of Fish and Wildlife as well as academic scientists concluded:

> Our results indicate that water demand for marijuana cultivation has the potential to divert substantial portions of streamflow in the study watersheds, with an estimated flow reduction of up to 23% of the annual seven-day low flow in the least impacted of the study watersheds. Estimates from the

> other study watersheds indicate that water demand for marijuana cultivation exceeds streamflow during the low-flow period. In the most impacted study watersheds, diminished streamflow is likely to have lethal or sub-lethal effects on state-and federally-listed salmon and steelhead trout and to cause further decline of sensitive amphibian species.
>
> (Bauer, et al., 2015)

The environmental damage is so significant that the cost of remediating most of the damaged lands has been too exorbitant for the public land agencies to absorb. Only a small fraction of the identified grow sites are remediated. Usually, the plants, trash, pesticides, and hazardous materials are removed along with the pipelines. Other than alteration to the landscape, bear, deer, and other animals are poached and consumed on site. Long-term damage to the forest lands and to the sensitive public lands are extensive and as marijuana use continues to increase, the environmental impacts on the forest lands is expected to escalate (Bauer, et al., 2015; Milestone, et al., 2012).

Between 2005 and 2014, 19 million marijuana plants were seized according to the Law Enforcement and Investigations Managerial Attainment Reporting System (LEIMARS). In 2013, more than 118,901 pounds of trash, 80.5 miles of plastic tubing, 244 propane tanks, and 61 car batteries were removed from grow sites. Additionally, 17,091 pounds of fertilizer, nearly 40 gallons of liquid pesticides, and over five gallons of banned poisons were recovered from grow sites (Boehm, 2014). Both of these data sets occurred only in national forests in California. The state and forest which produce the second largest amount of marijuana is the Daniel Boone National Forest in Kentucky where illegal marijuana grows have an annual street value of $1 billion (Horng & Yu, 2009).

The list of pesticides and hazardous chemicals found on illegal grow sites includes insecticides such as Lorsban 480 EM, Sevin carbaryl and Malathion, the rat poisons Bromethalin and Brodifacoum, Acetylcholinesterase inhibitor which can be used as a pesticide, and plant hormone concentrate Hormoviton Calor. Marijuana growers generously spray their plants with highly concentrated insecticides such as carbofuran, a neurotoxin that can seep through soil and enter ground water. Carbofuran is listed as one of the most toxic pesticides and was banned in the United States by the Environmental Protection Agency (EPA) in 1994. The reason for its ban is because it is highly toxic when it is inhaled or is absorbed through the skin. It causes respiratory damage as well as contact burns to the eyes and skin. Lastly it produces poisonous gases when exposed to open flames. Additionally, Furadan, an EPA banned toxic insecticide that is prohibited for use on any crop that is consumed by humans, has been found on public land grows.

The amounts used are so large and widespread that a study conducted in 2015 by Integral Ecology Research Center discovered that of 101 fisher (*Martes pennanti*) carcasses that were studied 85% tested positive for rat poison, as did 67% of spotted owl (*Strix occidentalis*) carcasses. Fishers are mammals related to otters, minks, and weasels and are an indicator species as they can only thrive in a healthy forest. Currently they are being put forward to be listed as an endangered species due to their collapsing population size. Mountain lion (*Puma concolor*) carcasses are testing positive for rodenticide at a rate of 95% (Gabriel, et al., 2013). The animals ranged on public lands in California and Nevada. In 2017, out of 22 carcasses tested, 100% tested positive for rodenticide. Water samples taken from streams in national forests in California and Nevada are testing positive for rodenticides Bromethalin and Brodifacoum at a rate of 40% (Lohan, 2019).

Rat poison has been found in the carcasses of black-tailed deer (*Odocoileus hemionus columbianus)*, bears (*Ursidae*), fox (*Canidae*) and ravens (*Corvus*). Researchers who study animal populations on public lands have had their lives threatened and one of the primary researchers, Mourad Gabriel, returned home to find his pet dog killed via rat poison (Gabriel, et al., 2013). Many research studies of endangered species have been canceled due to the presence of the drug cartels responsible for the marijuana grows. They often set hidden traps in the area where they operate their illegal activity which further creates hazards and damage to human and wildlife populations.

Concentrated insecticides have been found in tuna and cat food cans that are placed near water diversion pipes and water catchment areas. In times of drought, animals are drawn to these water sources. To prevent them from chewing on the water hoses, marijuana growers have placed these tainted food sources to kill off the wildlife to prevent them from damaging the water lines or consuming the water. The tuna and cat food draw in ravens, bears, and foxes. In the process of bioaccumulation, the animal that eats the bait dies, then the animal that consumes it – usually a bird of prey – then succumbs and also dies from the secondary digestion of the poison. The potency, due to the high concentration of the poisons applied, has led to insects that feed on the carcasses of the animals to die. Thus, a domino effect of environmental destruction is put in place when marijuana growers cultivate their products on public lands.

Disturbingly, animal baits aren't used to repel wildlife, they are used to attract them. Rather than using repellents, drug-trafficking organizations place bait that lures wildlife with the intention of killing the wildlife on site. Researchers found hot dogs soaked in concentrated methomyl, a highly toxic pesticide, strung up on fishing hooks around the perimeter of one grow site (Gabriel, et al., 2013). Storage of chemicals, misuse or overuse and spillage of the chemicals are neither a concern nor addressed by the illicit growers. These compound to create long-term effects that persist for years after the grow is eradicated.

Regarding freshwater systems, over 1 billion gallons of water are illegally diverted in California each year. This is likely an underestimate as the forest service officers believe they identify between 20% and 50% of the illegal grows. Each marijuana plant consumes 900 gallons of water per growing season (Helmer, 2019). In 2017, California forest service officers removed 1.25 billion plants which means that more than 1.1 billion gallons of water were illegally diverted. Each year in California, 9 billion gallons of water are illegally diverted to illicit marijuana grows on public lands. This is enough water to supply 35,000 homes for a year.

Court Cases

The environmental harms have been considerable enough to prosecute several federal cases on violations of environmental laws in addition to the narcotics violations. In *United States v. Cruz Soria* No. 1:12-CR-00283 (E.D. Calif.), (2014), a case involving illegal marijuana grow in the Canebrake Ecological Reserve in eastern California was adjudicated leading to a five-year prison sentence following a plea of guilty. In the case of *United States v. Hernan Cortez Villaseñor*, No. 1:12-CR-00184 (E.D. Calif.), (2014), Hernan Cortez Villaseñor was sentenced to serve ten years plus five years of probation due to a marijuana grow in the Greenhorn Creek area of the Sequoia National Forest. The grow included destruction of a grove of native oak trees to make room for the 9,000 marijuana plants he cultivated in the forest. Villaseñor used more than thirty containers of the Mexican rat poison, Fosfuro de Zinc, on the site. He was found guilty of the cultivation of marijuana in addition to violating the Federal Insecticide, Fungicide, and Rodenticide Act (FIFRA). In the same year Chris Boehm, the assistant director of law enforcement investigations of the United States Forest Service testified before the United States Sentencing Commission:

> Last year [2013] in California alone, 17,091 pounds of fertilizer, almost 40 gallons of liquid pesticides, and over 5 gallons of banned poisons were recovered prior to use from grow sites. These numbers, although alarming themselves, represent only a small portion of the chemicals introduced into the fragile ecosystem. It is unknown how many tons of fertilizers, gallons of toxic liquids, or pounds of solid poisons are applied and used during the cultivation process on our public lands. However, we do know that the impacts are significant and far reaching.
>
> (Boehm, 2014)

The harms are not limited to wildlife and the environment. Alongside the siphoning of water from wildlife, in California the marijuana grow sites also deprive municipal water systems of more than a billion gallons of water. Siphoning and diversion of water depletes supplies as source sites are drained and the water is diverted to marijuana grows. Water inputs for the cities of San Francisco and Sacramento in California are at greater risk of contamination from highly concentrated amounts of rodenticide and insecticide. Concerns of rat poisons entering ground water and seeping into wells in rural areas are also increasing.

The reason that California is the source of much of the data is because this state accounts for 82% of the federal forest service's seizures. In part, California has more national forests than other states. The largest national forest is in Alaska and Maine has the largest forest cover, yet, California has the most amount of national forests. Fifty-seven percent of California's forest cover is federal forest land (Forests Unlimited, n.d.). This amounts to 19 million acres of national forest. There are an additional 14 million acres of forest land, much of it private, some owned by local or state agencies (USDA, n.d.). Aside from the large land holdings by the US Forest Service, California is a state with a high level of organized criminal activity.

Even in cities or suburban areas where there are illegal marijuana grows there are substantial environmental harms. The demand for water use is not diminished in indoor grows. With the cultivation of marijuana in residential or industrial buildings, there is a high demand for electricity and water. To prevent detection of the high powered grow lamps and industrial sized ventilation systems, many of the growers illegally tap into neighbors' electricity inputs. Areas with large grows experience blown transformers and blackouts. Growers often steal power by illegally wiring directly into the municipal power system, which drives up the price of electricity for legitimate customers and creates a significant fire hazard (Young, 2021). Additionally, the home or structure becomes a hazard as the high humidity necessary for the grow leads to mold growth.

Scientists and forest service officials hope that the increase in prosecution and public notices of criminal cases will generate public awareness of the environmental crimes associated with marijuana cultivation. Marijuana cultivation is a billion-dollar industry that often involves organized crime. Even in legal enterprises most of the businesses operate under investment-owned companies. Big Marijuana is no different than Big Tobacco with lobbyists, public relations firms, advocacy groups promoting legalization at the local level, and commercial marketing. Both licit and illicit marijuana grows involve substantial natural resource inputs. Outdoor grows, particularly those on public lands, threaten animal and plant species and involve large-scale pesticide, herbicide, and rodenticide applications. Indoor grows employ high rates of herbicides, pesticides, and nematicides.

Organized crime, mainly Asian organized criminal enterprises and Mexican cartels, drive much of the illegal market (Boehm, 2014). In June 2021, twenty-one Chinese nationals were indicted by a grand jury in Colorado. They got a license to grow "medical marijuana" in Haskell County, Oklahoma. But police officials found firearms, more than a million dollars, and cultivated marijuana on the property in Colorado (Tabachnik, 2021). Law enforcement officers seized and destroyed more than 10,000 marijuana plants and nearly 100 pounds of processed marijuana. These amounts grossly exceed accepted amounts of cultivation under the legal marijuana grow regulations. Like many illegal distributors, the marijuana was cultivated in a state that permits lawful grows but was grown in amounts well beyond what is permitted. The growers expand their cultivation to sell on the black market in states where the price of marijuana is higher. The money from the illegal grows is laundered and becomes part of a broader criminal enterprise. In 2020, despite coronavirus and massive wildfires, one million marijuana plants were eradicated from national forest service lands (Attorney General of California, 2021).

Marijuana, both legal and illegal, mirrors other natural resource crimes. While portions of sales or harvesting may be legal, the trade often expands via organized crime to an illicit market. This should not be surprising as the same effect is seen in other vice crimes. When prostitution is legalized, the illegal market for prostitution expands. Thus, a demand is created for sex trafficking victims. Both illicit prostitution and illegal marijuana grows, often with other illicit narcotics distribution, tend to fall under the control of criminal enterprises as prostitutes can become carriers and distributors for both currency and narcotics. For Mexican cartels, the excessive accumulation of wealth has led to the development of illegal zoos for cartel members (Sanchez, 2022). These zoos are inhabited by animals that are illegally acquired and transported to Mexico in violation of CITES. The Mexican cartel and Chinese organized crime trade in illegal wildlife trafficking (Mistler-Ferguson, 2022). In this manner, the cultivation of marijuana is an environmental crime that fuels financing of other environmental crimes and street crimes.

Costs of Enforcement

Conservationists, hunters, anglers, and recreational users of the forest have joined law enforcement groups in demanding better funding for marijuana grow suppression, eradication, and remediation of the land. Law enforcement budgets are persistently strained. Several had been considerably reduced throughout the country as progressives have demanded their cities "defund the police." This defunding political platform was promoted in California which suffers disproportionate environmental impacts from marijuana grows, affecting local police both at the municipal and county level. Given the climate of de-regulation of marijuana and reduced public support for police, California sheriffs have been unable to constrain illegal grows. Officials from local law enforcement agencies coordinate with federal law enforcement agents to remove firearms and disarm booby traps, in addition to coordination from local fire agencies that work to remove and identify fire hazards.

According to reporting by the Research and Development Unit of the Department of Agriculture, remediation attempts are complicated by a constellation of factors.

> Many grow sites are in remote locations and difficult to access, making remediation efforts challenging and costly. Helicopters must be used to air-lift tons of garbage and miles of irrigation piping. Partial HAZMAT protocols must be followed, and decontamination kits used to contain and clean up the waste.
>
> (Sullivan, 2017)

Funding for remediation is insufficient. Often, local volunteer groups assist with replanting a former grow site once the area is cleared of hazards. The federal forest services along with other public land agencies such as the National Park Service and the Bureau of Land Management have consistently been underfunded. Much of the budget of the U.S. Forest Service has been directed toward fighting wildfires. The budget of the law enforcement unit within the forest service is a small portion of its total budget. This impeded the agency's capacity to suppress, mitigate, and remove illegal marijuana grows. The problem is too large for any one agency to handle.

The National Forest Service budget for maintaining cooperative law enforcement agreements with 500 county, local, and state law enforcement agencies is

$23.97 million per year. In comparison, the amount for wildfire suppression and wildland fire management is $9.7 billion for the year (United States Forest Service, 2023). Congress pressures the Forest Service to have at least 10,000 firefighters on staff yet the number of law enforcement officers is 650 personnel (United States Forest Service, n.d.).

The law enforcement component of the U.S. Forest Service is not able to compete with the other demands put on the agency. Thus, it is incumbent on states and other law enforcement agencies such as the Drug Enforcement Administration to assist. Unfortunately, these agencies have other demands placed upon them ensuring that eradication of illegal marijuana grows on public lands is not prioritized. In part, the political climate of tolerance and support of marijuana consumption makes the pursuit of marijuana grows unappealing to politicians who determine budgets. In this manner, this environmental crime appears like other environmental crimes. Voters and citizens claim to want clean environments and protections for wildlife but when it comes to enforcement of laws to reach these objectives, many are non-committal. The consumer wants inexpensive marijuana and, for many, the local dealer is more accessible than a lawful dispensary which may be dozens of miles away. It becomes a calculation of free market; however, the market isn't free. It is the result of theft of public resources at the expense of the environment, neighboring communities, downstream communities, and wildlife.

United States versus Lumber Liquidators

The Lacey Act (16 U.S.C. §§3371–3378), originally signed in 1900, addresses illegal trafficking of wildlife, fish, and plants. The 2008 Farm Bill amended the Lacey Act and extended its protections to a broad range of plants and plant products, making it unlawful to import into the United States any plant or plant product that was illegally harvested (Customs and Border Protection, 2022). The legal definition of a plant includes any part or derivative product of any wild member of the plant kingdom, including trees harvested from plantations. This includes all wood products, such as paper, pallets, furniture, essential oils, tool handles, or types of fabric. Any product that is made with wood or plant material must be declared. The declaration must include the scientific name of the plant, import value, plant quantities, and nation of where the plant was harvested. It is illegal to take a plant, including trees or their parts, where they are protected such as a nature preserve. It is illegal for any company to purchase then import any stolen plant. Additionally, it is illegal to import any plant or plant product without paying royalties, fees, or taxes that are associated with the harvest, transportation, and commerce of the originating nation. Illegal logging rates are widely varied by country of origin and plant species. According to the Environmental Investigations Agency, for some countries approximately 80% of exported timber is believed to be illegally harvested (Environmental Investigation Agency, 2010).

In this way, the amended Lacey Act is an attempt to combat illegally sourced natural resources such as timber and prevent illegal logging. Common cultivars such as corn, cotton, or cut flowers are excluded from the Lacey Act. The focus is on wildlife and wild flora. The intent is to preserve the ecosystem from which the plant originates. The Animal and Plant Health Inspection Service (APHIS) unit of the federal Department of Agriculture, the National Marine Fisheries Service, and the U.S. Fish and Wildlife Service (USFWS) enforce the Lacey Act. APHIS is responsible for collecting declarations for imported plants and plant products, and defining the scope of plant materials that require a declaration. The Fish and Wildlife Service has a 100-year history of investigations of Lacey Act violations. The Department of Homeland Security, that controls U.S. customs and monitors the borders through Customs and Border Protection, supports these investigations.

There are two ways an import company can get into trouble with the Lacey Act, leading to either criminal or civil penalty. The company can knowingly engage in malfeasance by falsifying import declarations or through purchasing illegally sourced wood. These are criminal actions under the Lacey Act. If a company imports illegally sourced wood unknowingly, it can be held civilly liable based on failed due diligence required by all import companies. If the company can prove that it had multiple steps in place to prevent the importation of illegally sourced wood but that they accidentally did so without intent, the company can be held civilly liable for its actions. This often includes the forfeiture of the assets and fines. If the company failed to exercise due care and imported illegally sourced wood then it can be held both civilly and criminally liable for their actions. Corporations have an obligation to follow the provisions of the Lacey Act on any importation of wild flora or fauna into the United States. Failure to follow the law can lead to significant penalties. The case of Lumber Liquidators Inc., a hardwood flooring company, is illustrative of what happens when the Lacey Act is applied to those who knowingly import illegally sourced wood products.

The first federal case to prosecute a company for unlawful importation of illegally sourced lumber was the case of Lumber Liquidators Inc. (*U.S. vs. Lumber Liquidators, Inc.*). Lumber Liquidators pled guilty and was charged in October 2015 in the Eastern District of Virginia with one felony count of importing goods through false statements and four misdemeanor violations of the Lacey Act. The Lacey Act was violated as it is a crime to import timber that was taken in violation of a source country's laws and to transport falsely labeled timber across international borders into the United States.

The company was sentenced in federal court in the eastern district of Virginia. The case concluded with the company paying $13.15 million, including $7.8 million in criminal fines, $969,175 in criminal forfeiture and more than $1.23 million in community service payments (United States Department of Justice, 2016). The $13.15 million criminal penalty was the largest financial penalty that resulted from a Lacey Act violation. Lumber Liquidators received a sentence of five years of organizational probation and mandatory implementation of an environmental compliance plan that is overseen by the federal government. The compliance plan is subject to third party, independent audits. The $1,230,825 in community service payments were given to government created programs: the National Fish and Wildlife Foundation (NWFW) and the USFWS Rhinoceros and Tiger Conservation Fund.

Additionally, some of the funds were used to develop a tool that will identify wood types as they come across the United States borders. The tool is a technological development that will assist investigations to occur as soon as timber products arrive to the United States and will permit quicker enforcement of the Lacey Act. The device is being developed to identify high risk and other timber species that are listed on the CITES Appendices, including the species that were involved in the Lumber Liquidators case. Other funds will be applied for conservation programs for the Siberian tiger, Amur leopard, and the east Russian forests where they dwell.

In 2013, Lumber Liquidators imported Mongolian oak (*Quercus mongolica*) from far eastern Russia. This location has the unique ecosystem that supports the habitat of the last remaining Siberian tigers (*Panthera tigris altaica*) and Amur leopards (*Panthera pardus orientalis*) in the world. The company declared on its paperwork that the Mongolian oak was Welsh oak (*Quercus petraea*). Lumber Liquidators also imported merpauh (*Swintonia spp.*) from Myanmar that the company declared was big leaf mahogany (*Swietenia macrophylla*) originating in Indonesia. Lumber Liquidators understood that mahogany importation would be complicated as mahogany trees are listed as a high-risk species. Mahogany trees throughout the world are limited in the commercial market due to decades of illegal logging and overharvesting. The three species of mahogany trees (*Swietenia sp.*) are listed by the International Union for Conservation of Nature (IUCN) as endangered. Indonesia has a reputation for illegal timber harvests and their lumber products are scrutinized as high risk on the import market. Despite Indonesia's reputation Lumber Liquidators ordered its Chinese supplier to declare falsely that it was importing big-leaf mahogany that was of Indonesian origin. Indonesia was chosen as the fraudulent origination point because mahogany from South or Central America is regulated by the Convention on the International Trade in Endangered Species (CITES).

The charges levied against Lumber Liquidators described the company's use of timber that was illegally logged, then deliberately mislabeled on import declarations that were used to obfuscate the true species and origination point of the timber. Other violations included using the same permit multiple times to the point where the take on the timber was 800% over the lawful limit declared on the timber permit. Prosecutors were able to document that Lumber Liquidators employees knew that timber from the Russian Far East was considered to likely be illegally sourced because the region is known for its political corruption and illegal harvesting.

According to U.S. Fish and Wildlife Service Director Dan Ashe who oversaw the case at the time:

> By knowingly and illegally sourcing timber from vulnerable forests in Asia and other parts of the world, Lumber Liquidators made American consumers unwittingly complicit in the ongoing destruction of some of the world's last remaining intact forests. Along with hastening the extinction of the highly endangered Siberian tiger and many other native species, illegal logging driven by the company's greed threatens the many people who depend on sustainable use of these forests for food, clean water, shelter and legitimate jobs. These unprecedented sanctions show how seriously we take illegal trade, and I am grateful to the Service special agents and wildlife inspectors, Homeland

> Security agents, and Justice Department attorneys who halted Lumber Liquidators' criminal acts and held the company accountable under the law.
>
> (United States Department of Justice, 2016)

According to records submitted to the court, between 2010 and 2013, Lumber Liquidators consistently failed to adhere to an internal system set up to alert the company of suspicious supply chain concerns. The company willfully ignored its own audit systems. The audit systems identified and alerted "imports from high-risk countries, imports of high-risk species, imports from suppliers who were unable to provide documentation of legal harvest and imports from suppliers who provided false information about their products" (Department of Justice, 2016).

United States versus Gibson Guitar

In August of 2012, Gibson Guitar Corp. entered into a criminal enforcement agreement with the federal government in order to end an investigation into criminal actions in violation of the Lacey Act. Gibson Guitar illegally purchased and imported ebony wood (*Diospyros ebenum*) from Madagascar and India as well as rosewood (*Dalbergia latifolia*) also from India. A criminal enforcement agreement permits the company to stop the criminal prosecution by agreeing to facts into evidence at the court, by paying fines, and by adjusting its company policies. The agreement is established to prevent Gibson Guitar from engaging in more criminal violations of the Lacey Act.

Gibson Guitar paid $300,000 in fines as well as an additional community service payment of $50,000 to the National Fish and Wildlife Foundation (NFWF). The NFWF funds are to be used to promote conservation, identification, and propagation of protected tree species and their associated forests. The forests targeted are those which were illegally sourced for wood used in the musical instrument industry. Gibson Guitar has to initiate and operationalize an internal audit and compliance program designed to strengthen its compliance controls and procedures as set forth by the federal government. In related civil forfeiture actions, Gibson will end its claims to the seized shipment of illegally obtained wood in the course of the criminal investigation, including Madagascar ebony from shipments with a value of $261,844.

The federal government intended to criminally charge Gibson Guitar with criminal violations of the Lacey Act, but with the legal agreement, as long as Gibson Guitar complies with the government's orders to stop all imports of Indian and Madagascar ebony and rosewood from India, the criminal prosecution is permanently suspended. Part of the stipulation is that Gibson Guitar will conduct regular audits of its buyer, supply chains, and import specialists to ensure that new violations do not occur.

A statement released by the Department of Justice as written by Assistant Attorney General Moreno of the Middle District of Tennessee included:

> As a result of this investigation and criminal enforcement agreement, Gibson has acknowledged that it failed to act on information that the Madagascar ebony it was purchasing may have violated laws intended to limit overharvesting

> and conserve valuable wood species from Madagascar, a country which has been severely impacted by deforestation. Gibson has ceased acquisitions of wood species from Madagascar and recognizes its duty under the U.S. Lacey Act to guard against the acquisition of wood of illegal origin by verifying the circumstances of its harvest and export, which is good for American business and American consumers.
>
> (United States Department of Justice, 2012)

Madagascar Ebony is a slow-growing tree species and supplies are considered threatened in its native environment due to over-exploitation. Both legal and illegal logging of Madagascar Ebony and other Madagascan tree species have substantially reduced Madagascar's forest cover. Madagascan government officials banned the logging of ebony and rosewood in protected areas in 2000. The harvest of ebony in, and export of unfinished ebony from, Madagascar has been banned since 2006. Illegal logging operations were funded in advance and included payments to corrupt local officials. The funds were derived from payments for future shipments by Chinese brokers and by loans from international banks. Demand for these woods come from Chinese furniture makers and from European and American demand for high-end musical instruments, of which Gibson Guitar was knowingly a participant in the illegal logging (United States Department of Justice, 2012). Wood buyers who were employees of Gibson Guitar took trips to Madagascar to specifically identify and purchase illegally harvested woods that the company knew were banned from export from Madagascar. Enforcing the Lacey Act was not only welcomed by conservation groups and American foresters who oppose illegal logging but also by non-profit organizations in Madagascar who are working to maintain the nation's unique wild flora and fauna.

What makes the Gibson Guitar case unique is not the malfeasance by the company but its immediate public relations campaign which launched following federal officials' enforcement of the Lacey Act. Company officials contacted the press to announce that the United States government "raided" its facilities in Tennessee and sent their employees home so that the government could take over the Gibson manufacturing facility (Havighurst, 2011). Even while purposefully misleading statements were being made to the press, Gibson Guitar employees knew and had documented that they had acquired illegally obtained ebony and rosewood in 2008. Internal documents showed that employees understood that the ban against ebony export from Madagascar was in effect since 2006. Documents about the employees' travel to Madagascar were stipulated as facts for the court. Gibson Guitar created a media stir by alleging that the "out of control government" was targeting an innocent company (Havighurst, 2011). The amount of evidence the governments of both Madagascar and the United States had was insurmountable against Gibson Guitar as both nations' officials had seized company warehouses with banned ebony products. Nonetheless Gibson Guitar executives proclaimed that they couldn't wait to make their case in a court of law to show their innocence and the depravity of the Department of Justice (Havighurst, 2011). Despite its intentional public deceit, Gibson Guitar voluntarily entered an agreement with the federal prosecutors to avoid an open court hearing or trial.

In a proclamation to reporters, Gibson Guitar CEO Henry Juszkiewicz declared: "We had a raid, with federal marshals that were armed, that came in, evacuated our factory, shut down production, sent our employees home and confiscated wood." He added:

> We're in this really incredible situation. We have been implicated in wrongdoing and we haven't been charged with anything. Our business has been injured to millions of dollars. And we don't even have a court we can go to and say, "Look, here's our position."
>
> (Havighurst, 2011)

Juszkiewicz made these statements to the press on August 30, 2011, knowing that the federal government had filed court papers in June of that year.

Independent auditors from the Environmental Investigations Agency (EIA) concluded that Gibson Guitar executives knew in advance that they imported prohibited wood products. In the independent audit by the non-profit organization, Andrea Johnson who conducted the investigation stated:

> Gibson clearly understood the risks involved. Gibson was on the ground in Madagascar getting a tour to understand whether they could possibly source illegally from that country. And made a decision in the end that they were going to source despite knowing that there was a ban on exports of ebony and rosewood.
>
> (Havighurst, 2011)

There is no evidence to support CEO Juszkiewicz's claim of "losing millions."

This application of intentional duplicity by Gibson Guitar executives, as a move to protect its brand, is not uncommon in white collar crime cases. Gibson Guitar executives were well aware of banned exports of various woods and understood that the trees being logged were in national parks. This is because the mahogany trees outside of protected areas were already logged by 2007. The only mahogany groves remaining in Madagascar were those inside nature preserves and national parks. The Gibson Guitar executives portrayed themselves as victims of government overreach and abuse knowing and documenting their criminal activities in internal communications. In this case, potential punishment resulting from of a criminal trial would have been much worse for the company. Thus the executives who persistently declared that they needed their day in court were working prudently to keep themselves out of court.

Challenging the legitimacy of authorities and condemning the condemners are part of Gresham Syke's and David Matza's neutralization theories. The language used by the Gibson Guitar executives showed that they not only tried to portray themselves as victims and condemn the actions of the government, but they also denied that there were victims in this case. The people of Madagascar are indeed victims since Gibson Guitar executives' actions contributed to an environment of corruption within the leadership in Madagascar. Additionally, substantive damage is done to conservation areas since ebony trees are notoriously slow growing and have already been over-exploited. Each tree felled is a substantive injury to the ecosystem of Madagascan forests. Residents of Madagascar strongly rely upon tourism which is diminished when nature preserves are damaged through illegal logging.

Government officials at the agencies charged with protecting wildlife as well as those who work in the Natural Resources Division of the U.S. Department of Justice know that when they file against a large company which is protective of its marketing brand, they will face a backlash of criticism and false allegations. White-collar criminals like CEO Juszkiewicz rarely acknowledge that their greed creates damages to others. They feel fully entitled to act in their interests without scrutiny and perceive the government's oversight as an intrusion on their business practices and profitability. This is one of the many challenges in enforcing environmental crime statutes. White collar crimes are notoriously difficult to prosecute because those with substantial resources like Gibson Guitar Corporation employ public relations teams, lawyers, and marketers to broadcast their supposed innocence, thereby skewing and tainting a potential jury pool. No person at Gibson Guitar expressed remorse at violating the laws of the United States or Madagascar. They failed to acknowledge publicly their engagement in environmental crime as part of their profit-making scheme. Instead, they continue to promote themselves as victims even after they signed court agreements acknowledging their criminal violations of the Lacey Act.

Conclusion

Globally illegal logging is the most profitable environmental crime. Illegally sourced timber accounts for approximately 10–30% of global timber trade. While the U.S. is not a net exporter of illegally harvested timber, there are cases of illegally imported timber such as the Gibson Guitars and Lumber Liquidators cases demonstrate. The biggest impacts to U.S. forests, which are highly regulated for timber harvest, is the destruction of forest land for illegal marijuana grows. California, Oregon, and other states have failed to effectively address this burgeoning and ongoing crime of large-scale illegal marijuana cultivation. The environmental damages from these grows are wide scale ecological destruction to soils and wildlife as well as long-term as they often involve the applications of pesticides that have prolonged effects in the environment. The failure of state and federal governments to address this specific crime creates domino effects of biodiversity loss, collapse of riparian systems, and clearcutting sections of the forest. This unique forestry-based crime leads to greater expansion of organized crime which in turn generates other street crimes. The increasing trend of illegal grows in multiple states from California to Maine has significantly expanded the presence of Chinese, Russian, and Mexican organized crime within the United States. The exploitation of public lands does not appear to have a limit under current federal leadership and the state natural resource systems are too underfunded and under sourced to adequately address the current trends.

Discussion Questions

1. What does Gibson Guitars' public ridicule of federal agents and investigators tell you about the public's perception of offenders who profit from deforestation?
2. The public often has a negative perception of timber and paper product companies' role in deforestation but side with companies like Gibson Guitars and Lumber Liquidators. Why is one industry which does not have a history of criminal behavior (paper products) targeted by environmentalists whereas Lumber Liquidators and Gibson Guitars don't suffer sales loss after they are found guilty of criminal charges?
3. California's marijuana grows are impacted by high rates of violent crime and significant environmental harm. Why do the media or environmental groups not focus on these harms when discussing environmental concerns?
4. How can state, tribal, and federal forest conservation agencies address harms done by illegal marijuana grows when more states are moving toward legalization of marijuana?

Further Reading Recommendations

1. Environmental Investigation Agency (2016, February 1). Lumber Liquidators sentenced for smuggling illegal wood into the United States. http://us.eia.org/press-releases/lumber-liquidators-sentenced-for-smuggling-illegal-wood-into-the-united-sta/.
2. Kaplan, A., Adou-Sabe, K., & McFadden, C. (2021). "We're one cigarette away": Illegal marijuana farms pose wildlife risk in California's parched national forests. *NBC News*. http://nbcnews.com/news/us-news/fire-guns-poison-illegal-marijuana-farms-pose-deadly-risks-californias-rcna7153.
3. McDaniel, P. (2019, August 29). Illegal cannabis farms still scarring public lands, two years after Prop. 64. *Los Angeles Times*. http://latimes.com/environment/story/2019-08-28/cannabis-california-national-forests-environment.
4. Mowbray, S. (2022). Legal and illegal cannabis: A cause for growing environmental concern. *Mongabay*. http://news.mongabay.com/2022/legal-and-illegal-cannabis-a-cause-for-growing-environmental-concern.
5. Patel, N., McGinnis, R., & Moody, S. (2022). *Narcofornia* [Video]. *Daily Caller*. http://dailycaller.com/stream/narcofornia.

Note

1 Radical environmental groups are unlike conventional environmental groups such as the Sierra Club, Audubon Society, Nature Conservancy, and the Wilderness Society, which advocate community education and engagement, advocacy, and filing legal cases in courts. The traditional environmental groups do not seek provocation or engage in illegal behavior and they condemn the use of violence including property destruction.

References

African Press Organization (APO) (2012). From illegal logging to timber laundering: Organized crime trade worth over US$30 Billion responsible for up to 90% of tropical deforestation / Report spotlights almost 30 ways of procuring and laundering illegal timber compromising security, climate mitigation and sustainable development efforts.

Associated Press (2012, August 7). Tennessee: Deal with guitar maker ends case on illegal import of wood. *New York Times*. https://www.nytimes.com/2012/08/07/us/deal-with-gibson-guitar-corporation-ends-case-on-illegal-import-of-wood.html.

Attorney General of California (2021, October 17). Attorney General Bonta announces eradication of more than one million marijuana plants as part of interagency effort to combat illegal grows. https://oag.ca.gov/news/press-releases/attorney-general-bonta-announces-eradication-more-one-million-marijuana-plants.

Balliett, J.F. (2010). *Environmental issues, global perspectives: Forests*. Routledge.

Bauer, S., Olson, J., Cockrill, A., Van Hattem, M., Miller, L., Tauzer, M., & Leppig, G. (2015). Impacts of surface water diversions for marijuana cultivation on aquatic habitat in four northwestern California watersheds. *PLOS One*. https://doi.org/10.1371/journal.pone.0120016.

Bisschop, L. (2012). Out of the woods: The illegal trade in tropical timber and a European trade hub. *Global Crime*, *13* (3), 191–212. https://doi.org/10.1080/17440572.2012.701836.

Boehm, C. (2014). Marijuana cultivation and the environmental impacts on public lands, 113th Congress. *United States Sentencing Commission*. https://www.ussc.gov/sites/default/files/pdf/amendment-process/public-hearings-and-meetings/20140313/Testimony_Boehm.pdf.

Cain, J. (2021, July 7). $1.2 billion in illegal marijuana seized from Antelope Valley farms, authorities say. *Los Angeles Daily News*. https://www.dailynews.com/2021/07/07/1-2-billion-in-illegal-marijuana-seized-from-antelope-valley-farms-authorities-say/.

Carah, J., Howard, J.K., Thompson, S.E., Gianotti, A.G.S., Bauer, S.D., Carlson, S.M., Dralle, D.N., Gabriel, M.W., Hulette, L.L., Johnson, B.J., Knight, C.A., Kupferberg, S.J., Martin, S.L., Naylor, R.L., & Power, M.E. (2015). High time for conservation: Adding the environment to the debate on marijuana liberalization. *Bioscience*, *65* (8), 822–829. https://doi.org/10.1093/biosci/biv083.

Chaudhuri, S. (2015, July 30). IKEA is getting deeper into the woods. *Wall Street Journal. Europe*. https://www.wsj.com/articles/ikea-gets-deeper-into-the-woods-1438310691.

Conway, J. (2022, May 24). Legal vs illicit cannabis sales in California, United States 2019–2024. *Statista*. https://www.statista.com/statistics/1075946/legal-vs-illicit-cannabis-sales-california-us/.

Customs and Border Protection (2022, May 2). Guidance on the Lacey Act Declaration: Article number 000001841. https://help.cbp.gov/s/article/Article1841?language=en_US.

Environmental Investigation Agency (2010, October 5). 'Rogue traders' in timber smuggling exposed. https://eia-international.org/press-releases/rogue-traders-in-timber-smuggling-exposed/.

Environment and Natural Resource Division (n.d.). The Wilderness Act of 1964. *Department of Justice*. https://www.justice.gov/enrd/wilderness-act-1964.

Felbab-Brown, V. (2021, April 12). Pot, water farms, and environmental harms in the US and Mexico. *The Brookings Institution*. https://www.brookings.edu/blog/order-from-chaos/2021/04/12/pot-and-water-theft-and-environmental-harms-in-the-us-and-mexico/.

Forests Unlimited (n.d.). California forest statistics. https://www.forestunlimited.org/resources/california-forest-statistics/.

Gabriel, M.W., Wengert, G.M., Higley, J.M., Krogan, S., Sargent, W., & Clifford, D.L. (2013). Silent forests: Rodenticides on illegal marijuana crops harm wildlife. *The Wildlife Professional*, *7* (1), 46–50.

Havighurst, C. (2011, August 31). Why Gibson Guitar was raided by the Justice Department. *National Public Radio* (NPR). https://www.npr.org/sections/therecord/2011/08/31/140090116/why-gibson-guitar-was-raided-by-the-justice-department.

Hawkins, D. (2017, February 27). We wanted them to live in fear: Animal rights activist admits to university bombing 25 years later. *Washington Post*. https://www.washingtonpost.com/news/morning-mix/wp/2017/02/27/we-wanted-them-to-live-in-fear-animal-rights-activist-admits-to-university-bombing-25-years-later/.

Helmer, J. (2019, June 18). The environmental downside of cannabis cultivation, wide-scale cannabis cultivation is causing environmental damage. Federal regulations could change this. *Daily JSTOR*. https://daily.jstor.org/the-environmental-downside-of-cannabis-cultivation/.

Horng, E., & Yu, K. (2009). The Bluegrass State's number one cash crop: Dope. *ABC News*. https://abcnews.go.com/Nightline/kentucky-drug-trafficking-daniel-boone-national-forest/story?id=8935635.

Hwang, G. (2021, August 20). Examining extremism: Violent animal rights extremists. *Center for Strategic and International Studies*. https://www.csis.org/blogs/examining-extremism/examining-extremism-violent-animal-rights-extremists.

KCAL News (2021, July 7). LA County Sheriff announces largest marijuana bust in department history. *CBS News*. https://www.cbsnews.com/losangeles/news/la-county-sheriff-announces-largest-marijuana-bust-in-department-history/.

Liddick, D.R. (2011). Crimes against nature: Illegal industries and the global environment. Bloomsbury Academic.

Lohan, T. (2019, February 15). Endangered wildlife are getting dosed with rat poisons. *The Revelator/Center for Biological Diversity*. https://therevelator.org/wildlife-rodenticides/.

Los Angeles County Sheriff (2022, May 17). Los Angeles County Sheriff and other officials announce crack down on illegal marijuana operations. https://www.cbsnews.com/losangeles/news/la-county-sheriff-announces-largest-marijuana-bust-in-department-history/.

Luna, D. (2021, July 21). Why we must confront the growing threat to national security posed by illicit economies and cesspools of corruption and organized crime. *Morning Consult*. https://morningconsult.com/opinions/why-we-must-confront-the-growing-threat-to-national-security-posed-by-illicit-economies-and-cesspools-of-corruption-and-organized-crime/.

Milestone J.F., Hendricks K., Foster, A., Richardson, J., Denniston, S., Demetry, A., Ehmann, M., Cuvelier, C., Schifsky, D., & Fireman, D. (2012). Continued cultivation of illegal marijuana in US western national parks. In S. Weber (Ed.), *Rethinking protected areas in a changing world: Proceedings of the 2011 George Wright Society Biennial Conference on Parks, Protected Areas, and Cultural Sites*, 209–216. http://www.georgewright.org/1138milestone.pdf.

Mistler-Ferguson, S. (2022, April 14). Mexico's cartels corner the Chinese market for illegal wildlife. *Insight Crime*. https://insightcrime.org/news/mexico-cartels-corner-chinese-market-for-illegal-wildlife/.

National Public Radio (NPR) (2021). 5 Years after California legalized weeds, the illicit market dominates. http://npr.org/2021/11/07/1053387426/5-years-after-california-legalized-weed-the-illicit-market-dominates.

Odura, K.A. (2016). Ghana's high forests: Trends, scenarios and pathways for future developments. *Wageningen University*. https://doi.org/10.18174/378343.

Price. T. (2022). Harvesting on land. In *Ecology of a changed world*. Oxford University Press. https://doi.org/10.1093/oso/9780197564172.003.0020.

Quinney, R. (1965). Is criminal behavior deviant behavior? *The British Journal of Criminology*, *5* (2), 132–142. http://www.jstor.org/stable/23634650.

Quinton, A. (2016). California illegal marijuana grows killing wildlife, damaging environment. *California Public Radio/NPR*. https://www.capradio.org/articles/2016/12/15/california-illegal-marijuana-grows-killing-wildlife-damaging-environment/.

Sanchez, F. (2022, July 7). Mexican police haul off 200 big cats, other animals in sanctuary raid: 'Horrible situation'. *USA Today*. https://www.usatoday.com/story/news/world/2022/07/07/200-animals-mexico-sanctuary-raid/7831581001/.

Sullivan, C. (2017). Cleaning up illegal marijuana grows. *United States Forest Service*. https://www.fs.usda.gov/features/cleaning-illegal-marijuana-grow-sites.

Tabachnik, S. (2021, June 20). Black market marijuana grows are popping up faster than law enforcement can take them down. But is legalization the cause? *Denver Post*. https://www.denverpost.com/2021/06/20/black-market-marijuana-colorado-chinese-crime-rings/.

Trujillo, H.R., Jackson, B.A., Baker, J.C., Cragin, K., Parachini, J., & Chalk, P. (2005). The radical environmentalist movement. In *Aptitude for destruction, volume 2: Case studies of organizational learning in five terrorist groups* (pp. 141–176). RAND Corporation. http://www.jstor.org/stable/10.7249/mg332nij.13.

United States Department of Agriculture (USDA) (n.d.). Focus on forestlands in California. https://www.climatehubs.usda.gov/hubs/california/topic/focus-forestlands-california.

United States Department of Justice (2016, February 1). Lumber Liquidators Inc. sentenced for illegal importation of hardwood and related environmental crimes. https://www.justice.gov/opa/pr/lumber-liquidators-inc-sentenced-illegal-importation-hardwood-and-related-environmental.

United States Department of Justice (2012, August 6). Gibson Guitar Corp. agrees to resolve investigation into Lacey Act violations. https://www.justice.gov/opa/pr/gibson-guitar-corp-agrees-resolve-investigation-lacey-act-violations.

United States Forest Service (n.d.). USDA Forest Service law enforcement and investigations. https://www.fs.usda.gov/lei/job-opportunities.php.

United States Forest Service (2023). FY 2023 budget justification. https://www.fs.usda.gov/sites/default/files/2022-03/FS-FY23-Congressional-Budget-Justification.pdf.

Warren, B. (2021, December 19). Marijuana wars: Violent Mexican drug cartels turn Northern California into Wild West. *USA Today*. https://www.usatoday.com/in-depth/news/nation/2021/12/19/mexican-drug-cartels-move-in-on-californias-shadow-marijuana-industry/8960873002/.

Westervelt, E. (2019). Illegal pot operations in public forests are poisoning wildlife and water. *National Public Radio*. https://www.npr.org/2019/11/12/773122043/illegal-pot-grows-in-americas-public-forests-are-poisoning-wildlife-and-water.

Woodhouse, K.M. (2018). *The ecocentrists: A history of radical environmentalism*. Columbia University Press.

Young, C. (2021, June 1). Indoor cannabis grow centers draining electricity. *WBUR*. https://www.wbur.org/news/2021/06/01/indoor-cannabis-grow-centers-draining-electricity.

9 Pollution

Introduction

This chapter covers the main sources of pollution: water pollution, air pollution, and hazardous waste. These topics are often at the forefront of the public's mind as cases of malfeasance are often highlighted in the press. Pollutants in the air and water are often linked to exposure related illnesses. Throughout the world, wastewater often flows directly into rivers and riparian systems. Bacteria and parasites can breed disease when they permeate water systems. Spills from industrial manufacturing can lead to both water and air pollution. The recent case of the train derailment of in East Palestine, Ohio, which occurred on February 3, 2023, demonstrates the complicated and anxiety-inducing impact of a large scale industrial accident which causes significant air and water pollution. This chapter will cover some of the more famous pollution events and will address the legal processes available to prevent these events from occurring. Additionally, there will be a discussion of how the government seeks through the legal system to repair the environment after it is damaged.

Five Norfolk Southern train cars filled with vinyl chloride were intentionally burned through a government-initiated explosion. The explosion led to an evacuation of the area. According to the Centers for Disease Control and Prevention, chronic exposure to vinyl chloride can lead to liver damage (Sullivan, 2023). Officials from the EPA notified the residents the area was safe. Officials claimed they tested homes and the air and determined that there was no level of vinyl chloride detected. Yet, the chemical was detected in the area's creeks (Deliso, 2023).

This case shows us that even when officials from the EPA engage in mitigation efforts, environmental pollutants can still have deleterious effects and permeate fear throughout the community. If government officials can create harm through the attempts to constrain consequences of an accident, then not all environmental pollutant releases can be categorized as law violations. But when corporations do it, they run the risk of fines and audits. Accidents are not always preventable, but if they are, they can be classified as crimes of negligence. Many violations of the Clean Air Act or the Clean Water Act reflect a failure to abide by regulations. Some violations are deliberate actions such as the mislabeling of waste or the fraudulent recording of pollutant releases.

DOI: 10.4324/9781003241201-9

Water Pollution

Water pollution is defined as the contamination of water by products, chemicals, bacteria, viruses, or gases that can impair human use such as drinking water, recreation, and irrigation. Water pollution is most common in the form of runoff from ground surfaces into riparian systems. Runoff can transfer nutrients, sediments, toxins, and organic materials into freshwater and littoral waters. Areas of concern include lands and water systems downstream from agriculture, construction sites, septic tanks, waste treatment facilities, underground injection wells, urban environments, extraction from gas and oil wells, and construction sites. Water pollution includes both subsurface and surface waters. Storms accelerate drainage and can overwhelm water treatment and diversion systems. Municipal water systems are second to industry in contaminant release into rivers. The pollution from cities rivals the amount of pollution created by factories and industrial areas. In locations like Seattle, Washington, where there are persistent rain patterns, there is substantial water pollution of the Puget Sound due to runoff from urban environments where oil, antifreeze and other auto fluids, paint, and fertilizer from streets as well as human waste from faulty septic systems, animal waste, and trash are regularly washed into the Sound (Dutch, 2022; Landahl, et al., 1997).

Point source pollution is pollution that can be identified from one specific source such as a discharge pipe, a shipping vessel which is leaking waste, or waste discharge from a specific manufacturing facility that is adjacent to a waterway. Non-point source pollution is defined under law as anything that is not defined as point source pollution under section 502(14) of the Clean Water Act.

Water pollution became a part of the public consciousness as part of a broader awareness of the environment and pollution that took place in the 1960s. In 1952, the Cuyahoga River in Ohio caught fire due to accumulation of fuel sources on the water's surface. It again caught fire in 1969, this time under greater scrutiny of the national press. In the period from the 1950s through the 1970s, the leaders of states adjacent to the Great Lakes were the drivers of attention to water pollution. The Great Lake states had large-scale industrialization which led to long-term pollution from the manufacturing that employed heavy metal manufacturing, industrial chemicals, and solvents, as well as plasticizers from automotive and its related manufacturing (Boissoneault, 2019). Decades' accumulation of large-scale industrial manufacturing with limited pollution controls compelled the government officials of the Great Lake states to be the leaders in demanding federal response to water pollution (Newton, 2007).

In 1968, Governor Otto Kerner of Illinois joined governors from Michigan, Indiana, and Wisconsin to discuss pollution in the Great Lakes. This was in response to the Federal Water Pollution Control Act of 1948 which was the precursor of the Clean Water Act of 1972. There were nineteen sessions where business leaders, scientists, and state government officials gathered to generate recommendations to the federal government. There were 9000 pages in the 20-volume set of findings and recommendations. The Great Lakes had been polluted for decades and had documented findings of chlorides, oils, phenols, sulfates, polychlorinated biphenyls, and phthalate plasticizers amongst other pollutants (Newton, 2007). Pollutants had been discharged into riparian systems and into the lakes directly. The recommendations included compelling industry and agriculture to treat water before discharge and to distance discharge from the lakes.

One of the problems of water pollution is bioaccumulation and impacts to drinking water sources. Bioaccumulation occurs when pollutants are incorporated between the natural processes. The soils on lakebeds, sea floors, and sediment of riparian systems become infiltrated with waste that is absorbed by plants that are eaten by fish, which are in turn eaten by other fish that may later be consumed by humans. A recurring challenge of water pollution investigation is that the damage is done before investigation can begin. Ideally, through regulatory schemes, water pollution can be abated before it becomes an identifiable problem.

Phosphorous in the form of inorganic phosphates instigate eutrophication. Nitrates, particularly in the form of runoff from agricultural production, accumulating in water systems also cause eutrophication. Eutrophication is defined as nutrient accumulation that stimulates algal blooms that in turn causes oxygen levels in the water to drop – creating hypoxic environments – which in turn causes fish death. Ultimately this process leads to dead zones. Eutrophication in turn sets off another set of consequences. Once the process of eutrophication begins with an overabundance of plants and algae, these plants will decompose and release carbon dioxide. As carbon dioxide increases, the waters acidify. This process is called acidification. "Acidification slows the growth of fish and shellfish and can prevent shell formation in bivalve mollusks. This leads to a reduced catch for commercial and recreational fisheries, meaning smaller harvests and more expensive seafood" (NOAA, n.d.).

Another contemporary issue of water pollution is leakage of chemicals from hydraulic fracturing as well as deep underground liquid waste disposal. Deep wells and deep well disposal present a number of potential sources of water pollution. According to McCaull and Crossland the possible sources of underground water pollution through deep wells are:

1. Improper pressure monitoring resulting in the failure of injection equipment.
2. Mining, excavations, or additional wells might lower subsurface pressures. This could trigger escape of waste fluids from the disposal zones (into other formations, water reservoirs, or to the surface).
3. Wastes under pressure can escape through abandoned and improperly plugged oil, gas or water wells nearby.
4. Corrosion of wells with age, allowing fluids to escape.
5. Natural or induced fractures in rock formations through which wastes can escape.
6. Corroded or broken casing through which wastes can escape.
7. Corrosion break in injection tubing, allowing wastes may escape.
8. Poor cement job. Wastes under pressure can break out between outer casing and the surrounding geological formation if outer casing is not adequately cemented to formation.
9. Leaky or faulty packer, allowing wastes to enter annulus.

10. Several wastes injected together can react and form new compounds. Wastes can also react with the injection formation, or with other wastes injected into nearby wells which share the same disposal area. Such reactions could create toxic fluids or poisonous gases in some cases.
11. Fluid could invade injection zone by means of osmosis, with resulting rise in pressure and fracturing of zone.
12. Clogging of injection tubing or disposal formation can cause pressures to rise abruptly, with consequent possibility of rupturing of tubing or fracturing of formation and consequent escape of wastes.
13. Wastes under pressure can reduce friction between rocks under stress, triggering earthquakes.

(McCaull & Crossland, 1974)

Water pollution in subsurface waters has the potential to linger much longer than in surface waters due to the hydrological cycle that moves water in different forms indefinitely. The accumulation of subsurface water pollution is difficult to detect and measure when compared to surface water pollution. Areas adjacent to mining areas, agricultural production, and urban and suburban areas experience water pollution through runoff. The water discharges that occur in these areas occur through runoff, exacerbated during periods of precipitation. Discharged or waste water is not dispensed through pipes as it is from industrial manufacturing sites. It is discharged through diffusion of surface and subsurface seepage, a.k.a. non-point source pollution. Even if legislation could address non-point source water pollution, water pollution would still exist. Examples include the production, manufacturing, and use of plastics. If a plastics manufacturer abided by all laws and regulations, the use of plastics miles away from the initial source can later pollute waterways and plasticizing chemicals are dispersed through the air which can eventually pollute water as the chemicals disperse and find their way to riparian systems.

Enforcement

The range of environmental crimes requires a different approach than other crimes. Murder, arson, kidnapping, burglary, robbery, and illicit narcotics sales are always illegal. Many environmental crimes have a range whereby some pollution is permitted, some fish catches are permitted, mining, most timber harvest, and animal hunts are permitted through regulation. These events become illegal when a ceiling limit is breached: there is a violation of a constraint of time, specific parcels of land are infringed upon, or limits to catch or harvest are exceeded. Environmental crimes, specifically pollution related crimes, are complicated by the fact that the actions often reflect permitted actions which are lawful actions formalized by the state.

Like many areas of environmental regulatory enforcement, development of land requires multiple environmental permits. In the case of development of land that can be considered wetlands, development is scrutinized under the Clean Water Act. In order for an individual or company to develop a parcel of land that is considered a wetland a number of steps must be taken and any step which is missed can be considered a violation. Most violations are handled administratively rather than criminally.

There are limitations to enforcement through regulatory schemes as some of the restrictions imposed through Congressional statutory language narrow the scope of enforcement activity. Often missed in policymakers' provisions is that the scientific, economic, and technological standards don't align with political aspirations or public demand. As a result, compliance with environmental laws is less consistent than with other laws. Reasons aren't due to willful flouting of the laws; rather, it is the misalignment of political desires, court decisions, and shifting statutes through amendments to the original acts.

> Full compliance with all applicable environmental laws is consequently the exception rather than the norm. Just as the EPA rarely meets congressional aspirations in meeting all of the deadlines in environmental laws – industry rarely meets all of those aspirations as reflected in the deadlines – industry rarely meets all of those aspirations as reflected in the statutory and regulatory requirements themselves. Nor does government itself or its contractors.... strictly comply with environmental requirements. In a recent survey, two-thirds of all corporate counsel reported that their companies have recently been in violation of applicable environmental laws.
>
> (Brickey, 2008)

In environmental crimes, as in many white-collar crimes, the distinguishing mark between legal and illegal can be blurred. The activities in question, such as securities exchanges, investment schemes, and fund transfers, are all lawful, yet they can violate criminal statutes when extended beyond legal thresholds. Since statutory language shifts and intent and/or knowledge can be required, failure of compliance becomes more frequent. In areas of environmental law and finance law, agencies tend toward administrative law enforcement before civil and criminal enforcement takes place. While some advocacy groups or members of the public may persuade policymakers to expand criminal codes to include more criminal sanctions in environmental laws, the government as an institution has always been wary of criminalizing actions that are lawful and necessary – such as waste dumping.

In the area of environmental laws, the political wishes of those who pursue more restrictive laws ignore the uncertainty of the science that underpins their demands. This reality compels more enforcement through civil and administrative laws rather than criminal codes. Traditionally for the Clean Water Act, any spillage into a waterway must compel two requirements: the waterway must be navigable and the chemical or product being released is considered via statute to be a "pollutant." The federal government assert jurisdiction via the navigable element yet this seemingly straightforward legal definition recently changed.

On January 18, 2023, a revised definition of "waters of the United States" was published in the Federal Register. It took effect on March 20, 2023 (Federal Register, 2023). The rule is operative across the United States with exceptions granted to Idaho and Texas. The revised definition states that the EPA now has jurisdiction over "waterbodies that Congress intended to protect under the Clean Water Act" (Environmental Protection Agency, 2022). The revised definition expanded authority of the government to have jurisdiction over "upstream waters that may significantly affect the integrity of downstream waters" (Environmental Protection Agency, 2022). This revised definition expands authority and power of the Environmental Protection Agency. The agency now has authority over the traditional navigable waters, impoundments of "waters of the United States," tributaries to traditional navigable waters, jurisdictional-adjacent wetlands, and intrastate lakes, pond, streams, or wetlands (Federal Register, 2023).

In the case of *United States v. Weitzenhoff*, United States Court of Appeals for the Ninth Circuit 35 F.3d 1275 (1993), the court found two executives guilty of six violations of the Clean Water Act although the government charged the men with thirty-one violations. The East Honolulu Community Services Sewage Treatment Plant was permitted under the National Pollution Discharge Elimination Sewage System (NPDES) to discharge treated waste into the ocean. Michael H. Weitzenhoff and Thomas W. Mariani, two managers of the treatment facility ordered workers to dump an additional 436,000 pounds of activated sludge into the ocean at night. The plant was required to transport the waste to a different waste treatment facility for processing if they could not process the waste appropriately on site. The treatment plant had more waste and sewage than it could effectively treat so workers dumped the excess that exceeded the plant's capacity into the ocean. The two managers were investigated by the FBI and charged in criminal court for substantive violations of the Clean Water Act and conspiracy to violate the Clean Water Act (33 U.S.C. §§1251 et seq.). Mr. Weitzenhoff was ordered to serve 21 months in prison and Mr. Mariani was ordered to serve 33 months in prison. The plant managers appealed their case claiming that they had a valid permit and were unaware that they had violated the NPDES permit.

The Ninth Circuit found that the case *United States v. International Minerals & Chem. Corp.* (402 U.S. 558, 91 S.Ct. 1697, 29 L.Ed.2d 178 (1971) would apply. This case was tried in the Supreme Court where the justices held that when a person or company "handles wastes and dangerous materials, knowledge of the regulations is assumed." While this was a win for the EPA in bringing a case on violations of the Clean Water Act, the dissenting judges in the *Weitzenhoff* case made striking remarks that demonstrate differing views within the courts and governing officials.

The dissenting judges of the Ninth Circuit wrote that ignoring "a criminal state of mind" (*mens rea*) in the pursuit of social goals through the application and authority of the criminal justice system causes imprisonment to lose "its moral opprobrium and our criminal law becomes morally arbitrary." The court found that:

> We have now made felons of a large number of innocent people doing socially valuable work … NDPES permits are often difficult to understand and obey. … The wrongful conduct was violating the NPDES permit by discharging 26,000 more pounds of waste than the permit authorized during the fourteen months.

The court made the declaration that violating the Clean Water Act "by exceeding the limits of a permit should not veer into criminal sanctions." Regarding *mens rea*, the appellate court ruled that the government was not required to prove that the defendants knew their acts violated the permit requirements or the Clean Water Act, only that the defendants "knowingly engaged in the conduct." Thus the defendants' conviction and punishments imposed by the lower court were valid (Justia, n.d.).

Like many areas of environmental regulatory enforcement, land development requires multiple environmental permits. In the case of development of land that can be considered wetlands, development is scrutinized under the Clean Water Act. In order for an individual or company to develop a parcel of land that is considered a wetland, a number of steps must be taken for compliance for development. Any step which is missed can be considered a violation of regulatory compliance but is not yet a violation of criminal law. The government regulations specify that a criminal prosecution can take place only if the violator disobeyed a compliance order and a government official has to show that the violation caused environmental degradation.

Property rights advocates have claimed that the government usurps authority of the land owner through enforcement of the Clean Water Act. Through continued amendments during reauthorization acts starting in 1995, the government through the EPA defined waters to include bodies of water that are adjacent to traditional waters (*U.S. v. Mills*, 33 C.F.R. §328.3(b); 40 C.F.R. §230.3(t)). Under this rule, wetlands, bogs, marshes, and swamps could not be filled, but the expansive authority of the law now prohibits arroyos and ditches to be filled with dirt if they fall under the revised definition of waters. Thus an individual could be imprisoned for a statutory offense of "discharging pollutants into the navigable waters of the U.S." (*U.S. v. Mills*). In the case, *Solid Waste Agency of Northern Cook County v. Army Corps of Engineers*, the Supreme Court held that non-navigable waters must directly abut navigable waters to be covered under the Clean Water Act (531 U.S. 159 (2001). Under the newly revised definition, this no longer applies.

The purpose of the environmental regulations is to specify standards and encourage compliance. Criminal law is applied when there is sufficient evidence to suggest that willful negligence toward the environment led to irreparable harm. Criminal law is applied when the administrative or civil law has been insufficient to stimulate compliance. In the case of regulated development through laws such as the Clean Water Act the government generates distrust and rejection of laws if it moves to protect more lands and waters over a truncated period of time. Additionally, if government regulations increase the cost of operations for industry, agriculture, or development, then there are often filings against the government in court. While officials are expectant of these effects, there is little acknowledgment of the fact that deterrence has never been regarded in the legal realm as the sole justification for criminal penalties. Yet, civil and administrative procedures compel more compliance thereby having a net positive effect on environmental safeguards. The government must always balance the cost increases it imposes on industry through environmental compliance and the cost of environmental enforcement. The water pollution cases demonstrate how nuanced and complicated achieving this balance can be.

Air Pollution

Air pollution is caused by solid and liquid particles and certain gases that are suspended in the air. These particles and gases can come from car and truck exhaust, factories, dust, pollen, mold spores, volcanoes, and wildfires. The solid and liquid particles suspended in our air are called aerosols. Aerosols come from various places, such as ash from an erupting volcano. Dust, pollen from plants, and mold spores are also examples of aerosols.

Indoor Air Pollution

Volatile organic compounds (VOC) are chemical compounds with carbon that vaporize at or near ambient temperatures. This lack of stability provides the etiology of the term. VOCs are released by paints, cleaning and supplies, pesticides, some furniture or carpeting whose fabrics are coated with fire retardant chemicals or have epoxies that release VOCs, and epoxies used in craft material. Other sources of indoor VOCs can include paints, composite wood products, vinyl flooring, carpet, cleaning products, tobacco smoke, and dry-cleaning chemicals left on clothing (Environmental Protection Agency, 2023).

Because these chemicals can have negative impacts on human health, the manufacturing, storage, and distribution of these chemicals are highly regulated. VOCs and other air pollutants are monitored and regulated by the Environmental Protection Agency. The EPA regulates the amount of VOC outdoors because they are photochemically reactive, meaning they release fumes when exposed to sunlight. VOC labeling for indoor products is not regulated by the EPA if the chemical is not going to be exposed to sunlight or if they are not photochemically reactive. Sources of indoor pollution that draw concerns are volatile organic compounds that are released from common products such as paints, fire retardants, pesticide use, cleaning products, and furniture.

Outdoor Air Pollution

According to the World Health Organization, air pollution leads people to be exposed to fine particles in polluted air that penetrate deep into the lungs and cardiovascular system, causing diseases including stroke, heart disease, lung cancer, chronic obstructive pulmonary diseases, and respiratory infections. Industry, transportation, coal power plants, and household solid fuel usage are major contributors to air pollution. Current analyses by the EPA demonstrate that the Clean Air Act has had a substantive impact on air pollution concentration averages, specifically regarding levels of carbon monoxide, lead, nitrogen dioxide, ozone, particulate matter, and sulfur dioxide (Environmental Protection Agency, 2020).

Outdoor air pollution is a mix of hazardous and potentially hazardous substances from natural and manufactured sources. The pollution sources most often considered and addressed include vehicle emissions, fuel oils and natural gas to heat homes, waste or byproducts that result from manufacturing, power generation such as air emissions from coal-fueled power plants, and emissions from food, agricultural, and chemical production. Natural sources of air pollution come from wildfire smoke, ash and gases from volcanic eruptions, and gases, like methane, which are emitted from decomposing organic matter in soils, riverbeds, or the ocean floor. Several of the most serious concerns that capture the public's attention come from traffic related pollution which includes ozone pollution and manufacturers' pollution.

Air pollution that is emitted from vehicular traffic involves a mixture of gasses and particles. Compounds that are released from vehicle exhaust include various forms of carbon, nitrogen oxides, sulfur oxides, volatile organic compounds, polycyclic aromatic hydrocarbons, and fine particulate matter (Health Effects Institute, 2010). The particulate matter is often in the form of chemicals that are nitrates, carbon, mineral dust, or sulfates. They originate with vehicular and/or industrial emissions. They can also be found in wildfire soot, cigarette or wood smoke, and any engine or motor that employs fossil fuel combustion. Fine particulate matter is measured as thirty times thinner than a human hair and can be inhaled deeply into the lungs where it can produce asthma or other lung diseases. It is notated as $PM_{2.5}$ because they are 2.5 microns in diameter (Health Effects Institute, 2010).

Polycyclic aromatic hydrocarbons (PAH) are chemical compounds containing carbon and hydrogen. PAH are released via combustion and various industrial processes, such as iron, steel, and rubber product manufacturing, but they can also be found on meats that are charred or grilled and in fumes from asphalt when it is freshly laid. PAH can be found in particulate matter. In general, PAH have low toxicity in humans. The problem is when people are exposed at higher rates. Smokers have higher rates of PAH in their urine than non-smokers (Goldman, et al., 2001).

Noxious gases, which include carbon dioxide, carbon monoxide, nitrogen oxides (NOx), and sulfur oxides (SOx), are elements of vehicle emissions and derivatives of industrial processes such as the production of iron. Noxious gases have had a history which prompted governments to restrict their emission and control manufacturing. These gases are considered noxious because they have the potential to create damage to human tissues, impairment to the central nervous system, and severe illness if a person is subjected to significant exposure. The most common gasses that affect people include carbon monoxide (CO – which can be released from poorly vented furnaces and boilers, kerosene heaters, leaking chimneys, automobile exhaust that enters homes, or tobacco smoke), solvents (such as chlorofluorocarbons, benzene, hexane, and chlorine) ozone (O_3), and hydrogen sulfide (H_2S – found in gas/oil refining, paper manufacturing, rayon manufacturing, mining, and tanning). These chemical compounds can be problematic if they accumulate in the environment; both indoor and outdoor air pollution can have environmental impacts.

Any particle that gets picked up into the air or is formed from chemical reactions in the air can become an aerosol. Many aerosols enter the atmosphere when we burn fossil fuels – such as coal and petroleum – and wood. These particles can come from many sources, including car exhaust, factories, and even wildfires. Some of the particles and gases come directly from these sources, but others form through chemical reactions in the air.

Certain gases in the atmosphere can cause air pollution. For example, in cities, a gas called ozone is a major cause of air pollution. Ozone is also a greenhouse gas that can be both good and bad for our environment. It all depends where it is in Earth's atmosphere.

In more recent times, concern about the effects of atmospheric pollution has widened to include damage to buildings and materials, crops, forests, animal species, freshwater ecosystems, and even the stratosphere. Certainly, much progress has been made in reducing the problems caused by many sources of pollution, especially those arising in industry (Environmental Protection Agency, 2020).

Governments introduced systems to monitor and restrict emissions into atmosphere, in order to resolve conflicts of interest between the emitters of pollutants, often industrial firms, and the neighboring population who were subject to the effects. These control systems were commonly aimed at achieving a balance between the costs imposed on the industrial processes and the resultant benefits to the community at large. The nature of the problems which have come to the forefront of attention in recent years makes such a balance much more difficult to attain.

Federal Cases Relating to the Clean Air Act

On October 12, 2016, four Texas-based companies pled guilty to violations of the Clean Air Act. They also agreed to pay a fine totaling $3.5 million for criminal violations that occurred in two oil and chemical processing facilities (United States Attorney's Office, 2016). The companies KTX Limited and KTX Properties released hazardous air pollutants after a tank explosion on their property in Port Arthur, Texas on March 31, 2011. One worker was killed and two others were injured. The explosion was the result of a falsified work permit which was required by the Occupational Safety and Health Act (OSHA). The workers initiated welding on a tank that had not been drained, isolated, and decontaminated as required by industry standards and OSHA requirements. This caused vapors to ignite when welding started. The tank exploded and released hazardous air pollutants.

On April 17, 2017, Volkswagen AG was sentenced on three felony counts. The company was charged with conspiracy to defraud the United States and violate the Clean Air Act, obstruction of justice, and importation of merchandise by means of false statements. The German automotive manufacturer agreed to pay $2.8 billion, the largest criminal fine against an automotive company (Dooley, 2017). The criminal prosecution stemmed from a ten-year scheme to sell diesel powered vehicles which employed software designed to cheat required emissions test. Volkswagen also paid an additional $1.5 billion in civil penalties to the Environmental Protection Agency. James Robert Liang, a Volkswagen engineer, was sentenced to forty months' imprisonment for his role in the criminal violation (Environmental Protection Agency, 2017).

Hazardous Waste

Hazardous waste is of particular interest in environmental regulation due to its potential to cause ground and surface water contamination and air pollution. Seepage of hazardous waste can occur when it is not disposed of or treated correctly. Large-scale industries such as chemical manufacturing and metal manufacturing as well as timber, fish, and agriculture industries face mounting operational costs in a highly competitive global trade environment. One of the most consistent high costs includes compliance with hazardous waste disposal in compliance with EPA regulations. While companies can reduce hazardous materials through treatment such as incineration, chemical decomposition, and biological treatments, these processes add to the operational costs. Additionally, costs of proper dumping through a lengthy permitting and inspection process add costs through storage, permit applications, and payment for disposal. Thus cases of night time dumping and on site disposal are notorious methods of hazardous waste disposal for the unscrupulous operator.

There has been historical association between organized crime and hazardous waste hauling and disposal. Many of the beliefs relating to the links between the two came from a book entitled *Poisoning for Profit: The Mafia and Toxic Waste in America*. The book was authored in 1984 by Alan Block and Frank Scarpitti: both authors had been social scientists who focused on organized crime. They made an assertion that organized crime syndicates controlled hazardous waste hauling through infiltration of trade associations and through corruption of criminal justice agencies such as the New Jersey state prosecutors' office. Hazardous waste generation and transportation, as well as recycling, treatment, and disposal of hazardous waste, are covered under RCRA (Resource Conservation and Recovery Act) Subtitle C. Solid waste management is under RCRA Subtitle D, and underground storage tanks, particularly as they relate to the petrochemical industry, are regulated under RCRA Subtitle I.

The *Poisoning for Profit* book asserted that prosecutors, politicians, and law enforcement officials colluded with hazardous waste criminals to create opportunities for syndicates to maximize profits while creating environmental harm. Characteristics of a successful RCRA violator included skills in timing regulatory inspections, rigging environmental tests by dumping chlorine or other cleaning agents into a tank from which samples would be drawn, and sending samples to laboratories that were known to conclude with desired outcomes as some laboratories were run by unprincipled owners who themselves were looking to maximize profit. While these characteristics were true for violators of RCRA, connecting these characteristics with organized crime and corruption of legal officials was wrong. As a result of the book release, the book's publisher, William Morrow and Company, and the authors were sued. The publisher, sued by Waste Management, Inc., agreed to destroy all copies of the book while the director of the New Jersey Division of Criminal Justice, Edwin Stier, sued the authors (Rebovich, 2015). Block and Scarpitti had to make public apologies to the officials in New Jersey and to Waste Management, Inc.

Errors in the book stemmed from relying heavily on statements from unreliable witnesses who had their own motives for their false assertions. Another issue was the timing of the authors' research. They highlighted a time period which experienced an uptick in RCRA violations. They did not have the full understanding of hazardous waste disposal and labeling. They were so ignorant of the industry, how violations occurred, and habitual violators that they drew the wrong conclusions. Explanations for some of the assertions made against political and legal officials were dispelled in a House Committee Meeting held in Washington, D.C. Yet, the impression that their text made was amplified by media and fictional portrayals of Italian organized crime in New York, New Jersey, and Pennsylvania. To this day, hazardous waste, RCRA, and the role of criminals is still poorly understood by most criminologists, politicians, and reporters.

In reality, the characteristics outlined earlier are true of RCRA violators but not as part of an organized syndicate or conspiracy. In 1992, Donald Rebovich published a study in which he gathered data from four states: Maine, Maryland, New Jersey, and Pennsylvania. Data was collected from hazardous waste incidents from state attorney generals' offices. Interviews of offenders and prosecutors were conducted (Rebovich & Curtis, 2020). The states were selected due to their variation in industry most likely to pollute: Maine had textile, wood, and fishing industry waste; Pennsylvania and Maryland had hazardous waste from metal treatment processes such as galvanizing; and New Jersey hazardous waste that stemmed from chemical production and petrochemical industrial waste. The states were also selected because Maryland, New Jersey, and Pennsylvania have shared borders. If organized crime were operating, as it often does across state lines and across multiple jurisdictions, studying these states for the same time period would be useful.

The study revealed that is was uncommon (approximately 13% of the cases) that a middle level manager or employee would violate environmental laws for self-enhancement. In cases where an employee in a waste generating company would conspire with a waste disposal employee through acts, such as mislabeling wastes, falsifying manifests, improper billing, or improper storage of waste, it was most often for the benefit of the company for which they worked. They did not obtain private profit from the illegal acts.

According to the study results:

> Surprisingly enough, the study has found that, most commonly, the criminal dumper is an ordinary, profit-motivated businessman who operates in a business where syndicate crime activity may be present but by no means pervasive. The research uncovers a criminal world of the hazardous waste offender unlike any theorized in the past. It is a world where the intensity, duration and methods of the criminal act will be more likely determined by the criminal opportunities available in the legitimate marketplace than by the orders of a controlling criminal syndicate.
>
> (Rebovich, 2015)

The study also informs us of patterns of criminality and crime characteristics that we see throughout white collar crime, which is to say offenses that occur within the context of one's occupation. Donald Rebovich started studying the hazardous waste industry's link to organized crime in 1986. He found that while there is evidence to suggest that some organized crime syndicates attempted to make inroads into hazardous waste dumping crime, they were largely unsuccessful. This is because most treatment, storage, and disposal facilities (TSD) and transportation firms are disconnected from each other and the industry is inherently fragmented (Rebovich & Curtis, 2020).

Routinely, fines for dumping improperly affect smaller operators more often than larger corporations or firms. Paradoxically, the cost of permitting and compliance are the most prohibitive for smaller firms. In this manner, some small firms may choose merely to exceed their permits as their most efficient mechanism for both following and not following the law. In the minds of these violators, they have tried in earnest to fulfill the laws but cannot be competitive as entrepreneurs if they fully comply with environmental regulations at all times. By contrast, the largest companies are more overt in their violations of regulations due to their capacity to pay fines and settle lawsuits. The cost avoidance in non-compliance is balanced through the payment in fines.

Case Examples

In December of 2021, Walmart was sued by the Attorney General Rob Bonta of California in Alameda County for dumping approximately eighty tons per year of hazardous waste into municipal landfills each year since 2015. Walmart was accused of dumping lithium batteries, pesticides, latex paints, electronic waste, aerosol cans, LED lightbulbs, and toxic household cleaners into unprepared landfills that are not designed or designated to handle hazardous material. This was the second case California officials filed in court against Walmart for complaints that Walmart was not properly disposing of hazardous waste. In 2010, California officials received a settlement of $27.6 million from Walmart for illegal storage of hazardous material in Walmart stores throughout the state.

In May 2013, Walmart pleaded guilty in federal criminal court to charges of dumping hazardous waste in sixteen different counties within California. As a result, the Walmart Corporation was required to pay $81.63 million in fines for illegally dumping fertilizer and various other hazardous wastes (Wohl, 2013). Between 2003 and 2005 Walmart employees inappropriately discarded hazardous waste in a manner that violated hazardous waste laws. Walmart officials explained their employees' action by stating that their workers were not appropriately educated on identifying potential hazardous waste. The company was found to be criminally negligent.

These are some of the larger settlements for hazardous waste violations. Unfortunately, several companies have had to pay substantial fines for similar actions and they do so repeatedly. Home Depot paid $9.9 million to the State of California in 2007 for failing to properly store and transport hazardous material (Skipitares, 2007). In 2018, Home Depot agreed to pay California $27.4 million for illegal disposal of hazardous waste including batteries, electronic waste, aerosol cans, and paints (State of California Department of Justice, 2018). In May of 2022, 3M agreed to pay $2.8 million for failure to properly handle hazardous waste at the company's incinerator in Cottage Grove, Minnesota (Minnesota Pollution Control Agency, 2022). 3M paid the State of Minnesota $80,000 for improper storage of hazardous chemicals in Cottage Grove in May of 2021 (Bjorhus, 2021). The aforementioned sums reflect agreed upon settlements, handled directly by state environmental compliance agencies.

In 2015, Congress implemented an increase in criminal penalties for violations of the environmental laws such as RCRA. In 2022, the costs for RCRA violations are the highest they've ever been: for not following a compliance order, 3008(a)(3) 42 U.S.C. 6928(a)(3), the fine is $109,024 per day; violation of a corrective action compliance order, 3008(h)(2) 42 U.S.C. 6928(h)(2), is $65,666 per day; violating RCRA Subtitle C hazardous waste program, 3008(g) 42 U.S.C. 6928(g), is $81,540 per day; failure to comply with an order to monitor for the presence or release of a hazardous waste, 3013(e) 42 U.S.C. 6934(e), is $16,307 per day; and violations of failure to notify state/local agency of the existence of an underground storage tanks subject to RCRA Subtitle I, 9006(d)(1) 42 U.S.C. 6991e(d)(1) is $26,269 per day. These substantive fines are intended to infer upon companies that breaches of RCRA are serious and will impact companies, particularly small businesses, in a serious manner.

Despite an increased fines system for violations of hazardous waste management, the types of cases uncovered by state and federal agencies are not likely to be sufficiently addressed. For most companies, the likelihood of being caught during an inspection or audit is slight. The cost of compliance with regulations can exceed the cost of the fines. Additionally, in a global marketplace with competition for goods being produced in countries like India, China, and Russia, which have the least stringent environmental laws, compliance becomes a burdensome cost that leads to imbalanced trade. The demand for goods creates the production of hazardous waste and the treatment of hazardous waste is not without flaws. In hazardous waste production, storage, and disposal, there are tradeoffs as there are in other forms of environmental regulations. Many of the trade-offs are overlooked as focus tends to be either on environmental impacts or on demands on industry. Congressional leaders have yet to fully articulate how to balance the competing interests and how to create laws which balance the trade-offs derived from this tension.

Conclusion

Environmental harms that result from pollutions may seem obvious for a government to attempt to constrain. Not all harms are preventable. Accidents occur. Lack of oversight and audit create opportunities for those who seek to minimize operational costs of industrial processes. Sometimes this creates incentives for shortcuts which can include not properly disposing of waste or releasing pollutants into water systems or the air. When corporations engage in this behavior routinely and with intentional concealment, they engage in criminal violations of the Clean Air or Clean Water Acts. The government must balance the cost imposed on businesses and the preservation of the environment. To some extent, there will always be some form of pollutant wherever human society exists. There will be human waste and waste from food production, home construction, and industry. When there is demand for technological production, there will be greater industrial production through expanded mining and manufacturing. Inevitably this will lead to more pollutants and waste. Innovation to recycle or mitigate waste will be more effective at overall reduction in pollution than adjudication of non-compliance when harm is created and measurable. The aim is to reduce the creation of pollutants in a manner that is cost effective for the manufacturer. Compliance with government rules will prevent more pollution and maintain the integrity of the environment. Audits and assistance from government agencies to industry officials would be the most effective way to reduce pollution. For companies that are unwilling to abide, criminal enforcement of the Clean Water and Clean Air Acts have been effective at creating deterrence in the industry and restitution covers the cost of pollution remediation.

Discussion Questions

1. Is it fair to associate hazardous waste crimes with organized crime?
2. Which criminal theories are most applicable to criminal violations of the Clean Air Act?
3. Are the permitting process requirements for construction and industry an effective tool for reducing pollutants and preventing environmental crimes?
4. If there is continuous or increased demand for consumer goods, housing, and technology, how are societal demands met without an expectation of greater pollution?

Further Reading Recommendations

1. Brusseau, M., Pepper, I.L., & Gerba, C.P. (Eds.) (2019). *Environmental and pollution science* (3rd ed). Elsevier Book.
2. El-Gendy, N. (2022). *Sustainable solutions for environmental pollution: Air, water and soil reclamation.* Wiley Publications.
3. Hill, M.K. (2020). *Understanding environmental pollution.* Cambridge University Press.
4. Spellman, F.R. (2021). *The science of environmental pollution* (4th ed.). CRC Press.

References

Bjorhus, J. (2021, May 12). 3M pays $80,000 over handling of hazardous waste in Cottage Grove. *Minneapolis Star Tribune*. https://startribune.com/3m-pays-80-000-over-handling-of-hazardous-waste-in-cottage-grove/600056538/.

Boissoneault, L. (2019, June 19). The Cuyahoga River caught fire at least a dozen times, but no one cared until 1969. *Smithsonian Magazine*. http://smithsonianmag.com/history/cuyahoga-river-caught-fire-least-dozen-times-no-one-cared-until-1969-180972444/.

Brickey, K. (2008). *Environmental crime: Law, policy, prosecution.* Aspen Publishers; Wolters Kluwer Law & Business.

Deliso, M. (2023). East Palestine derailment: Timeline of key events in toxic train disaster. *ABC News*. http://abcnews.go.com/US/east-palestine-derailment-timeline-key-events-toxi-train/story?id=97522161.

Dooley, E. (2017, January 10). Volkswagen near $4.3 billion settlement, guilty plea in emissions scandal. *ABC News*. https://abcnews.go.com/US/Volkswagen-43-billion-settlement-guilty-plea-emissions-scandal/story?id=44696227.

Dutch, M. (2022, January 7). 'Everyday chemicals' found at the bottom of Puget Sound. *State of Washington*. http://ecology.wa.gov/Blog/Posts/January-2022/Everday-chemicals"-found-at-the-bottom-of-Puget-S.

Environmental Protection Agency (2023, March 15). What are volatile organic compounds? https://epa.gov/indoor-air-quality-iaq/what-are-volatile-organic-compunds-vocs.

Environmental Protection Agency (2022, December). Final rule: Revised definition of "waters of the United States": Fact sheet. https://epa.gov/system/files/documents/2022-12/Public%20Fact%20Sheet.pdf.

Environmental Protection Agency (2020). Our nation's air: Air quality improves as America grows. https://gispub.epa.gov/air/trendsreport/2020.

Environmental Protection Agency (2017, April 21). Summary of criminal prosecutions. https://cfpub.epa.gov/compliance/criminal_prosecution/index.cfm?action=3&prosecution_summary-id=3009.

Federal Register (2023, January 18). Revised definition of 'waters of the United States.' https://federalregister.gov/documents/2023/01/18/2022-28595/revised-definition-of-waters-of-the-United-States.

Goldman, R., Enewold, L, Pellizzari, E., Beach, J.B., Bowman, E.D., Krishnan, S.S., & Shields, P.G. (2001). Smoking increases carcinogenic polycyclic aromatic hydrocarbons in human lung tissue. *Cancer Research, 61* (17), 6367–6371.

Health Effects Institute (2010, January). Traffic related air pollution: A critical review of the literature on emissions, exposure and health effects. https://www.healtheffects.org/system/files/SR17TrafficReview_Exec_Summary.pdf.

Justia (n.d.) *United States of America, Plaintiff-appellee, v. Michael H. Weitzenhoff; Thomas W. Mariani, Defendants-appellants*, 35 F.3d 1275 (9th Cir. 1994). https://law.justia.con/cases/federa/appellate-courts/F3/35/1275/605693.

Landahl, J.T., Johnson, L.L., Stein, J.E., Collier, T.K., & Varanasi, U. (1997). Approaches for determining effects of pollution on fish populations of Puget Sound. *Transactions of the American Fisheries Society (1900), 126* (3), 519–535. https://doi.org/10.1577/1548-8659(1997)126<0519:AFDEOP>2.3.CO;2.

McCaull, J. & Crossland, J. (1974). *Water pollution*. Harcourt Brace Jovanovitch, Ltd.

Minnesota Pollution Control Agency (2022, May 26). MPCA investigation: 3M mismanages waste at Cottage Grove facility dating back to 1996. https://pca.state.mn.us/news-and-stories/mpca-investigation-3m-mismanages-waste-at-cottage-grove-facility-dating-back-to-1996.

National Oceanic and Atmospheric Administration (NOAA) (n.d.). What is eutrophication? http://oceanservice.noaa.gov/facts/eutrophication.html.

Newton, D. (2007). *Chemistry of the environment*. NetLibrary.

Rebovich, D. (2015). *Dangerous ground: The world of hazardous waste crime*. Routledge.

Rebovich, D. & Curtis, G.E. (2020). *Crimes against the environment*. Routledge.

Skipitares, C. (2007, October 16). Home Depot to pay $9.9 million to California counties. *Mercury News*. https://mercurynews.com/2007/10/16/home-depot-to-pay-9-9-million-to-california-counties/.

State of California Department of Justice (2018, March 8). Attorney General Becerra: Home Depot agrees to $27.84 million settlement for violations of California's hazardous waste laws and customer privacy requirements. https://oag.ca.gov/news/press-releases/attorney-general-becerra-home-depot-agrees-2784-million-settlement-violations.

Sullivan, B. (2023). What to know about the train derailment in East Palestine, Ohio. *National Public Radio*. http://www.npr.org/2023/02/16/1157333630/east-palestine-ohio-train-derailment.

United States of America v. Weitzenhoff (II). 35 F.3d 1275 (9th Cir. 1993). https://www.hawaii.edu/ohelo/digests/Weitzenhoff(II)Summary.htm.

United States v. Weitzenhoff -35 F.3d 1275 (9th Cir. 1993). Lexis Nexis. http://lexisnexis.com/community/casebrief/p/casebrief-united-states-v-weitzenhoff.

United States Attorney's Office (2016, October 12). Four Texas companies agree to pay $3.5 million for criminal violations of the Clean Air Act at two oil and chemical processing facilities. *Department of Justice*. https://justice.gov/usao-edtx/pr/four-texas-companies-agree-pay-35-million-criminal-violations-clean-air-act-two-oil-and.

Wohl, J. (2013, May 28). Wal-Mart pleads guilty in U.S. hazardous waste cases, to pay $82 million. *Reuters*. https://reuters.com/article/us-walmart-hazardouswaste-idUSBRE94ROY720120528.

10 Conclusion

This text demonstrates a variety of environmental laws and regulations and their enforcement in the United States. The collections of laws covered reflect priorities by state and federal agencies whose jurisdictions include mitigating environmental harms, protecting plant and animal species by limiting their exploitation, and preservation of human health through limiting toxic exposures. While there are many texts that expound on environmental degradation caused through human activities, there is utility in examining the effects of the current regulatory schemes.

> The air we breathe in many urban areas is far healthier than before. According to a recent E.P.A. report, aggregate emissions of the six principal air pollutants monitored since 1970 have decreased by 25 percent, while energy consumption has increased by 43 percent, vehicular miles traveled by 149 percent, and gross domestic product by 160 percent. Waterways that were no better than open sewers once again support healthy aquatic ecosystems suitable for recreation. Two-thirds of the nation's surveyed waters are currently safe for fishing and swimming, compared to half that number in the early 1970s. Waste disposal, especially the disposal of hazardous wastes, is closely regulated, and waste sites are being cleaned up.
>
> (Lazaris, 2004)

The creation and implementation of the Clean Air Act, Clean Water Act, and Endangered Species Act have had a remarkable effect on enhancing the quality of life for human society and their surroundings. There is no data to show that these laws are insufficient but there are indicators that suggest that state and federal conservation agencies are inadequately funded. While many cases highlighted in the text reflect federal enforcement actions, a significant portion of enforcement occurs at the state level. Funding at the state level is grossly inadequate to effectively monitor and regulate environmental crimes.

Environmental law is extraordinarily complex involving criminal, administrative, and civil law. Historically, the federal government has relied on regulatory compliance through administrative enforcement. For those interested in advocating for environmental conservation, these actions are inadequate at addressing

DOI: 10.4324/9781003241201-10

environmental harms. Demands for enhanced penalties and more criminal enforcement by the United States Department of Justice have resulted in more referrals to criminal court. There has not been an equivalent demand at the state level. There have not been enhanced enforcement efforts by the states due to the lack of prioritization of environmental crimes prosecution in part due to budgetary constraints and political determinants.

In the enforcement of environmental law there have always been competing political and economic interests which result in complex regulatory schemes. Congressional modification of existing laws creates confusion, and cost and noncompliance by those in the commodities industries. When the cost of legitimate operations rises, inducements for illegitimate enterprises expand. A clear example in the field of environmental crime is the extensive negative environmental impacts of illegal marijuana grows. The alteration and damage to riparian systems in critical watersheds, water theft, threats to biodiversity, and alteration and destruction of forests are all environmental harms caused by a high demand product. The regulatory schemes applied to lawful marijuana products and sales are undercut by illegal grows. The cost of illegally grown marijuana is substantially less than the cost of regulated marijuana.

The high demand created by legalization has created a market where the illicit and the licit comingle. Legalization provides cover to the buyer who helps conceal the illicit supplier. Failure to enforce environmental regulations on public lands created a profitable industry for organized crime. Federal and state forest agencies do not have adequate resources to monitor and effectively prevent large scale grows. Failure by both state and federal governments to consistently apprehend and adjudicate rogue actors and criminal enterprises exacerbate environmental damage as these grows are a low risk, high reward enterprise.

This example demonstrates the complex role of the state. Governments have the power to make and enforce rules. In this case, state governments expanded markets for illicit trade of a lawful product through insufficient enforcement. The public interest and activist demand for legalization accompanied by willing politicians directly led to environmental damage. The harms to public lands were unsurprising given the under-sourced and often inconsistent management of public lands. Failure to establish code enforcement of this new market intensified these consequences. There was adequate data on narcotics usage to predict a rapid acceleration of demand; yet the newly formed regulatory scheme inhibited sufficient supply to meet demand. Thus, extensive long-term environmental damage to state and national forests is the result of illicit suppliers meeting market demand.

The government as both a stimulant and a deterrent to crime was foreseeable to criminologists. To the environmentalist, complexities of incentives and human behavior are frequently overlooked in pursuit of added regulations. Examples in this text show that societal demands can be duplicitous and no amount of government sanctioned restrictions will eliminate crime. "For the most part, how transnational, organized and criminal a market activity is depends largely on the commodity involved and the associated legal and financial risks" (Andreas, 2004). The illegal marijuana cultivator exploiting public lands faces minimal financial risk and the commodity is the newly legalized narcotic. Organized crime is the expected outcome of the inadequate regulatory scheme.

When poaching, illegal wildlife trafficking, illegal mining or deforestation occur, the local economy is harmed. Proper taxes are not paid. Smaller sized enterprises cannot compete in the market if they conduct lawful trade and abide by all regulations. Revenue streams are harmed, security and the rule of law are compromised, and little, if any, profit remains in the local economy. Partly, the regulatory schemes drive up the operational costs for both the licit and illicit enterprise. If the regulatory mechanisms for lawful businesses are too burdensome, the illegal market can flourish. If there are no restrictions, the tragedy of the commons can ensue which permits catastrophic collapse of a species or biome. This happened famously with the carrier pigeon. The government must artfully create enough deterrent to dissuade would-be entrepreneurs who are willing to operate outside of the bounds of the law without creating so much restriction as to dissuade obedience to the law.

Conversely, to some extent, the constraining apparatus of government enforcement can stimulate risk-taking maneuvers by criminal enterprises.

> Most laws against money laundering and trading in endangered animals and wildlife are of relatively recent origin. While not always terribly effective, it is the very existence and enforcement of state controls that necessitate that smuggling groups devise such creative and elaborate evasion schemes.
>
> (Andreas, 2004)

Mitigation of crime is the optimal outcome. Expansion of government regulations to different aspects of human behavior will not necessarily lead to the desired results. If one is inclined to preserve ecosystems or specific species, or conserve resources, understanding economic incentives and legal standing is as important as understanding motives for law creation. Recognizing that environmental laws can be some of the most effective because they can be addressed through various courts and legal remedies is imperative. This category of crime enables governments to work cooperatively with industries to reduce the extent of violations. The environmental record demonstrates that applying the laws reviewed in this text has yielded more stable and productive environments.

Engineering students at West Virginia University who worked with Dr. Arvind Thiruvengadam, an assistant professor, discovered and proved that Volkswagen officials lied about diesel exhaust systems in various vehicles they manufactured. In 2015, Volkswagen officials admitted to using illegal software to cheat emissions tests in their Porsche, Audi, and Volkswagen vehicles. Their vehicles emitted forty times the amount of allowable emissions in direct violation of the Clean Air Act (Shepardson & Poltz, 2020). The unlawful pollutants were emitted from vehicles sold in the United States for over ten years. Volkswagen marketed their products as "clean diesel" while the company had installed software in the vehicle that would drive in one mode when the vehicle was being tested, versus a different mode when the vehicle was being driven in standard conditions (Glinton, 2015). This software was designed and installed by Volkswagen executives and engineers working out of their Michigan office. Nine executives were charged with obstruction of justice, falsifying documents, and customs violations in addition to violations of the Clean Air Act. The United States Department of Justice charged the company executives with criminal conspiracy to sell approximately 590,000 diesel vehicles which they knew would violate emissions under the Clean Air Act. As a consequence, Volkswagen paid a $2.8 billion criminal fine and $1.5 billion in civil penalties (United States Department of Justice, 2017).

It was not environmental organizations or non-governmental organizations that made this finding. It was not environmental think tanks or sustainability programs at more elite institutions and universities that detected the fraud. It was students in Appalachia accompanied by a faculty member at West Virginia University who revealed the criminal intent of executives from one of the largest international companies. Due to the university students' work, Volkswagen executive Oliver Schmidt was sentenced to seven years imprisonment in addition to paying a $400,000 fine and engineer James Liang was sentenced to forty months and a $200,000 fine (O'Kane, 2017). The West Virginia engineering laboratory shows us that U.S. laws are adequate and scientific inquiry can effectively address environmental threat and harms. The laboratory tested other vehicles produced by German manufacturer BMW and found no emissions violations. The fines and imprisonment of a large corporation's executives reflects the seriousness of U.S. environmental regulations. The Volkswagen case also shows us that relying on the federal government to systematically enforce and audit compliance agreements yields uneven results.

Environmental crimes are different from other categories of crime in that most environmental violations are addressed through administrative and civil courts rather than through criminal courts. Environmental crimes are diffuse in that they cover a broad range of industries, business practices, administrative agencies, international markets, and criminal actors. Many of the crimes that are committed are deviations from normal trade and industry practices. Fishing, logging, whaling, wildlife trade, mining, hazardous waste shipments and disposal, and waste discharges are legal. Even limited trade in elephant ivory and rhinoceros horn is legal within the United States. These characteristics make environmental crimes appear more like white-collar crime than street or violent crime categories. Embezzlement is always illegal but many financial transactions that appear to be intentional fraud may upon investigation be the result of disorganization, system failure, or incompetence. Similarly, environmental crimes can be willful such as poaching, trade in endangered species, or willful deceit on trade manifests but a hunter can accidentally shoot at a deer that is undersized or an angler catch a fish that is undersized. These ambiguities lead to many investigations that do not result in criminal prosecutions. Similar to white-collar crime offenses, the most efficient government approach is to generate compliance to reduce future crimes and ensure cooperation between industry and government officials.

While there are reports that environmental crimes such as the global trade in wildlife presents a substantial scourge for society, it is important to consider the costs of illegal trade in wildlife in comparison to trade in other commodities on the illicit market. Wildlife trafficking is the fourth largest illicit trade globally, behind narcotics sales, guns trafficking, and counterfeit goods trade. The range between the first and fourth largest illegal trades are substantive. Worldwide narcotics smuggling is estimated to be between $426 billion to $652 billion annually while wildlife trafficking is estimated to be worth $23 billion annually. Counterfeiting, a property crime, is estimated to be valued at $923 billion to $1.13 trillion. The most valuable natural resource crime is illegal logging valued at $52 billion to $157 billion (Mavrellis, 2017).

To place environmental crime in perspective, the U.S. government exports on average $7 billion of cotton each year, $6 billion of wheat per year, and the global timber trade was valued at $625 billion in 2022 (Meyer, 2023; Business Wire, 2022).

> Indeed, the value of the illegal wildlife trade is now dwarfed by the larger crimes against the environment. The illegal wildlife trade is by some estimated at 7–23 billion USD per year. Environmental crime is now estimated to be approximately 91–258 billion USD (2016) annually, a 26% increase from previous estimate in 2014. Environmental crimes are rising by 5–7% annually – 2–3 times the rate of the global economy. Losses of government revenues through lost tax income due to criminal exploitation account for at least 9–26 billion USD annually. Forestry crimes including corporate crimes and illegal logging account for an estimated 51–152 billion USD; Illegal fisheries an estimated 11–24 billion USD, Illegal mining estimated at 12–48 billion USD; Waste at 10–12 billion USD.
>
> (Nellemann, et al., 2016)

It is difficult to know the exact value of the trades in illegal harvests, mines, and trade of wildlife and plants. Partly the reason is because the value of natural commodities is constantly in flux. Additionally, because many of the illegally garnered goods converge with the legal products in the global trading system. Even in the United States, the illegally grown marijuana is sold alongside the lawfully grown marijuana. The illicit product is not often distinguishable from the licit product. The blurring of these products enables political leaders to avert responsibility for better regulation. In California, the permeation of unlawful pesticides and herbicides in water wells as well as the high volume of water theft is unaddressed. Political and administrative leaders routinely discuss climate change but do not address the consequences of water and land use policies. Accountability is deflected through political distraction – at the cost of the environment and local residents. Their discourse on atmospheric issues produces a veneer of environmental sensibilities while diverting from measurable and considerable environmental damage resulting from a negligent state apparatus. This demonstrates that public discourse can divert attention from resolvable environmental problems.

There are many approaches to the study of the environment and the study of crime, much less to the study of the convergence of these two topics. For some, the framing of environmental concerns as crime may not be particularly useful (Halsey, 2004). For those who may be interested in work as conservation officers and resource managers, understanding the limits and capacity of governments is advantageous. For those who are interested in policy formation, understanding the complexities of trade, human behavior, and industry in both licit and illicit classifications may prove useful. Regardless of which perspective or aim one seeks, the federal and state government systems have yielded encouraging results to further a cleaner and more sustainable environment.

References

Andreas, P. (2004). Illicit international political economy: The clandestine side of globalization. *Review of International Political Economy, 11* (3), 641–652.

Business Wire (2022, September 21). Insights on the timber & wood product global market to 2027 – Ongoing demand for aesthetic furniture and from paper and pulp industry presents opportunities. https://www.businesswire.com/news/home/20220921005577/en/Insights-on-the-Timber-Wood-Product-Global-Market-to-2027---Ongoing-Demand-for-Aesthetic-Furniture-and-from-Paper-and-Pulp-Industry-Presents-Opportunities---ResearchAndMarkets.com.

Glinton, S. (2015). How a little lab in West Virginia caught a big cheat. *National Public Radio.* https://www.npr.org/2015/09/24/443053672/how-a-little-lab-in-west-virginia-caught-volkswagens-big-cheat/.

Halsey, M. (2004). Against green criminology. *British Journal of Criminology, 44* (6), 833–853.

Lazaris, R.K. (2004). *The making of environmental law.* University of Chicago Press.

Mavrellis, E. (2017, March 27). Transnational crime and the developing world. *Global Financial Integrity.* https://gfintegrity.org/report/transnational-crime-and-the-developing-world/.

Meyer, L. (2023). The World and U.S. outlook for 2023/2024: Interagency Commodities Estimates Committee. *United States Department of Agriculture.* https://www.usda.gov/sites/default/files/documents/2023aof-Meyer.pdf.

Nellemann, C., Henriksen, R., Kreilhuber, A., Stewart, D., Kotsovou, M., Raxter, P., Mrema, E., & Barrat, S. (Eds.) (2016). The rise of environmental crime: A growing threat to natural resources, peace, development and security. *United Nations Environment Program.* https://reliefweb.int/sites/reliefweb.int/files/resources/
environmental_crimes.pdf.

O'Kane, S. (2017). VW executive given the maximum prison sentence for his role in Dieselgate. *The Verge.* https://www.theverge.com/2017/12/6/16743308/volkswagen-oliver-schmidt-sentence-emissions-scandal-prison.

Shepardson, D. & Poltz, J. (2020). U.S. judge approves transfer of jailed VW executive to Germany. *Reuters.* https://www.reuters.com/article/us-volkswagen-emissions-idUSKCN24H367.

United States Department of Justice (2017, January 11). Volkswagen AG agrees to plead guilty and pay $4.3 billion in criminal and civil penalties; Six Volkswagen executives and employees are indicted in connection with conspiracy to cheat U.S. emissions tests. https://www.justice.gov/opa/pr/volkswagen-ag-agrees-plead-guilty-and-pay-43-billion-criminal-and-civil-penalties-six.

Index

Note: Locators in **bold** indicate tables.